Opera, or the Undoing of Women

Opera,
or the Undoing
of Women

Catherine Clément

Translated by Betsy Wing

Foreword by Susan McClary

University of Minnesota Press, Minneapolis

The University of Minnesota Press gratefully acknowledges translation assistance provided for this book by the French Ministry of Culture.

Copyright © 1988 by the University of Minnesota

Originally published in France as *L'opéra ou la défaite des femmes* by Bernard Grasset, copyright © 1979, Editions Grasset & Fasquelle.

Published by the University of Minnesota Press
2037 University Avenue Southeast, Minneapolis MN 55414.
Published simultaneously in Canada
by Fitzhenry & Whiteside Limited, Markham.
Printed in the United States of America.

Library of Congress Cataloging-in-Publication Data

Clément, Catherine, 1939-
  [Opéra. English]
  Opera, or The undoing of women.

  Translation of: L'opéra, ou, La défaite des femmes.
  Bibliography: p.
  Includes index.
  1. Women in opera. I. Title. II. Title: Opera.
III. Title: Undoing of women.
ML2100.C613   1988   782.1'09   87-34322
ISBN 0-8166-1653-1
ISBN 0-8166-1655-8 (pbk.)

The University of Minnesota
is an equal-opportunity
educator and employer.

For Claude Lévi-Strauss and for my son, Michel

Contents

Foreword
The Undoing of Opera:
Toward a Feminist Criticism of Music
Susan McClary

Feminist criticism has been a central concern in literary, art, and film studies for nearly twenty years. This has not been the case, however, in music. In a recent book surveying the present state of musicology, Joseph Kerman noted that feminist criticism is still strangely absent from the discipline.[1] And in separate articles in the past few months, critics Edward Said and Gregory Sandow both have expressed exasperation over that continuing absence and have offered preliminary sketches of what feminist criticism of opera might look like.[2]

At a recent meeting of the American Musicological Society, an open caucus of women scholars was held for the purpose of setting agendas in feminist scholarship. Among the areas discussed as having highest priority for women scholars of music were biographies of women composers, editions of their works, and the status of women in present-day music institutions. When the possibility of feminist criticism was raised, a puzzled and somewhat anxious silence was the response — in part because criticism *of any sort* is strangely absent from musicology, but also in part because women scholars still feel themselves to hold a precarious position with respect to the discipline: a position that overt criticism might jeopardize. Thus the feminist work that is produced tends to operate within a marginalized ghetto that adds fragments of information concerning women to the already existing canon but that does not dare tamper with the outlines of the canon itself. It is significant that the voices calling for a feminist criticism are those of well-established men. Women in musicology tend to read such appeals not as open encouragement but as taunts, as invitations to professional suicide.

One very powerful example of a feminist criticism of music has existed since 1979—Catherine Clément's *L'opéra ou la défaite des femmes*—although it is largely unknown to most of the American cultural critics who are concerned about the dearth of serious feminist criticism in music. And it is no doubt significant that Clément identifies herself as a literary critic rather than as a musicologist, for the literary community gives her the institutional grounding necessary for the undertaking of this project. A female musicologist writing such a book, at least in the United States, would resemble Clément's archetype of the woman who leaps into the void.

Clément's writing sometimes recalls the figure of the Freudian "hysteric" that plays an important role in the book she coauthored with Hélène Cixous, *The Newly Born Woman*:[3] when faced with a disconcertingly large number of young women, all of whom claimed to have been seduced by their prominent fathers, Freud took refuge in the position that such pervasive abuse by the very pillars of patriarchal society could not be true, that these "hysterical" women were lying.[4] In *Opera*, as Clément subjects one cultural treasure after another to feminist scrutiny, the reader may begin to clutch at Freud's displaced solution: What? Could they all be guilty of misogyny? All my pretty ones? The woman must be hysterical! Yet, as we are beginning to discover with respect to victims of incest abuse, the accuser may be telling the truth about a phenomenon that has long been protected by the foundations of phallocentric culture. Do we really need to ask why there is no feminist criticism of music?

Clément begins with a prelude—which is not the same as the preface an American reader might ordinarily expect. Her prelude seems to owe little to standard academic procedure: it more closely resembles the web spun by a first-rate storyteller, the free-association ramblings of a subject on the psychoanalytic couch, a piece of music. Rather than setting forth the premises of her volume forthrightly, Clément composes an overture that foreshadows many of the operas she eventually addresses, that pays homage—stylistically as well as intellectually—to several of her own cultural influences (including most obviously Lévi-Strauss, Freud, Lacan), and that introduces obliquely many of the leitmotivs she later develops. If the resulting prose is somewhat disorienting, its rhythms often evocative rather than expository, that very effect is central to Clément's concern: music likewise bypasses the modes of logical argumentation to catch the listener unawares. By simulating in language the seductive undertow of music and then repeatedly pointing up the kinds of agendas that slip past unnoticed in its wake, she makes her point far more forcefully than would be feasible through a positivistic account.

Some of the allusions in Clément's text are perhaps more accessible to the French reader. For instance, the strategy of patterning intellectual prose after musical structures is indebted to Claude Lévi-Strauss.[5] A more obvious homage to him is the ethnographic account of the Bororo village and the brilliant parallel she draws between it and the Paris Opera. For what Clément is attempting here is nothing less than an anthropology of high European culture.

Anthropology was first developed as a tool for understanding — and thereby controlling — racial Others. In the nineteenth century, it provided information concerning native customs and beliefs [i.e., superstitions] that facilitated imperialist missions and that enhanced widespread feelings of Western superiority. For in the West, we do things rationally, naturally, and in line with "universals"; we see things "as they really are." To turn the questions of anthropology on *ourselves* is, thus, an especially disconcerting enterprise. In many of her descriptions, Clément distances and alienates those forms that seem to us most natural, universal, and even sacred. The question of gender organization, for instance, is central to most ethnic studies. But to examine European middle-class constructions of gender and sexuality and to turn to opera as a suitable source of information is threatening on several fronts.

Significantly, she refuses to separate the art form from its means of consumption. Just as in any anthropological investigation, these cultural objects and rituals are studied not as autonomous entities in and of themselves but as constructions that reveal a great deal about the values of the people who produce, preserve, and transmit them. Both the operas themselves and the rituals of the audience fall under her examination, both are understood as spectacles operating through very similar premises. The comfort of the listener/viewer's anonymity is thus withdrawn, the artificial partition separating political and aesthetic spheres is collapsed.

Clément's scrutiny includes even herself, and it is in part the candid presentation of her own ambivalences that makes her discussion so compelling. For she freely admits the influence opera has had on her life: the extent to which she modeled herself after favorite heroines when she was young; the obvious love of opera she still maintains; her desire to transmit to her son some sense of opera that does not passively accept the stories it articulates; and yet, of course, the recognition that "her kind" are the inevitable victims of an art form that demands the submission or death of the woman for the sake of narrative closure. Her book is marked throughout by the anguish of one who has been betrayed one too many times by a lover, by the torment of an addict trying to kick a cherished if deadly habit. This is not at all, in other words, a savaging of despised objects. Clément tries to locate and extricate the roots that opera has buried deep within her; or, if extrication is impossible, to convert to some positive end those elements of herself that have been shaped by her lifelong exposure to opera.

Certain Marxian assumptions also inform Clément's treatment of opera. She recognizes, for instance, that the modes and purposes of culture changed in postaristocratic European society: the bourgeoisie, in other words, demanded new venues, new forms, new themes, new operas. The operas about which she is concerned were virtually all designed for a middle-class public.[6] Yet the ornate temples within which these operas are produced and the lavish apparel deemed appropriate for opera attendance reveal a deep-seated desire on the part of the bourgeoisie to emulate the nobility, to traipse about in pseudoaristocratic drag. Because a large part of opera's appeal is to this elitist urge, their original social contexts are often mystified. Thus to call attention to the fact that these pieces were written for the middle class is to deflate a central fantasy. Questions of political economy and opera are almost as disconcerting as those of anthropology.

Clément's (as well as Said's and Sandow's) strategy of beginning a feminist criticism of music with opera is appropriate, for at least it is clear in texted and dramatic music that women are being represented, that gender is understood explicitly by composer and listener alike to be an issue. In her careful analyses of operatic plots and characters, she presents what is finally a formidable, irrefutable indictment of at least the literary and theatrical dimensions of opera. Indeed, other very recent studies make it clear that such readings emerge almost invariably, once one turns questions of gender on opera.[7] Moreover, it becomes apparent that it has only been through tremendous force of general cultural will that these questions have been held at bay for so long.

The main body of Clément's text is organized after the model of countless opera-lovers' handbooks that relate succinctly the plot and highlights of each opera. The principal difference is that her synopses are told from the woman's point of view. As she shatters the sacrosanct cultural frames that have protected these pieces from scrutiny, she lays bare not only the gender politics that require the death of the heroine but also the racism and imperialism that opera often so unapologetically celebrates. (See, for instance, the discussions of *Madame Butterfly*, *Carmen*, *Turandot*, *Norma*, *Aida*, Wagner's *Ring* . . .)

The strategy of relying on texted music, however, is always vulnerable to the charge that one is finally dealing only with words (which we already knew were socially contaminated) and that music itself—in particular the "Absolute Music" of the classical symphonic repertory—remains essentially pure, ineffable, and emphatically not concerned with such mundane issues. Indeed, the music theory classes by means of which musicians are trained rarely deal with texted music at all; or, if they do, they pointedly ignore the words or dramatic situations, precisely because it is only in the absence of words that music can really be examined "on its own terms."

Clément does not leave the music itself untouched, even though she claims to be particularly interested in examining the words and stories that get washed over and submerged by the music. Her reluctance to deal technically with musical detail makes the book more accessible to readers who care about opera and the cultural problems she addresses but who are not proficient at reading musical notation. Although Clément's primary concentration is on the verbal dimensions, her frequent references to music shed considerable light not only on the operas she is dealing with but also on issues of instrumental music and Western culture's privileging of musical discourse.

First, Clément's occasional sorties into musical semiotics prove to be extraordinarily insightful, especially since so little work has been done in this area. For instance, she notes that the "impure," indirect chromaticism characteristic of Isolde's musical discourse is informed by a set of traditional metaphors that link such gestures with a seductive yet deadly form of feminine sexuality. Isolde, for instance, sings with melodic inflections that refuse to be contained within the rational scalar system of tonality, that play maddeningly in its gaps, that are given to slippage rather than direct statement. "That is what catches them [operatic heroines] in a social system that is unable to tolerate their presence for fear of repudiating itself. Always, by some means or other, they cross over a rigorous, invisible line, the line that makes them unbearable; so they will have to be punished. They struggle for a long time, for several hours of music, an infinitely long time, in the labyrinth of plots, stories, myths, leading them, although it is already late, to the supreme outcome where everyone knew they would have to end up" (p. 59). Eventually, in other words, a tonal piece must establish closure, must resolve that slippery, fragrant chromaticism to the security of a rational tonic triad.

Clément's reading of Isolde's chromaticism provides a key to far more than Wagner's *Tristan and Isolde*. Indeed, *Carmen* might be considered an even better example of the deadly seductive quality of chromaticism. Carmen makes her first appearance with the slippery descent of her "Habañera," and it is her harmonic promiscuity—which threatens to undermine Don José's drive for absolute tonal closure at the conclusion of the opera—that finally renders her death *musically* necessary.

This explication of chromaticism also helps to unlock some of the gender politics of "Absolute Music." The second theme of Tchaikovsky's Symphony no. 4, for instance, is thoroughly informed by this code: it is the sultry, slippery, seductive female who taunts and entraps, who needs to be brought back under tonal domination and absorbed. The fact that this theme is not, in fact, quashed contributes to the paranoid quality of the movement's narrative.[8]

Clément's analysis helps make sense of a very recent phenomenon as well: several current women musicians and composers have picked up on that traditional semiotic relationship between chromaticism and female eroticism and have appropriated precisely those signs for their own use. For instance, "Langue d'Amour," Laurie Anderson's ironic retelling of the Adam and Eve story, plays continually in the cracks—that is, in the chromatic inflections that escape diatonic scalar control and in rhythmic pulsations that defy regular metric organization. And the music of Sweet Honey in the Rock likewise often refuses to submit to metric or scalar order; rather, it lingers deliciously in the erogenous zones of inherited musical discourse.

This is not, of course, to suggest that there exists some kind of feminine essence. Rather it is an example of how a discourse as apparently abstract as music can be fundamentally informed by prevailing attitudes of "how women are," of how these attitudes are metaphorically articulated in musical imagery, and of how these images can be wielded either as weapons of misogyny or as signs used out of context in ironic, self-empowering strategies. In other words, what might have been initially a cultural truism concerning women became in subsequent stages an empty formalism (when acknowledging its implications became socially embarrassing), and finally a politically charged image — the meaning of which is to be fought over.

Another of Clément's insights concerns the anaesthetic quality of music per se. As she explains why the plots and characterizations in opera have been so consistently overlooked, she moves into the transcendentally-significant-yet-meaningless terrain that Western music has become. Music (whether classical or popular) tends to stimulate the listener so strongly — as though without mediation — that texts which might otherwise be viewed as silly or offensive are embraced without critical reflection. Indeed, operas are often sung in unknown tongues, and fans seem to prefer it that way. Those who have worked with opera singers know the extent to which verbal meaning fails to inform most performances. It is, in other words, the seductive pull of the music itself rather than the content of the verbal text that typically compels people to devote themselves to musical genres. And because most members of society have no methods for dealing cognitively with strictly musical imagery and meaning, listeners (and performers) get to experience intense emotional narratives without being consciously aware of what is at stake, thus without seeming to be accountable.

Yet the music is not an innocent accompaniment — ignoring the text does not mean that one avoids the potentially questionable dimensions of the pieces. The instrumental introduction to the "Habañera" tells us how to regard Carmen before she even opens her mouth. And it is precisely the overpowering necessity of diatonic closure that causes audiences *to desire her death*: the tonal cards are stacked against her from the outset. Indeed, nineteenth-century opera's demand for blood sacrifice, which marks it as different from most drama or literature of the day, is grounded in "purely" musical, tonal procedures. Cadence at all cost.

Now to be sure, most audience members have no idea how Bizet causes their pulse to race more quickly or to suspend breathing in anticipation of the final cadence/stabbing. Because they can claim to be paying less attention to the action per se than to the beauty of the music, they can leave the hall feeling edified — not as though they had just witnessed a snuff film. Clément's book insists that one focus on what the music compels us to swallow and affectively to celebrate.

A crucial part of Clément's argument concerning the acknowledgment/denial of music's power is tied to the Freudian-Lacanian psychoanalytic models that French intellectuals tend to take for granted.[9] Because American readers usually reject such models out of hand, the sections of the book marked by psychoanalytic influences might well be viewed with suspicion or even passed over. Such a response would be most unfortunate, for the issues Clément addresses through these models are extremely insightful, if fundamentally disturbing.

At stake is the question of why we in Western culture wish, on the one hand, to deny that music has social meaning and, on the other, to ascribe to it transcendental significance. It is precisely this contradictory attitude that protects opera from the sort of scrutiny Clément is attempting. A psychoanalytic model permits the following sort of explanation: music is able to simulate that state when the infant still feels itself to be coextensive with the mother's body, a state in which all sensation appears to be authentic—before the alienating social codes of language and culture intervene, before one is even aware of being an individual separate from the mother. Musical patterns act upon most listeners in ways that are not rationally explicable; it is as though one is connected to the subjectivity of another *without mediation*—as though still linked directly to the mother's body. This medium is therefore privileged above others (all of which bear more obviously the signs of their social, symbolic constructedness) because of that illusion of authentic communion.[10] Just as those infantile feelings antedate social meaning and thus are held to be infinitely superior to it, so music's power lies in its simultaneous transcendental meaningfulness/meaninglessness.

Already I can hear scoffing—I too was conditioned with a reflex to gag at such explanations. Yet American musicology simply accepts this privileged position of music and refuses to explain why. I suspect that Freudian models are distasteful to Americans in part because they call into question the beloved myth of individual autonomy. Semiotic models meet with similar resistance, since these approaches too assume that music is a social discursive practice, that one neither invents nor controls objectively the self and its responses. The American musicological world is grounded on the contradiction of simultaneous positivism (the obsessive search for facts) and radical mystification (belief in the divine inspiration and ineffability of great music). It goes to extraordinary lengths to avoid confronting those aspects of music that move either the emotions or the body, those aspects that provoke anxiety.[11] Music itself is treated much like Carmen: that which is alluring and seductive about it also threatens a world of rational order and control. It can be enjoyed and even adored in private, but in the public realm it must be knocked down and pinned to the Schenkerian graph so as to show who's boss. And once pinned to the graph, it yields up the radiant image of transcendental significance—that which is perfectly ordered without apparent social intervention.

If one follows Clément's arguments concerning cultural resistance to music criticism, it becomes obvious that far more is at stake than the portrayals of a few women characters in a few nineteenth-century operas. If, as she suggests, music serves as a kind of cultural security blanket, confronting that issue could be devastating far beyond strictly musical circles. Are deconstructions of religion, language, literature, or philosophy feasible only as long as there is some secure place to stand from which to launch those attacks? Some place that is as reliable, authentic, and unmovable as the memory of the mother's body? Music?

This argument goes a long way toward explaining the waves of disciplinary—and even interdisciplinary—hysteria that tend to greet most semiotically based analyses and attempts at music criticism. If we are not dealing with a psychological universal here (and I strongly doubt that we are), we at least seem to be tapping a much loved and cautiously protected myth.

It could be argued that a book such as this, which deals with an art form of the past, has little to do with present-day culture. This would be to deny, however, the fact that the institution of the opera house continues to exist, with the exploitive patterns Clément points out still intact. My students are often shocked by evidence that in the Renaissance, for instance, women who sang in public or who tried to publish their poetry were regarded as courtesans and were pressured to grant sexual favors in exchange for being permitted to participate in cultural production. Unfortunately, conditions have not changed as much as we would like to think. Clément traces these same attitudes as they have affected the lives of famous divas, reaching from Malibran to Maria Callas: the ways in which the figure of the prima donna is a male-constructed fantasy image (indeed, an image that often approaches that of the campy female impersonator); the demands of the public that the singer conform to their ideals of femininity, temperament, sexual behavior, beauty, and weight; and the viciousness with which the inevitable decline of her singing ability is greeted by her former idolaters.

Another book exists that presents many of the same ideas, but from a very different point of view. Ethan Mordden's *Demented: The World of the Opera Diva*[12] celebrates the ritual of alternately worshiping the artificial construct of the opera star and tearing her to bits. His title refers to an either/or mode of judging prima donnas, which he claims was fashionable for a while at the Met: when a diva is in good form on stage, she gives the appearance of being thoroughly demented; anything less than that and she is filth.[13] I have colleagues who gleefully invent names of abuse for fading sopranos—names such as Miss Piggy and others too hurtful to mention—and who glory in sending bouquets of dead flowers to their dressing rooms before performances. This is supposed to be hilarious, and it is a large part of the sport that opera has become (or still is). The old custom of the *droit du seigneur* is also alive and well—conductors who demand sex from aspiring sopranos in exchange for casting them in roles and who then condemn those same women for having slept their way through their careers. As a professor in a school of music, I have witnessed many an idealistic young singer get devoured as soon as she leaves the ivory tower. We somehow neglect to tell them about the "real world."

To claim that opera is a phenomenon of the past is to deny the extraordinary prestige and influence it still exerts. Public television revels in its operatic broadcasts. Everyone from flamenco companies to Godard contributed their versions to a *Carmen* orgy a few years ago. In the summer of 1987, the Pepsico Corporation presented an entire festival celebrating Mozart's *Don Giovanni*, for which the centerpiece was a new production of the opera by avant-garde wunderkind Peter Sellars, surrounded by a cluster of newly commissioned theater pieces on the theme by leading experimental artists and writers. These pieces have become our archetypes: as Clément suggests, they continue to inform our plays, our movies, and even some of our popular music (see, for instance, Malcolm McLaren's album *Fans* or the Canadian rock group Dollie de Luxe). Opera's premises need to be examined more urgently, then, than even classic literature's or theater's.

And, in fact, many of the renderings of the beloved masterpieces just mentioned do precisely that: in keeping with a postmodern aesthetic, many artists are reengaging with icons of the past. But rather than transmitting them as sacred objects, they are deconstructing them—laying bare their long-hidden ideological premises—and yet reenacting them, so that one experiences a shared heritage and its critique simultaneously. The sounds of whiplash, the masochistic rap, and the controlling phallic pulse that bombard "Un bel dì" in McLaren's "Madame Butterfly" tell us a good deal more about what is at stake in that opera than any traditional production. In Richard Schechner's contemporary production of *Don Giovanni*, the action was repeatedly ruptured by discussions that forced the audience to focus on the patriarchal violence perpetrated by that beautiful musical text. In my recent music-theater piece *Susanna Does the Elders*, a musicologist is seduced by and entrapped in her own presentation of a seventeenth-century oratorio by Alessandro Stradella and is obliged to come to terms with the politics of sexual representation.

In the final pages of *Opera*, Clément delivers an invocation for all the women victims of the operatic stage. For she loves them, has felt their magnificent, subversive voices to be inspiring and powerful—despite the law that has demanded their deaths. What she hopes for the future is the emergence of women who (like Carmen) can enjoy their erotic energy and still say no when they please but who (unlike Carmen) are permitted to survive—women who form a sisterhood that can sing freely and who cannot, *will not*, be driven underground.

And perhaps this hope is not in vain. Such women artists exist, although one is not likely to encounter them on the stage of the Met. The blues queens of the 1920s (Ma Rainey, Bessie Smith) pioneered in creating their own musical images of a feminine erotic—against all odds and often in demeaning circumstances—although women of the white middle class tended until recently to overlook their contributions.

In the last few years, women of all kinds have emerged to participate in every sphere of musical production, to construct various models of femininity. Aretha Franklin's popular and gospel albums reveal her as a descendant of the great blues queens—a woman who sings with extraordinary power and physicality of longing, of satisfaction, of faith, of survival. Composer/performance artist Diamanda Galas draws upon the traditionally taboo figures of the madwoman, the temptress, the amazon to enact the ancient Mediterranean ritual of keening—for the politically oppressed and for victims of AIDS. Janika Vandervelde's piano trio *Genesis II* both deconstructs the phallic violence that underlies much of classical music and articulates an alternative erotic impulse that she identifies as feminine.[14] And in the popular sphere, Madonna throws into confusion the virgin/whore dichotomy that has divided and contained women in Western society for centuries and takes on the figures of the seductress Lulu, the exotic Carmen, the martyred Monroe, and leads them all to a moment of self-possession and open celebration. No longer simply victim, toy, or dangerous essence, no longer forced to play dead within a male-controlled frame, this figure skips, dances, sings, and invites the audience—made up largely of young girls—to join in the festivities.

The games that Franklin, Galas, Vandervelde, and Madonna play are still fraught with difficulties: to what extent are these spectacles still informed by the masculine gaze? Can a woman give voice to the erotic in a mixed public performance and escape being consumed as a commodity or reduced to the traditional stereotype of the woman who is trapped in her sexuality? Are there possible solutions other than the drab suppression of sexuality that informs much feminist art or the "for women only" contexts that have sheltered some recent experimentation with feminine erotic imagery?

These problems are central to performance today, and they have yet to be satisfactorily resolved in either "high" or "popular" art. As Clément recounts both the splendor and the tragic ends of her operatic heroines, she provokes nostalgia but also a desire for new, even more powerful images. Opera was one of the principal media through which the nineteenth-century bourgeoisie developed and disseminated its new moral codes, values, and normative behaviors: that central ideological function was responsible for opera's vitality in the past, but it also marks the historical limits of its effectiveness. Today—in the aftermath of a revolution in gender organization—we often find ourselves looking to the performing arts for new paradigms of how women and men can live freely and openly together. Traditional opera is not the answer, but neither is it irrelevant: our processes of reformulation demand a thorough critique of the prestigious models we have inherited through opera. Clément offers us the beginning of such a critique.

Opera, or the Undoing of Women

Prelude

Lasciatemi morir

A great house, a strange one, in the heart of the city. Nightfall, going to the opera. Changing worlds. Trading the working world for one of fantastic, fleeting leisure. Climbing giant staircases. Bronze women proffer fake torches, ceilings full of goddeses and gods watch with indifference; evening cloaks trail their velvet hems with old-fashioned grace on the marble floor; bit by bit a dull roar swells the festive house.

By day it is a gigantic edifice, decorated with columns and statues, useless. Fauns dance with their nymphs in an eternity of well-worn stone; a half-naked Orpheus lifts a lyre; and Muses in procession, futile dancers, look down on the city. At night, it all comes to life. The house with its Greek pediment—the temple for music—begins to quiver. Coaches, carriages, cars, taxis, subways discharge a delighted populace. Sometimes official retinues led by helmeted motorcycle escorts arrive in pomp. The brilliance of all the chandeliers is visible through the tall windows.

Entering the opera. Passing one by one through the gates of ritual; buying tickets, presenting them, letting oneself be guided by a woman who opens the doors, penetrating the heart. The immense room, red and gold, white and gold, blue and gold: always the gold of the balconies, the garlanded gold. In this architecture can be read a whole, no longer existent, world. The ghosts of a society wander here in a dream. There the fragile young duchesses so beloved of Balzac in *Scènes de la vie parisienne* let themselves be seduced by dubious dandies;

3

there, Mme de Vandenesse, Mme de Rochefide, the Princess de Cadignan, the women with their blond curls, hardhearted heroines with their nervous fans plot against their friends. In this loge where there is sitting today one of those pale girls who still go out with their parents, Mathilde de La Mole felt her heart catch fire for Julien Sorel, feeling so sorry she treated him badly. . . . And there, feverishly, she repeated the lilting, Italian words that had just crystallized her pride: *"Devo punirmi, se troppo amai"* [If I loved too much, I should be punished]. There died the Duc de Berry, pierced in the heart by Louvel, dying in the wings, while, with great difficulty, they hauled Louis XVIII in his cripple's chair to come and close the Duke's dying eyes, because only he had the right to do so. . . . At the opera attempts are made on the lives of powerful men; there is burning and killing; passions are kindled and snuffed out.

Remember *Senso* and Visconti's somber brilliance. When the curtain goes up on a performance of *Il Trovatore*, bouquets are falling from high above, and their colors are those of the future Italy then in the midst of gestation. White, uniformed Austrian officers, defeated and undone by the opera, leave in retreat; but in one of the loges there is (like in an opera) a woman already in love with one of these enemy officers. *Se troppo amai . . . devo punirmi.* She will be punished. Remember something else, closer to us. A woman in black, her gaze burning with sadness, watches a newly engaged couple from afar. The man leaves his loge and meets the woman in a long corridor that is white, deserted. That was called *Prima Della Revoluzione.*[1] These are goodbyes: to a disappointed hope, to a revolution that never comes, to youth. In the theater, the show goes on, while the young fiancée, stiff as one must be on a velvet seat, a butterfly pinned to the performance, watches and listens. Opera is the place for intrigues, love affairs, glances that intersect and never meet again.

Theater house and stage are a match for each other, reflecting the same golden image: the long gowns, the pomp of festive bourgeois in search of a forgotten nobility, correspond to the brilliant spectacle and the stage costumes. All around, motionless statues extend their polished arms. Beneath the great staircase a nymph in the image of Castiglione's beautiful duchess dips a foot, rubbed gently so often that it glows, into an empty basin; she laughs, and all her teeth are bronze. Peristyles in the ancient manner have false mosaics to support their columns; above there are levels and more levels, until you come to the meeting-place known familiarly as the foyer.

But it is rumored that underneath lies a black, impenetrable lake, where sometimes the phantom of the Opera[2] comes by boat to carry off a golden-voiced singer with the name of a Greek goddess, Christine Daaé. There is a whole world of hideouts where stolen goods are received; a world of secret exchanges, petty trafficking, where stories of love and stories of death circulate before the very eyes of an audience whose attention is elsewhere.

The lights, slowly and imperceptibly, go down. The noises of the crowd are hushed. A few coughs surface; these are people, after all. The orchestra tunes up, improvising; for an instant, on the horn, a sad melody from the third act lingers. The curtain is going to rise: the heavy painted curtain whose gold-tasseled velvet always opens onto a light cloth. Trompe l'oeil: flying in the breezes there are two golden giantesses holding back the stage. Trompe l'oeil: there is a huge velvety conch with thousands of eyes looking out in fascination. Trompe l'oeil: the curtain goes up on a forest of gauze and wood, on a palace of cloth. Always it grows cooler when the curtain rises; a breath of air moves from the stage into the audience. And the voices begin their rise.

A great house, a strange one, in the heart of the Bororo village, in a tropical Indian forest, destroyed today by our roads and our germs. In the center, there is this great house covered with dried palms. They call it: the men's house. The women's huts radiate from it like a wheel. Families live in the huts: women and children. But in the central house, the men spend the day dressing and adorning themselves, making musical instruments and hunting implements, singing. If a woman, by chance, dares to enter the house, she is attacked—often mortally. There the great ritual ceremonies, in which women play no part, are prepared; there simmers the delicious dish of men's culture. This is all different from the world we live in; but . . . Yes, allocation of roles is different: women do the rough work, with no ornament except uniforms that scarcely vary. Men, on the contrary, are like great, painted birds, covered with feathers and shells; they are stylish. Social structures are different: women give the male children their family name, and, as part of their daily routine, the men spend a bit of time in their wives' huts. But despite the distances and societies, despite the upside-down codes, there is still this large, strange house in the central place, at the heart of the assembled group: a men's house, forbidden to women, where men's voices sing.

Opera is not forbidden to women. That is true. Women are its jewels, you say, the ornament indispensable for every festival. No prima donna, no opera. But the role of jewel, a decorative object, is not the deciding role; and on the opera stage women perpetually sing their eternal undoing. The emotion is never more poignant than at the moment when the voice is lifted to die. Look at these heroines. With their voices they flap their wings, their arms writhe, and then there they are, dead, on the ground. Look at these women who fill the theater, accompanied by penguins in uniforms that scarcely vary: they are present, they are decorative. They are present for the dispatch of women like themselves. And when the curtain closes to let the singers take the last bow, there are the women kneeling in a curtsey, their arms filled with flowers; and there, beside them, the producer, the conductor, the set designer. Occasionally, a . . . But you wouldn't know how to say it: a produceress? A conductress? Not many women have access to the great masculine scheme surrounding this spectacle thought up to adore, and also to kill, the feminine character.

In the eighteenth century, during the period when harmonious worlds were being constructed in thought, while the monarchic power and the idea of divinity were being shaken, there were architects who passionately devoted themselves to dreaming of operas to correspond to this world in gestation. They were not wrong; opera, in its origins in the sixteenth century, was born from the meeting between court processions, accompanying the solemn entrances of kings into cities, and the mystery plays in front of cathedrals: two social perfomances to sustain two powers linked to God. This grand performance, born in the courts, represented also the hierarchy of a world in which the king alone had the position of sovereign eye. They were not wrong, Boullée, Ledoux, the utopian architects of the eighteenth century, to want this place built as a calculated reflection of their hopes. The eye carved by Ledoux for the project of the theater at Besançon—all that remains of this building—symbolizes this new gaze: society, within opera space, is to be able to look at itself. And the whole will be imagined as a circle. "Seeing a spectacle provided free for the people stimulates my imagination and enlarges my thoughts; I am going to unroll for you all the treasures of the human race; peoples of the earth, hasten to my voice, obey the universal law. Everything in nature is a circle . . . Inexhaustible source of the great impressions that are visually interesting, nothing can survive without your solemn splendor. There, yes, there, in the circle a man returned to his original state recovers the equality that he never should have lost. It is in this vast theater, balanced in the clouds, in circle after circle, that he unites with the secret of the gods." This is Ledoux's comment on the carved stage where an opera audience watches us through a giant, piercing eye. Prefiguring the great revolutionary festivals and the solemn arrangements surrounding the goddess Reason, the utopians' opera where stage and audience watch each other is a microcosm, it is the "immense circle of human affections."[3]

Yes. Where are the women in the structure of this edifice? In their place, of course. "Women make the front rows beautiful, with all the inherent graces of their sex; those who are strongest protect the weak; children cling to their father's body; others, sitting on their mothers' knees, give the effect of progressive tiers. All the tones are varied, it is all pyramidal. What sublime solemnity!" Tears form under the emotional lashes of the dreamer, and Greuze grabs his brushes. Women "make opera beautiful"; in the meantime, Boullée for his part exclaims: "By bringing together and assembling the fair sex, placed so that they take the place of bas-reliefs in my architecture, I believe I am certain to have stamped my tableau with the features of grace." Nothing comes along to disturb the social pyramid that makes the audience itself an ornament of the opera. Nothing will come later, in the nineteenth century when romantic opera flourished, to disturb the order reflected from audience to stage. In this order of human affections, women struggle, and from the moment these women leave their familiar and ornamental function, they are to end up punished—fallen, abandoned, or dead. The "fair sex" indeed.

This place of delights, where all the pleasures for ear and eye are gathered, this place where in the beginning Orpheuses lost their Eurydices with a single glance, gives rise to some very strange fantasies in which opera reveals its underside. Leibniz, the philosophical genius behind both infinitesimal calculus and Theodicy, outdoes all the rest with his. Is it coincidental or intentional? This text has come down to us with the following fiendish title: *A Funny Idea Relating to a New Kind of Representation*. Funny all right, this idea that popped up in Leibniz's overheated mind after a night of fireworks and fantastic contraptions on the Seine.[4] There was to be a great house where everything that could be presented in performance would be brought together. Everything demonstrating the glory of the divine architect, who calculates from his corner all the coincidences of this world, would be there—the best of course. All that would be necessary to begin is that "a few important people" be in agreement. You would see magic lanterns—eye, reflections, illusions—optical marvels; you would see the fortifications for war with a master of fortification who would explain everything. You would see a naval battle and concerts immediately afterward. You would see rope dancers, an anatomical theater, a garden of medicinal plants, Father Kircher's room, the fire-eater (who would come from England), the moon through a telescope, a game of chess, a mirror that sets things on fire, comedies of different sorts for every country, *carillons*, a menagerie. . . . What would not be there to see? The philosopher, in a fever of inspiration, reels off a rough draft that is a prodigious inventory of all the curiosities of his time.

But he thinks back. What did he leave out? An Academy of Games, also baptized the Academy of Pleasures. That would be essential: gambling, *lansquenet*, *trente et quarante*, cards. The dice. And the idea—the sublime idea.

"These houses or rooms will be built so the master of the house will be able to hear and see everything that is said and done, without his being noticed, by means of mirrors and pipes." Surprise! Now we have police and surveillance. And that ingenuous philosopher goes on: "That would be a very important thing for the State, and a sort of political confessional." And if someone asks, Where's the opera? here it is, next sentence: "And the opera, or the Academy of Music will be attached to it." Opera, to make the trick work, to add a powerful distraction. Opera, to seduce ears while hands toss money on the table, and while the "masters of the house," hidden in an invisible room, note everything well, hearing and seeing it all, the faithful who reflect the king first and then God. In Giacomo Puccini's opera *Tosca*, the chief of the Roman police sees all and hears all, in a room high in the Farnese palace, while the queen dances and while, in the next room, the secret revolutionaries are being tortured.

Yes, Leibniz, that philosopher, certainly had a funny idea. But it is a very coherent idea, one that transforms the opera, the men's house, into a place of artifice, a container of illusions and sciences of illusion—optics, war, theater, society—where police surveillance is in effect. It is a thought putting optics and acoustics to good use, deriving political advantage from the illusions themselves. Was that the danger Rousseau sensed? He detested opera and theaters; he hated the French royal celebrations and preferred simple ones, celebrations that spoke to the heart. He would banish harmony (still too close to a symbolic architecture of the unequal divisions of society) and have men and women sing melodies in unison, and more melodies. . . . And, in *La Nouvelle Héloïse*, Julie's enclosed world, a utopian space itself, peasants, servants, and masters join in singing the old songs beside a lake, at the foot of mountains, in the heart of nature, far from scenery of gauze and painted wood. Densely foliaged trees replace portals, unembellished voices replace arias, carefree clothing takes the place of feathers and embroidery. . . . How beautiful that would be. How beautiful that can be sometimes, a marvelous, unpretentious moment of celebration, an unexpected meeting, music with no harmony, unorchestrated!

But Julie dies of pneumonia, her face decomposes under its enveloping veil; she smells. The world is evil, the city perverse, and nature elusive. And Julie's garden, this natural paradise, is just a gardener's artifice. Can one dream within society? Not possible. The wonders of opera do not leave even Rousseau cold: "this strange theater." "All jumbled together we see gods and goblins, monsters, kings, shepherds, fairies, rage and joy, a fire, a jig, a battle and a ball." The inventory once again—the collection of pleasures and marvels. A whole, crowded world is talking to itself; a whole society watches its own dreams, its own struggles, and gazes at its gods descending in magnificent, heavy machines. And, if there is no king making his entrance into the city to receive the homage of the subjects he has finally conquered, it is because there is no need for it. The Nation is in existence. In the eighteenth century opera begins to trace the republican figure, still veiled in divine figures and machinery.

VERDI. A century later the letters forming the name of opera's most famous composer serve as a magic symbol for the incipient Italy, a nation, finally centered on a new-look king, Vittorio Emmanuele Re De Italia. And in Venice thousands of bouquets, thrown by thousands of hands in the white theater of La Fenice land on the white uniforms of Austrian officers. Visconti knew his history. But this historical overture is the introduction to the story of a woman. When the stage is set, what remains is the scene and the show that one has come to see. What remains are stories unwinding amid flat scenery and footlights. The operas remain.

I have seen these operas at work; if I am touched by them it is because they speak of women and their misfortune.

In the great house at the heart of the city, and with the greatest pleasure, I have seen and heard women caught in a network of cruel intrigues. I have cried with joy at the sound of voices, I have clapped my hands to express my happiness, I have dreamed and felt. Little by little dead women, suffering women, women who are torn, have appeared before me; it was like an immense plot coming out of the depths of time, created to make one see these women preyed on by their womanhood, adored and hated, figures who simulate a society that is all too real.

My first opera, when I was a little girl, made me laugh. Memory conjures up a so-so opera, a sort of operetta, with scenes that change before one's eyes, swirling costumes, sunny palaces, congenial inns, a raised dagger, black eyes. It was *Pelléas* and there was nothing like that in it. The persistent fog, the simplicity of the words, the foreignness of a sad story, and then this woman giving birth on the front of the stage—that was funny. For weeks I put our daily life to song, pseudo-Debussy, quasi-Maeterlinck. At the dinner table it amused the guests and family. I was taking my place in the bourgeois farce: making fun of an opera that is its reflection nonetheless, and laughing at the pastiches that opera is full of, without even seeing them. The joke lasted a long time. In a sense it is still there. But it is inside out, like a glove: like anamnesis in a psychoanalysis.

Later, opera made me cry. It was the same thing, minus the family dinner table. It was just the same, too much life. A little girl unconsciously making fun of herself by imitating adults, those unknown giants, or a woman who cries unaware of where the tears that come from nowhere are coming from, have the same physical reaction. It is the same emotion, revealed without warning by life's delayed reaction. There is nothing sillier than seeing a love story sung on stage. Opera is grotesque when one takes the slightest distance on it and sublime when one goes along with identification. The baroque perspectives through the sumptuous house, with its extraordinary richness, the scenery, the staircases, the hallways, all transform the spectator into a character participating in a comedy. And he participates not only as a decorative extra but as an actor caught up in an identification for which he has paid.

Risk-free identification: that is "music." The old Brechtian problem of distancing is thus relegated to the fog obscuring things that are true. No risk: the words in opera are seldom understood, either they are in another language, or they are made inaudible by the singing technique. No risk: one makes a pretense of not being interested in the plot, which is completely unimportant. So one is moved for no apparent reason, what bliss! This gift is attributed to grace, to the prima donna, to leisure, to the miracle of opera. It is most particularly important not to know one's position there. It is important to ignore it. When you leave it is all over. Outside it is chilly; it was a beautiful performance.

The unconscious, however, does not hear it with this deaf ear. It drills deep; it grasps the story's deep structure for the spectator; it finds the phrase, the word, or the gesture that precipitates identification and provokes tears of joy, that is to say, exultation in a make-believe, pointless pain. The music makes one forget the plot, but the plot sets traps for the imaginary. The plot works quietly, plainly visible to all, but outside the code of the pleasures of opera. It is totally dull, always setting in play vague philosophical premises, ordinary banalities, life-love-death; it is all familiar and forgettable. But, beyond the romantic ideology, lines are being woven, tying up the characters and leading them to death for transgression—for transgressions of familial rules, political rules, the things at stake in sexual and authoritarian power. That is what it is all about. A Gypsy loves whomever she pleases and goes off with the smugglers: *Carmen*. A Moor who is a foreigner in Venice marries one of the lagoon's daughters, too blond, too far-removed: *Othello*. A prostitute permits herself conjugal love: *La Traviata*. An *infante* of Spain loves his stepmother: *Don Carlo*. A one-eyed god quests after incest and absolute power: Wotan in the *Ring* cycle. A singer kills the chief of the Roman police: *Tosca*. A Spanish nobleman defies heaven and his father: *Don Giovanni*. That is what it is all about. What is played out for us is a killing—for our pleasure, with no risk. Whence the laughter, whence the tears. Whence, occasionally, pain and anguish.

Later, after having industriously learned all the theories, old and new, on the subject of opera, I knew, along with Brecht, that opera provided the more pleasure the more unreal it was; with Lévi-Strauss that, like any cultural production, it was a matter of family and structures; with the psychoanalyst Rosolato, that voice was related to drives and to genealogy. I felt a sort of shame and remorse when I read, in Adorno, that only Schönberg met with approval and that there were musical beauties that were bad for you. And I trembled listening to Tosca, and I loved the traviata's death; I felt guilty. Oh I knew some things, some useful, well thought out, true things, things inherited from a culture that so many others had duly thought: so many, who were men, had thought.

I did not know the same thing for myself. All that knowledge seemed deaf to something. Something was going on there, none of which they heard. When you turn the knob on a radio, seeking, not knowing what, absentmindedly turning, and suddenly a woman's voice rises, very high—that is happiness! When you walk in an Italian street, siesta time perhaps, in the hot sun, and hear a voice suddenly rise! All of opera is present in an instant. No matter where, here it is, alive again in all its splendor, all its display. The aria goes around, mouth to ear, and belongs to the people. A whole population will adopt it stripped of its nobility, even those who end up forgetting where it came from. When Sacco and Vanzetti began their last walk—to their execution, they sang Mario's aria from the last act of *Tosca*: "*O dolce baci o languide carezze . . .*". Oh sweet kisses, oh languid caresses, the prisoner sings in the moment of execution; in the opera it was a farewell to life. In the American prison where the two convicts were going to die, like the fictional Mario, from police abuse under a racist regime, it was a farewell to the Italy of their childhood, an operatic farewell. It was a disturbing way of saying one is foreign, affirming what one is dying for. In the street, the song stops; the street is as before. The rare passerby walks on the shady side.

Opera concerns women. No, there is no feminist version; no, there is no liberation. Quite the contrary: they suffer, they cry, they die. Singing and wasting your breath can be the same thing. Glowing with tears, their decolletés cut to the heart, they expose themselves to the gaze of those who come to take pleasure in their pretend agonies. Not one of them escapes with her life, or very few of them do . . .

Women like me from an earlier time, come. Come in procession, so your death at least will be triumphant. In dirty rags, in court robes, half-dressed, in an empress's rags, dressed like a geisha for innocent colonialists, you drag yourselves around when you are consumptive, you dance when you have been stabbed or suffocated under shields, you die strangled by hands that are black, you succumb to a princely kiss, you throw yourself from the top of a Roman palace, you jump into the fire. You cry, you laugh, you trill, you call out so far your voice cannot help but fail you. . . . You are faced with the spectacle awaiting, in that black hole full of eyes shining with joy. Just like in the circus, you will have to leap without a net and destroy yourself. You are there to enact only one thing: to die on stage, to die of fear, to pretend you do. You are there to demonstrate, with a splendor that is done for, the woman who is in front of men's mirrors. Those people are the ones who created you. This is just like a maze leading a desperate rat to the end predicted by the test, where his cheese awaits. A golden maze, made from exquisite statues, velvet loges and lights; where in front of the chandeliers and brilliant lights, the voice is conducted by ins and outs of scenery, by plinths and posts into its space; where the narrow passages of arpeggios and octaves lead to the sound the audience will give in return: applauding, killing, adulating, then forgetting.

There was a child, whose name was Maria Felicia Garcia. When her chance came to sing in the tragedy *Othello*, her father threatened to kill her on stage if she did not sing well enough. She became Malibran. This child, another one yet always the same, used to wander in her petticoats around the streets on the edge of Paris, in the alleys of Seville, and on the ramparts of a Nordic castle. She turns into a prostitute, she drinks the demimonde's lethal champagne; she works in a cigarette factory, smokes cigars, and tells her own fortune; she wanders in a forest, she has lost the crown, the crown he gave her; she is carried off on a boat full of men by an unhappy hero who is taking her to someone else in his kingdom. Touch them and they leap. Into the water, into the sea, into love, from the top of a prison. Touch them and they sing "*Lasciatemi morir*." Let me die. They sing it in a voice that touches the heart, a heartbreaking voice that makes you cry. This child, at the end, will die. Poor and tubercular; stabbed at the arena's gates while the cuadrilla makes its entrance; she will give birth to a baby girl and pass away in silence; she will leap on Tristan's body and die of sorrow, or joy. Between the childhood, left behind, and the deaths of Violetta, Carmen, Mélisande, Isolde, there will have been these spectacles. The women button up their gloves again—that was last century, but make no mistake, it is also today. The men, exhausted from listening, put on their coats and make their comments. Life once again takes on the value of an intermission. The women leave the stage and go off in turn to eat, talk, screw, and sleep. Until the next time they have to work on their scales: the scale of voices, the whole range of fears.

This perfect spectacle has finished the creative stage, and repeats in this century the love stories of the last. It has overflowed the theater and the stage and produces operatic effects all over the place: in the movies, in musical comedy, in theater and in the texts of novels. The song of these dead women and these prima donnas feeds the forms of a production endlessly trotting out the long story of its passions. No doubt we are at the end of the track, where we finally have to get out. Just when there is a rebirth of opera, when the halls are filled with spectators, old and new, is it possible to escape the heritage, to bank on something else? Is that what I want?

There however, in opera, the music of the court once linked with divine power to make an audience sit still before a story that was sung. There the triumphant bourgeoisie set its passive rear end down to watch these family stories, *prima della revoluzione*. There a marvelous legacy perpetuates new massacre, threaded through with history. There, perhaps, the nineteenth century, whose models, ideas, feelings, ways of loving we still drag around in our forgetful memories, finally comes to an end. There, as always, die the gods that Christianity interminably kills and resurrects. There sing the voices lifted in agony, forsaken, lost, never more powerful and disturbing than when all the illusions show us their sorrowful faces. Lost song for a dead opera; and song found again for an opera that is bursting forth, springing from sources that are always fresh: women suffering. . . . *"Lasciatemi morir."*

Duets on the Golden Calf

And so I am going to talk about women and their operatic stories. I am going to commit the sacrilege of listening to the words, reading the libretti, following the twisted, tangled plots. I am preparing not to follow in the great forebears' footsteps—I refuse to take such well-trodden paths; *initially* this is not to be about the music. What do I make of the music? It is everywhere of course, even in the words. The women sing and the melodies carry them away. However, I am determined to pay attention to the language, the forgotten part of opera. The part that always keeps to the shadows, although the words are still sounds and make music. But it is not that easy . . .

Often the men are musicians or musicologists. One of them plays a piano. The piano has almost a physical attraction for him; he caresses it, makes it glow like a woman brought to climax. He shines its black frame and golden insides, he manhandles it. He represents all those for whom the music comes first, as the invincible giantess, the supreme mistress, love in the absolute. And for him opera is perversion itself. We have had this discussion about opera hundreds of times, our lines so mechanical that often the soundtrack could run by itself, scratched, like an old record. Just the same old song somehow.

He says . . . the words of language are an unacceptable interference in music that cannot be permitted. It should be possible to banish them all. They prevent one's really hearing. They are parasites. Static. Angrily, he goes so far as to call it a penetration, as if the music were violated, pricked right through its virgin hymen. And this brilliant metaphor sheds a lot of light on this violent resistance to language. As a man he discovers in music something feminine that is more than woman, something feminine that will never let itself be penetrated, never be had. He turns both women and language into interminable plays on words; his readings take a Joycean turn and ally themselves with Freud, in his serious-minded dissection of the linguistic mischief of the unconscious. What gets away is perfectly obvious; the piercing of the hymen speaks volumes in fact. This perfect musician is a Don Juan who has invested the enveloping nature of music with the fantasy of an ever elusive, inviolate woman. Impenetrable; that is why he loves and protects her.

With all his might. Schubert makes him cry less with his lieder than with his piano music, and he can hardly stand the titles chosen for their works by a Rachmaninoff or a Chopin. He is relentless. From that tirade (longish already) he goes straight into the history of music. I will go along with it; lectures can be useful.

So I learn that there was polyphony in the sixteenth century; that counterpoint was born the way the alphabet book was born; and that opera made musical composition regress, arresting its development. We could just be coming out of this stage now that opera is exhausted and creates hardly any new productions. Still docile, I will go along with this. But I am thinking about those young composers, a bit desperate, yet full of musical energy, who search in opera's mythology, in its sources, for something with which to nurse their creation. Yes, nurse, the way one goes back to fresh milk, to a vital flow without which no image is articulated, no sound exists. This pianist in love with a particular music endlessly rehearses a repertoire that a single man has created, for an audience that is occasionally scarce, an elite whose ear is trained. Then I think about opera's audience, partially composed of fanatics who will not let one note of the score — which they sometimes bring with them into the theater — escape; partially composed also of innocents who have never read a single note on a single staff but who know how to listen, hearts thrilling, tears in their eyes, without understanding what moves them. I think of the great rite that completely eludes my good old pianist, of this social celebration where it is music nonetheless that reigns, a celebration conceived, from its beginnings, for the people. One that people have been able to appropriate for themselves.

The lecture continues.

A bizarre reasoning unwinds about a history that could be broken by the birth of opera, as if somewhere there existed a single history whose course could be thus interrupted. He is describing a dream. In some mythical space, it is the perfect and nonexistent history of a music in which opera would be only a childhood rash, a sort of measles. Anachronism bores me. I yawn. All around me flutter my favorite ghosts, Violetta's cries of pain as she says good bye to her lover; although he does not know it, Tosca's agonies, Carmen's provocations, ghosts that reach a certain point in the ear and soon are in the mouth. I often find I am singing to myself like this in real life. Sometimes the words of my heroines get lost. Sometimes even, for the brief instant of a possession releasing me from the ordinary, I don't know who is inhabiting me.

But with a little probing, I know why this tune, and this woman, have come to find me. A word the unconscious has caught in flight, a reply in a conversation, an unexpected association, or a latent conflict are calling. The melody comes back first; it is not separable from the words that make up its retinue. This man, impervious to an entire world, is finally getting on my nerves. Mozart wearies him, he detests Bellini, Puccini is vulgar, Verdi pretentious; and the whole thing is figurative, therefore, not musical. It is, he says, the Golden Calf.

The Golden Calf! Why did I not think of it sooner? The sacrilegious idol built by the Jews whom Moses abandoned, stands for the unclean, for debauchery. Golden Calf, money, wealth, the bank; Golden Calf, capitalism, bags bloated with dollars, prostitution. And for a musician, even more for a soloist, opera is truly the Golden Calf; it is facility, scenery, the image made of history. So this is my Moses, ascetic purity, aesthetic chastity, the artist's proud poverty, generations of Rimbauds, whole pleiads of the accursed. . . . The innocent beast with horns on his head and an Egyptian gaze symbolizes an opposition that was not born yesterday. Yes, the Golden Calf, something the people like, like opera. Yes, there is always some Moses to come down from his Sinai and destroy the idols. But it will be done at the expense of joy, at the expense of happiness, and for a religious mortification in which no image is to be displayed again, in which no pleasure is to be found except in the face, eternally invisible, of a hidden God. Like that music-woman — inviolate and inaccessible.

Talk talk talk. Bluntly, teasingly, this is for all the Moseses, all the censors. Talk talk talk, said the Jews to Moses, while they danced around their new god, and while he, the other, absent one, talked to himself on the top of the mountain. By a perfect coincidence it happens that one of the last operas in history is called *Moses and Aaron*. With perfect consistency Schönberg never came to the end of it; the opera is unfinished so that there, as everywhere else, there is no Promised

Land. Something very interesting is played out in it. For this borderline opera concerns the impossibility of opera itself. Two characters engage in dialogue: Moses, who does not sing but speaks and Aaron, his brother, who does not speak and who gets the singing part. In other words, the best part in opera. One defends idea and theory, by means of plain words, which have no place in an opera; the other defends image, figuration, and incarnation. Moses is a contradictory hero who resorts to talking in a place where only singing is expected; and Aaron, a heroic tenor with a flashy voice, retains the lyrical language that opera audiences of the period could recognize, like a beloved code. A dialogue between the people and their guide is developed on the stage of this opera, a dialogue between pleasure and asceticism, between the knotty music of speech and the divine, rare, exquisite, impossible word.

Impossible, in fact: Moses is defeated. Alone he is incapable of speaking to the people who do not understand him. He needs the support of Aaron, in other words, the support of music and magic: the stick turns into a snake, the water into blood, it rains frogs. . . . Only then, through the intermediary of phenomena that captivate the gaze, is the God of Moses acknowledged as omnipotent. But for Moses this God is an Idea and nothing else. Consequently, if it is necessary to go the route of images to convince the people of the existence of this Idea, it is a failure. Did Moses create an illusion, a fantasy for himself? His last words are those of defeat: "I created an image thus for myself, false as only an image can be. Thus am I defeated. Thus everything I thought was only madness. It cannot, must not be said. O word, thou, the word I lack." Schönberg stopped there. And this so-called unfinished opera came to the logical end compatible with its internal consistency.

An admirable representation on the opera stage of a divorce that is impossible: mere speech is powerless to convince through the force of the Idea alone. "I do not understand," says the pianist then. "You are searching for the meaning of the words in opera, and we have just had a whole tirade against Moses, the one who speaks, the powerless." Yes. That is because in opera there is no Moses and no Aaron. There is no naked speech and no song without words. Moses and Aaron represent well the two terms of an opposition brought together by opera, which moves endlessly from one to the other, never settling down. No word, even rapid, or isolated, has any value without the chord preceding it or the punctuation that follows. When Floria Tosca, in Puccini's opera, contemplates the body of the chief of police, stabbed by her and lying at her feet, and says, "And all of Rome trembled before him," this spoken speech, with no orchestra, is surrounded by an ample musical movement that calms the violence of the murder and subsides. And, as soon as the phrase is complete, the music starts up again, like a lingering echo, accompanying Tosca's flight. No music, even if it is interim music, played without the singers opening their mouths, has any value without the words that brought it on, and without those that are to follow. When Butterfly waits a whole night in silence for the man she loves, and whom she has not seen for three years, a long musical moment describes the sunrise on the port of Nagasaki; but it ushers in the day, the disappointed expectation of the little Japanese woman, and is the prelude to words of death. So much the better if opera is the Golden Calf. After all, for the Jews who were so long enslaved in Egypt, this bovine and glittering beast, made from everyone's jewelry, will be a real god, one as venerable as Yahweh.

Moses goes grumbling back to his piano and consoles himself by returning to the lovingly mystical relationship he maintains with his idol. Hot on his heels his brother Aaron shows up.

He is a good opera lover, like so many. He does not know music, at any rate he does not know its rudiments. (For an entire elite group, "knowing music" means knowing how to read a score, and being able to follow the complex developments of a specific writing throughout the history of music.) But this man loves opera. He invests all his passion in it. And tucked away safe and sound, he possesses all for himself, an immense knowledge about opera recordings. He could even recognize by ear Callas's voice singing in 1802 (his first tooth); Sutherland's accents singing in 1870 (his first long pants); Nilsson's sublime cries singing in 1914 (his first wife); and Malibran's sighs singing in 1950 (his first heartbreak). He has them all, every one. He has official recordings, great majestic subscriptions boxed sumptuously, rerecordings in mono where the voices are not very stable, but so very moving, faded and old-fashioned, as well as pirated tapes circulated under the cover of coats—everything. One might say that, frustrated in other knowledges that chance has prevented his acquiring, he pounced on this compilation and there finds his language for music. There he recognizes his emotions, transformed into living files; his memory fills a Borges-like library, where records are like books, true or false, that haunt the long corridors where day by day he classifies. His conversation is incredibly boring. You would say it was the slow maturation of a thesis whose critical notes are the essential thing. And words do not count for him either.

Oh, the words do not bother him. But does he even know they exist? That is not certain. Nobody listens to the words, nobody pays any attention to them. . . . Words—just incidental! What is all this about meaning? Nonetheless, he is capable of reciting a complete aria, after a fashion, with all these famous words-that-do-not-exist. See what a strange phenomenon this is! It is as if the words were in a foreign language. It is true that he likes neither *Carmen* nor *Pelléas* and that he is one of those people who thinks French opera is not successful. Of course, in one's own language it is rare that one can avoid the meaning. A French person singing Carmen understands the words of "a dark eye watches you," and "Toreador," and "love is a gypsy child." There is no getting around it. One has to understand. I think that that is the secret cause of resistance to French opera: meaning exists, no more mystery, so long exoticism. Mockery pours in through

this breach in the fascination of unknown language, and that grumpy Saint-Evremond (of all the men in the world the one most impervious to opera) comes
back. "Can one imagine a master who calls his valet, or gives him an errand by
singing; that one friend tells another friend a secret by singing; that a council
deliberates by singing; that orders one gives are expressed in song; and that men
are killed in battle with swords and javelins, melodiously?" Yet, in Italian, Count
Almaviva speaks to his valet Figaro, who replies: "*Se vuol ballare, signor
contino.*" If you want to dance, my little count, I will hold the guitar!

But Saint-Evremond is more bothered by orders that are sung than by the rebellious answers they can be given; even though, in fact, Figaro's lively and violent
song foreshadows the French Revolution. Is that another story, another history?
No, it is still the same. The least word bears centuries of history and culture
within it; the least word stirs up flocks of ideas, as birds are flushed when dogs
find them.

Our man knows neither the words, nor the stories. But he loves this psychotic
language. For many people it is made of Italian (and his body is roused by love);
for many of German (and, despite himself, his body bows in thought, kneeling
before Wagner's metaphysical aria); for a few of Russian (with onion spires hanging over crowds that are always subjugated); for a few this language is made of
Spanish, Czech, or English. It is an ecumenical language, where unknown musical words are strung together for the pleasure of an ear that is finally released
from meaning. He loves to say that music is what provides the meaning, which
is false; because, although it accompanies, completes, provokes, or slows it
down, it does not give meaning to words, which have their own power and their
own internal sense. He loves to say that the charm of opera is that nothing is
understood and that it is better that way. Silence. I wonder about that.

Am I somehow different from these other people around me who are wild
about opera? An opera whose words I do not know, draws me in and attracts me,
of course. But, when I know the words, the passions, what is at stake, then opera
wraps me totally in a world of fantastic clarity, of matchless life. The music is
then revealed in all its richness. There are two irreconcilable options, two irreconcilable ways of living—and of living opera: understanding it or not; enjoying
the effects of all the actual implications or being satisfied with what is not known.
The marschallin's long German monologue in *Rosencavalier* seemed sublime to
me, from the moment I learned that she was describing there her childhood and
the wrinkles now appearing at the corners of her eyes. The slow quintet of the
Meistersingers filled me with joy, when I was able to understand how old Hans
Sachs, the cobbler-poet, was expressing a cruel disappointment, masked by the
flights of music. But why deprive those who take pleasure in this mysterious language of their happiness? Why ruin something made not to be understood, made
to speak to that part of childhood that hears the mother, feels her close by, without yet knowing the meaning of those caressing words?

So I abandon Aaron, in the middle of a long discourse on the comparative merits of Caballé and Callas in the Aix-en-Provence and Los Angeles recordings. I could care less whether Maria Callas ever sang in California, and I take off. The opera lover plays with his amulets and wraps the Golden Calf with new garlands and his tender arms. The dead part of opera, language, is *my* problem.

Opera: it is a scene where words cannot be said except in sounds structured by music. It is a double scene where two languages, the spoken and the musical, employed by two authors, the librettest and the musician, play inseparably. The ineffable Saint-Evremond (him again) took this conjunction as reason for ridiculing opera: "poetry and music in a strange operation, one in which poet and musician, each one hampered by the other, go to a lot of trouble to create a poor product." Everybody ought to know about this combination; yet, in reality, what happens? *Don Giovanni* is Mozart's opera; *Otello* Verdi's opera, and the librettist, throughout opera's long history, is buried in the rubble of a text that was necessary but duly abandoned. I will not even mention what are generally agreed to be "bad libretti"; no doubt they exist. Instead, I will talk about the real writers like Da Ponte, the coauthor of Mozart's opera, of Boïto, coauthor of Verdi's best operas, and for good measure I will add those who are writers by profession who have devoted time to writing opera libretti: from Hofmannsthal to Hélène Cixous, with Maeterlinck between, they exist. But . . . at the most they are allowed a few good words, or a conscientious rediscovery. Sometimes on the radio one hears "Let us not forget." "We should not, however, forget that Da Ponte was an inspired librettist." Yes, he wrote the text of *Don Giovanni*, attributed eternally and to the end of time, to Mozart alone. Yes, the libretto of *Pelléas et Mélisande*, and Maeterlinck's words, so naked and so sad, heard with such pure lucidity, are an essential part of the opera. "We only know the underside of destinies, even of our own" and "I see a rose in the shadows" are unforgettable words. And could Leporello's aria (the one called the catalogue because he counts the beautiful women his master Don Giovanni has already seduced) even exist without "the scrawny one" and "the pudgy one," "the young one, just a novice," and the number "a thousand and three" so perfectly punctuated by the music? Opera music makes its empire and steals the glory, dispossesses half the authors, permanently strips them of their work — without which opera's song would have no place. And the libretti are orphans.

Opera's recent evolution produces yet another occultation. Now it is not even the musician who is the author. No, it is a third thief, who takes advantage of the other two: the director. I heard *Simon Boccanegra* called an opera by Giorgio Strehler. (This was so strange that I did not understand what was being said.) Pretty soon they will be saying that *Lulu* is an opera by Patrice Chéreau. An interesting development. I see there something like the latent return of the opera text. Because not every director is granted this prestigious paternity. Those who acquire it are the ones who reread the opera and who shape it; they pull from the words themselves, and from their surroundings, ideas that are capable of updating, or just plain bringing back to life, words that until then had only served as pretext for the song. This revival of opera through its staging does not give the authors of the words and story back their names; but Strehler's direction, and even more Chéreau's or Jorge Lavelli's, is first of all a work of reading.

These men know that an opera libretto is a history lesson. And that this lesson is not clear in the spectacle to be performed unless it is visibly taken from the *Zeitgeist*, the spirit of the times that gave rise to it. In this way *Simon Boccanegra* is restored to clarity, despite the extreme complication of its plot and despite its ellipses. The history of the people of Genoa and of the city's internal warfare produces the unfortunate destiny of the people's doge. With a single image, a sail hoisted and then lowered around the man who was first a sailor, explains the Genoan spirit that Verdi and the three successive authors of the libretto[5] wanted to communicate to ear and eye. One single gesture, discovered by the director, adds a sign to the many already in place.

This is a meditative period that we are in now, one in which opera, exhausted on the level of creation, is rediscovering its sources through a historical reading. The direction, whether distanced, critical, poetic, dreamy, or combative, develops the scenery, the gestures, and the objects, and gives the space a historical depth that it has doubtless never had before.

History lessons. All Verdi's operas are linked to a political or ideological struggle. Today *La Traviata* is no longer the story of an unhappy love between a prostitute and a slightly crazy young man, it is the cruel conflict between the family, its property interests, and the parallel world of prostitution. *Otello* is not simply a drama of jealousy, it is the racist conflict between a powerful city and a Moor the city needs. *Don Carlo* is not the moving tale of the thwarted love of two young people; it is a complex conflict between the Spanish Inquisition, the heir to Charles V, the people of Flanders, and, lost in all these obscure plots, are two young lovers made incestuous by a royal treaty. Verdi is obvious. Others, those to whom we have always attributed the song that is sung from the heart and stops there, are less so. For example, that is the stubborn mythology that goes along with "victim-women in Puccini's operas." It is an Épinal imagery (with its psychological gloss, naive characterology, shopgirls, and faded flowers) of an opera that is limited. As if "the heart," that powerful reality, could be separated from the story. As if every love story were not linked to how one married, the customs, the unconscious resistances, to the immense weight making each of us a pawn on culture's chessboard. Butterfly is first a Japanese woman, the unknowing prisoner of a tradition that obliges her to love a single man and to die of dishonor. That this man is an American sailor is not just a comic detail. It is the condition of the colonialist misunderstanding that leads Butterfly to suicide. When it is a matter of dreamlands (the case in *Turandot*, whose action takes place in a fictional China), we find the old projections of a Europe that, around the eighteenth century, began to make productions of China, setting there, in that faraway country, its own transgressions, fantasies and desires. None of these "women in Puccini's operas" can be understood without history. Perhaps no one knew better than he and his librettists how to show a destiny and a politics that were intimately inseparable, right down to their final crushing action.

There is landscape in opera. You see the sets and you will not forget that they are artifice and construction. But, look, in no time at all, surrounding the wonderful voices rending your heart, you see the forest where Mélisande is lost; it is the Middle Ages, the time of the sorceresses, no man can live there without fear, and the enigmatic Mélisande has lost a golden crown at the bottom of a spring. . . . Look at the dark pines and the shadowy spaces of an Altdorfer or a Dürer. Look, in Puccini's (and Giacosa's and Illica's) La Bohème, at a romantic Paris, its wretched poverty and the icy cobblestones where the barricades were born; look, beyond the conventional poetry of youth that adapts to everything, at a life destroyed by the lack of food and warmth. Look, in Bellini's (and Felice Romani's) Norma, at druidic foliage imagined the way imagination in a century in search of its origins would; look at Rome and Gaul, and the hesitant, empassioned quest that the nineteenth century was able to make in search of its cultural origins. Look at Poussin, where almost invisible at the foot of giant trees, there are tiny characters, wearing togas, tunics, blue cloaks blown by the wind: opera characters.

You think that it is the characters one must see, that they are stage center, that they fill it with their song, but their song itself, and the orchestra that expands the set ad infinitum, sets them in immense countrysides with lost horizons, where they are no more than little symbolic figures. They are tiny actors in a history where nature and culture seek, thwart, and marry one another—part and tear one another apart.

There are entire cities in operas. You can see Nuremberg in the fifteenth century, Renaissance Windsor, Moscow at the time of Peter the Great. When the Bolshoi theater produces operas, it does not skimp on history. Horses—real ones, like there used to be in Valkyrie—drag prisoners in chains or chieftains with armies to the front of the stage. The steppe inhabited by Tartars looms on the horizon, and Peter the Great's army marches in the snowy forest. No, this is not incidental. It is essential. These are the signs, the words of the complex language in which, according to the blissful theoreticians of the eighteenth century, all the arts were united. Fontenella went so far as to say: "I always imagine that nature is a great spectacle like that of the opera." What owes what to what is thus reversed; but opera has never stopped being a figure of the world and its conflicts. So why is music privileged?

Brecht, who put his mind to everything pertaining to spectacle, said some things on the subject that have always seemed convincing to me. "Opera's unreasonable side comes from the fact that there are rational elements employed there,

that *a certain* materiality and *a certain* realism are pursued there, whereas the
music nullifies all of that. . . . The music makes the reality vague and unreal.''
Yes, the fictional realism of forests, cities and closed up rooms does seem to drift
off in some powerful current that provides those boundless landscapes, those
exploded spaces, and those seas that go on forever. . . . Yes, the music and the
particular narrative it implies overflow theater's very real limits. You are present
at whole sections of story and history told by the music.

A double, inseparable scene: the words give rise to the music and the music
develops the language, gives it dialect, envelops it, thwarts or reinforces it. Conscious and unconscious: the words are aligned with the legible, rational side of a
conscious discourse, and the music is the unconscious of the text, that which
gives it depth of field and relief, that which attributes a past to the text, a memory,
one perceptible not to the listener's consciousness but to his enchanted unconsciousnesses. A word seeps through, an aria. This is the beginning of the opera.
You are not on your guard. The story advances. But at the moment of denoue-
ment, at the crucial moment when, in a flash, the conflict is played out in all its
violence, the tune comes back without its words. You are caught up in a musical
memory. And, even if you are not paying attention, you will have ''gotten it into
your head,'' as they say, you will have the barely formulated idea of this ephemeral word that is now returning in your unconscious. At the beginning of (Verdi's and Boïto's) *Otello*, the Moor embraces his blond, white wife and asks for a
kiss, and the music is all passion, everything light and pure, a wedding night.
But when he has killed her, the same music returns to complete the words that
he, stifled by death, is already no longer able to speak. That is how music works
on words.

The words are forgotten. An extraordinary paradox: in a world where the
unconscious takes up so little room, where so much is made of spoken words, as
if they meant what they said, with no past and no roots, we have the opera, where
the conscious part, the part played by words, is forgotten. No doubt it is because
opera is the place for unformulated dreams and secret passions, a place Brecht
saw as the link between pleasure and unreality. Consequently, the less one hears
the words, the greater the pleasure. . . . As if in a dream, I am just beginning to
understand the ambivalent fascination, the black and white magic — other people's opera. And I begin to give some more thought to the women: those massa-
cred women who are everywhere in the operas we love.

Women again. I hear a kind of irritated, ironic grumbling — the same old thing.
It is not very different from the timid, groveling objections that leave the talking
to women: you talk talk talk, you talk all the time. It is true that this can be annoy-
ing, this sometimes incoherent speaking. Too often it is dictatorial, with excesses
that are completely unjustified from the point of view of freedom's extremely
simple requirements. But one has to get used to it. We are in a period when soci-

ety, too long forgetful of those it has abandoned (who are right there, so close beside it), is rebuilding.

Women again. In opera, the forgetting of words, the forgetting of women, have the same deep roots. Reading the texts, more than in listening at the mercy of an adored voice, I found to my fear and horror, words that killed, words that told every time of women's undoing. It is perfectly obvious, you are vaguely listening to the story of a very unfortunate woman. But, so, they are love stories, and then, is that not women's fate? Oh voices, sublime voices, high, clear voices, how you make one forget the words you sing! How beautiful is suffering's melody, how good it feels to suffer an agreeable little sorrow, scratching the surface of the soul to give it depth, without really hurting it! I am not forgetting that is a prima donna who sings, and that she is playing a role, but I am too well-acquainted with the powers of spectacle not to watch fiercely with all my eyes and listen with all my ears to the stories repeated a thousand times by men who pursue women and reduce them to nothing. Do you know that *"lasciatemi morir"* means "Let me die?" It is the abandoned nymph's lament, the lament of every Dido and every Ariadne, the lament of woman. The only course open is death: that is opera's innermost finality.

These women have the most beautiful music; the glitter of spotlights is theirs. Adoration and sublimation, a formidable love that must forever be conquered and danger that is absolute are theirs. And the act of falling, the final gesture is theirs as well—and the voice in its death agony. When the men die or are defeated, it is because they have some unremarked traits deriving from a femininity unerringly detected by the opera. The ones defeated are the weak sons, the lame, the hunchbacks, the blacks, the foreigners, and the old men—those who are like women. The triumphant ones are the fathers, the kings, the uncles, the lovers. Authorities are triumphant, and so are Churches; above them a divine image is barely hidden. The defeated are the forces of the night, the forces of darkness, the forces of the weak and underprivileged. Defeated are paganism with its many gods, the rebellious, desirable existence of the sorceress, and any transgressions. Opera is pitiless. The nineteenth century extended the powers of opera, to love (this formidable and fatal mythology), but certainly, it is in the dawning of the eighteenth-century Enlightenment that the religious forces that brought opera into existence are to be found—along with, I would say, the struggle against God, through women who are crushed.

My passion is addressed to a man. To him, so that later he will be able to see and hear. To him, so that he will understand, and a bit of the reality of my life and his will change. Perhaps it is a man I love. Perhaps it is my son, who has never yet wanted to go to the opera, because his universe is elsewhere. But someday, no doubt, he will go, and then, perhaps, he will know something more about it. He is a young man. This is for him so that, when the time comes, he will love differently; so that the music and the words will be clear to him; so that his pleasure will be all the greater because he can understand the opera's story and history, and that of past centuries. . . . Perhaps it is you. It is you.

Chapter 1
Prima Donnas,
or the Circus of Women

*In which we see them flying, dying, and singing, in mirrors
deep inside mysterious castles; in which voices have their
source in fathers' threats and mothers' absences; in which
they collapse in tears; in which they kill and leap into the
void from prison tops: in their own darkest midnight hour.*

Listen. One day a wild-haired poet, in the dissipation of his old youth, wrote a
cantata for a choir of singers and a prima donna character.

The singers say:

> Young men are calling, calling
> Everywhere
> At the windows of the world
> On the brink of day
> They call for help.
> Places for the moon to sleep, the women dead of
> love . . .

The Prima donna answers without answering:

> See see how I can fly
> I can stay up alone
> Detach myself from earth
> Spin and rise
> Rise wingless, wingless
> Climb into the air the way you fall
> Gently
> In a whirl.[6]

Look. In the middle of the ring, a luminous circle lit by white spotlights and
a trainer wearing a ringmaster's uniform magnificently decorated, officer-style.

He holds a long whip in his hand as if to tame a wild cat. In fact he has a wild animal act. Here comes the wildest of all, the animal that spelled man's ruin: the snake. Enter the marionnette woman: this is the prima donna.

Her name is Lulu in Alban Berg's opera; she is one of those so-called femme fatales, you know, those evil women. Her name is Lola, in Max Ophuls's remarkable film, *Lola Montès*; she acts out her own life, her own part. The prima donna also, the prisoner of the circle of light that fixes her in place, lures her in and wounds her, exits into the fiery role assigned to her by the world. In the film *Lola Montès*, the tamer who is in love with Lola conducts her in living tableaux. Spangled, white, ostentatious, and golden, they spin out the dream life of a heroine who turns her real experiences into circus. Young men in uniform, wearing black masks, pass long-handled purses to the spectators, collecting the dollars that grant permission to question Lola. She replies in her blank voice, a living museum figure. "How many lovers has the countess had? Does the countess remember the past?" and the camera shoots dizzyingly away while Countess Lola dreams for herself; but that is not her role.

She will make it to the end of the performance. Right up to the dangerous moment when she has to jump, from the heights of the big top, and land in a basket. "Are you ready, Lola?" asks the trainer with his golden whip. She is ready. Everything around her is toppling, but she is ready. When the jump is over—this evening and every other evening to come—Lola in a flannel bathrobe, stripped of her tutus and the fragile, black swan's crown, is exhibited in a cage. Where wild animals are kept. Men can pay a dollar to touch one of the two hands dangling through the bars. And two endless lines wait to kiss this woman's hands, to kiss a bit of serpent. Here ends the story of a woman who, to make her living, acts out her life in performance.

This Viennese tale filmed under a dreamlike Barnum's big top is a perfect metaphor for the prima donna. The femme fatale, the empty woman, in costume, on stage, off stage, the bearer of a destiny that will never be merely a life because all around her opera's magic creates its powerful effects, swells all her actions to overflowing, transforming them into dramatic art. Remember la Castelfiore, whose caricature in *Tintin* reveals the truth about all prima donnas—the theatricality of her least gesture, the horrified cries delivered widemouthed in a stage voice: "EEE-EEE-EEE . . . ". Her head is completely surrounded by the cry and her fat body is ridiculously contorted. She makes her blunders in the grand manner, she flutters and she sings so loudly that Captain Haddock's cap falls off. And she wears jewels that will be stolen. She wears her Marguerite-in-*Faust* wig, whose false braids cast her as an eternal old maid. She is the sole important feminine character in this oddly homosexual realm, where an old kid in golf breeches and a drunken captain spend their time saving the world. What real, flesh and blood woman could be integrated into the stories of Tintin? None who might go along with any possibility of desire that would transform one of the heroes, young or old, into a lover. None who might simply be possible. Bianca Castafiore is impossible; she is not really a woman, she is a prima donna.

Listen some more; you know how much I like to tell stories. In the books you read as a child, do you remember those ghost women? Once upon a time, in a dark country haunted by vampires and black forests, there was a castle in the Carpathian mountains. The author, Jules Verne, says very specifically that this story is not "fantastic"; "it is *only* romantic." A young count from Telek is in love with a diva, the romantic Stilla. One day she decides to bid opera farewell—on stage at the theater San Carlo, in Naples. But when she comes to the scene in which the heroine dies, she sees a horrible head staring at her from a loge. She falters, her mouth becomes red with blood, she cries out, and "La Stilla is dead. . . . A blood vessel has burst in her chest. . . . Her song dies with her last breath!"

She is dead. But not quite. The young count nearly dies, as he should, but at the end of a long quest, a long voyage, he hears the beloved voice one evening, alive and singing in the Carpathian castle. He even sees her, white in her opera gown, still singing. . . . When she comes to the fatal note once again she stops, and once again she cries out. But she does not fall. The mirror reflecting her image smashes into thousands of glass splinters, and the machine that repeated the singer's voice breaks in pieces. The second Stilla was only an illusion, a ghost pieced together by a mad lover; she was integrated into a phantasmal machinery that caught up the desire of a man in love with only the voice of the dead woman. The castle is swallowed up in a violent explosion; the voice of la Stilla will never be heard again.

The prima donna is the prisoner of a machinery, and booby-trapped by a machination. She is a living doll to be carried off and taken around for one's personal pleasure. She takes the place of the child's object: a stuffed animal endowed with a maternal voice, a teddybear that, in her womanly weakness, will never get away.

Once upon a time in Paris there was a grand opera, newly constructed with tunnels, corridors, and a great, hidden, inaccessible pond.[7] There was also a debutante prima donna, Christine Daaé, surrounded because of her growing fame by favors and rumors. And there was a strange phantom, who haunted the velvet loges, killed the stagehands, who were discovered hanging behind the scenery, and terrorized the opera's little world. The phantom loved the prima donna, and, without showing himself, whispered in her ear to make her think he was the Angel of Music. And it is true that, aided by the miraculous voice of the faceless man, Christine Daaé sang marvelously. To ensure the glory of his beloved, the phantom of the opera went so far as to sabotage her rival's success. When the rival opened her mouth, at the very moment when the astonishing sound sure to guarantee her triumph was to come out, instead, out came a "toad." A horrible "couac." The opera director sat in the loge haunted by the phantom, loge number five. Listen, the phantom's voice whispers in his ear. "Tonight she is really going to take the chandelier down with her singing!"

Look up! The huge chandelier is coming loose, falling into the clamoring audience. It kills an innocent old lady, during her first night at the opera, with all its crystals. Voices bring down lights; they do things, they kill. But their power depends on a pitiless chastity. And like Stilla, Christine loves a man who is not the phantom. The phantom, to protect her singing, carries her away. (Same scene, same structure: a prima donna, a divine voice, an inhuman love linked to pure song, a human love that everyone knows will extinguish the singing fire, like a pail of water thrown on a blazing hearth.) The phantom carries her away, taking her into secret rooms where he has fixed himself a fabulous domain right underneath the opera. The phantom of the opera is another Leibniz: he has built listening rooms, halls of illusion, rooms for torture, where one believes one is dying of heat and thirst. He has built a powder keg that is poised to go off.

The prima donna will be saved, married, and silenced, deprived of her song. The poor phantom, because he showed her the face that even his mother could not look at, dies, the way a flame is extinguished. He is already dead; there is no skin hiding the death's head he has always had for a face. Christine Daaé and the phantom, or the eternal couple: Death and the Maiden. They loved each other with a pure love, Death and the Maiden, they loved each other as in Schubert's song, and their duo stemmed entirely from their two disembodied voices. Song, or horror of bodies. Christine when married will sing no more.

And once upon a time again, there was a poet named Hoffmann. He lived, he wrote, he composed, he died. But Offenbach made him the hero of his only opera, *The Tales of Hoffmann*—a wonderful one, which is not well enough known. He loves—all women. He loves—a memory, an arm seen in passing, a shadow seen in a window. The young, motionless silhouette sets him afire. . . . She barely speaks—an incredible attraction; she does not eat—an appealing proof of her good education. But she sings delectably, a little song she knows by heart, in a voice that is a touch inhuman. Everyone around him has caught on; but the smitten poet tries to touch his idol, press her hand, squeezes her arm. . . .

Then she explodes. Her arms fall off, her head rolls to the ground, smoke pours from her body. She was a doll, an automaton. There has been all this machinery surrounding prima donnas, and now—this performance where the prima donna herself becomes a machine. The prima donna is a phantom presence, whose body is expressed only by voice, whose existence is created only by voice: the new Eve, she is the place of illusion.

Listen. The poet of the dreamy stars, the author of the *Parents terribles* has the prima donna sing:

A prima donna
Is a column broken in two
That bleeds from top to bottom . . .

Callas and Malibran

When she died, discreetly, lost to a heart attack when no one was looking at her anymore, when she died her real death, the sad phenomenon of posthumous adulation began for her. A few months later, time to dictate and publish a few hurried words, there appeared some pathetic lovesongs glorifying Maria Callas.

They were all men, these eulogist clowns.[8] They sometimes developed theories of homicide. We are the ones who killed Maria Callas. "We" (speak for yourself) made her have to be thinner so her heavy silhouette would become the tragic will-o'-the-wisp, mad as Lucia di Lammermoor, inspired as Norma, consumptive as la Traviata. So there she was, figured and disfigured, eternally confused with her heroines. False tombs, word tombs, faithless from the beginning; she had been reproached for being a woman of flesh who loved ice cream and candy, and who loved with love. How could the real Maria Callas, whom I do not know, interest them? The men writing about her, necrophiles and necrophagiacs, revel in her trembling image on those old documents. Moving arms, a changing mouth, eyes that knew how to look down to better open wide, immense, in the blazing sun of stages, emerge there, living. What haste, what hatred drives them thus to reduce a woman to her image? They ramble on until they run out of words, about the voice lost along with the fat, about broken notes. Their pleasure is extreme, what violence! She is silenced by them, flattened as mortally as Dorian Gray was by his immortal portrait. A three-dimensional woman, living flesh, reduced to ashes (her wish).

She died a banal death. But her ashes were stolen from the Père-Lachaise cemetery; a pyre of books was built for her; hastily pressed records were sold in abundance.[9] Come on, men, shut up. You are living off her. Leave this woman alone, whose job it was to wear gracefully your repressed homosexual fantasies. Do not dress her up any more. Strip off all that false love and suffocating tenderness. Let those ashes that she wanted to be ashes have some peace. The only man who hid nothing from himself, loving her enough not to want to make song from her, Pier Paolo Pasolini, is also dead. But the remains of them and their encounter will be the image of a Callas surrounded by brilliant flames, a woman at bay whose face trembled slightly through the flows of expression caused by the burning heat. This blurred face of a Medea, speaking and no longer singing, that was Callas, in flames.

I am remembering—while, fugitive and sunk in calm oblivion, the arms that flutter around Callas's face turn into silent film—the image of a fat woman. A tremendous pile of meat that sings for us, and is alive. She is tremendous, a fat lady who knows how to turn her weight into opera. Her name is Montserrat Caballé. She weighs so much that she is incapable of expression; fixed superbly in her song, attentive to vocal perfection alone, she sings as if she sought to banish the memory of the one who sacrificed her voice to the perfection of a body that finally conformed to death. Oh Caballé, deformed idol, never get thin. Stay buried in life, in the anger that occasionally stirs you. Norma grown old, an imposing matron, be able to stay ugly. Thank you for being so, in the midst of those masculine wings, flapping their useless hands, their empty hands all around you. Never will there be anyone like you, gracelessly touching the ground at the end of *Roberto Devereux*, in the real despair of a useless, fat body. No one else will ever be able to tear off the abandoned Elizabeth of England's little crown and cry out her woman's aggression.

But this—what a coincidence!—is an opera in which the heroine does not die. The fat queen lives, disappointed, deceived, and cuckolded. And Maria Callas who knew how to die like a queen is dead. The prima donna has to appear the way men want her, like that other woman dressed up as a woman, Norma Jean, who was called Marilyn Monroe. And there is a lot of writing about them. Feathers, eyes rimmed by false lashes, artificial blondness, whimsy, and a body dressed as a woman. . . . Men have transformed these bodies according to their image. If one of them commits suicide or falters, the vultures are after their feathers. And the stink of their writing is stronger than the natural corruption of those dead bodies they dare to write about.[10]

And, silenced by emotion, I applaud. Next to me is the man I love; he looks at me, his eyes full of love, and is moved by my emotion. Anger, futile, furious anger comes over me. Ah, will I never be able to untangle myself from this two-hearted ambiguity that makes me, a woman, watch wordlessly as if I could not speak, the perfect, always perfect, putting to death of my people?

> I am bleeding from love, and no one
> Leaps forth to help me . . .

Do you know the story of Maria Malibran? One can no longer draw a line between dreaming and reality. Her father was an illustrious Spanish tenor, Manuel Garcia. She was a skinny little girl, whose portraits and descriptions resemble those of the tragic actress Rachel. In 1825 she was sixteen. Her father played the role of Othello in Rossini's opera, and they lacked a Desdemona. Manuel Garcia gave his daughter six days to learn that role. She did it. He warned her that if she was not perfect in the role, the first one in her life, he would actually kill her, during the performance. It was her real father—and a false lover. The evening that this fictional and real drama was played, she was so sure she was going to die that when her father took hold of her to strangle her, she grabbed his hand and bit it until it bled.

Later Malibran, now a diva, repeated this original scene in which she had played both her life and her voice in one body. She—a soprano—sang the role of Othello. And did she terrorize some unknown Desdemona? I do not know. The song of fear was definitely the only true one: the song sung under threat, torn out by paternal Law, with nary a shadow of loving mother there to help the prima donna. . . . Parents are terrible. The first thing they impart to these badly loved daughters, trained from childhood in the disciplined exercise of singing, is fear.

She died young, at twenty-eight. She had a riding accident and was wounded in the head. That very evening she played in Bellini's *La Somnambule*. For one last time she was sublime, wearing makeup and a wig that hid her bruises, in a role where the torpor of her injuries strengthened the strange, hallucinated aspect of the young girl who sings in her sleep. Then she lost her voice, and finally her sight. Six months later, still singing, in spite of everything, she died. Her corpse stirred up passion and song. Her body was dug up several times, and buried as frequently. The poor bodies of prima donnas—destined for desecration! What remains of her are a few verses by Musset and a harrowing film by Werner Schroeter, in which blood and snow become a sort of funereal finery for her to wear.[11]

Just as Callas had her opposite in the gentle Tebaldi, Malibran had her reverse double, a rival who was blonde and cold, whose name was Henriette Sontag. Malibran, Callas, Caballé, Sontag. . . . Strange, foreign names. The prima donna comes from somewhere else, as if exile were necessary for her to become famous. No doubt one can look for the sociological or technical explanations. But I see something else. Foreigners are necessary to assume the strangeness of a woman who is not really a woman, the perfect disembodied mannequin, whose voice is all that is alive. The Spanish Malibran, Austrian Sontag, Greek Callas, left their roots, finding in displacement and the loss of a birthplace the source of their mythic power. The successors to the *parents terribles* are the adoptive country and the vague paternity of a dangerous and adulating public—a symbolic and demanding father for whom they will go so far as to die of their singing. Yes, opera surrounds the prima donna with a family. A family with fearsome prohibitions: no marriage without approval, no love other than those spectacular loves, meant for display, that are part of their role. The same thing goes for toreros. In the bullfighting section of Madrid, it is not good form for a "real" torero to be seen in public with a woman he loves, with two exceptions: stars and whores.

This adoptive family watches over its golden daughters jealously, cloistering them in a web of lights that let nothing escape. Once, the great prima donna Cornelia Falcon became hoarse. She was treated, went to Italy to recover her voice, and finally dared return to the stage. But there was nothing; no sound, no voice. Charles de Boigne, who was in attendance that memorable evening, described it. "This performance, that should be a family party meant to celebrate the return of the prodigal voice, turned into an evening of mourning, where two thousand spectators sorrowfully saw the irreparable loss that art has suffered." She sang, nonetheless, sobbing on her partner's shoulder, trying between sobs to produce a voice that would sing only unspeakable sounds now. . . . She was never seen again.[12]

But de Boigne's words still speak. "A family party." "The return of the prodigal voice": the voice, the runaway child that has left the heart far behind. "An evening of mourning." The prima donna is a child-voice. If the voice disappears, the public mourns the child. Although a body remains, and a voice still able to speak . . . that does not count. The opera family displays its mourning, while Cornelia Falcon, having banished portraits of herself and scores, shuts herself away until her death. Maria Callas no longer went out in public, but remained cloistered, enclosed within an endless listening to a dead voice. She would not accept that it was time to mourn it, although the public long had done so. And this public finds other children, other voices sprouting to assuage its devouring affection.

One more step, over a fine line. . . . There are prima donna characters in opera itself. Because they are the objects of reflection, a place where mirages occur, they had to give rise to operas with their own character as heroine. Here is the queen of the dead prima donnas; here is sweet Antonia.

The story: Hoffmann, the poet—the real Hoffmann loves a real prima donna. While she performs on the opera stage, he projects onto her three memories of love that are haunting and destroying him. Three women: a prostitute in Venice who stole his reflection after making a pact with the Devil; an automaton who falls apart in his arms; and a young girl, Antonia, stricken with a lung disease that forbids her singing. Her father and her fiancé—Hoffmann—watch over her and promise her a calm, bourgeois, family life, without song. Then the Devil meddles; he raises the ghost of Antonia's mother, who was once a singer herself. The young girl surrenders to their temptation, sings, and dies because of it. Hoffmann drinks so heavily to forget his misfortunes that he collapses dead drunk on the table. When the real singer comes to meet him, he cannot even stand up. So she goes off with someone else.[13]

No one saw more clearly than the court jester in his old age; no one went further than Jacques Offenbach. To the point of putting on the stage both a real prima donna—who does not sing, the role is spoken—and a "false," dreamed prima donna, who dies from singing too much. The real prima donna (Stella-Stilla, the star of artificial nights) performs her job as singer; she is hardly seen. But Antonia . . . Antonia is the fantasy of singing in its purest form. Surrounding her are a prudent, kindly father, a cozy, flannel poet, and a whole future of marriage and children: Germany's three *K*'s, Kinder, Kirche, Küche. Children, church, and kitchen. A woman's life all in all.

But that was reckoning without the mother. For, like Christine Daaé, Antonia has no mother. Their childhoods were spent in the shadow of a possessive, abusive father. (Who was Maria Malibran's mother?) This father forbade singing. Because, the mortal threat lies where the hand rests on the heart. The vessel breaks, the heart fails, bursts, as if some invisible track of life linked voice and heart. As if pushing the voice too far made blood spurt out, as if the precious liquid in its turn rushed from the body. . . . Antonia is no longer able to sing. But first, her mother's ghost, raised by the Devil, grows insistent inside her, and then, all around her. The prima donna mother has only to call her daughter by name. . . . Another feminine voice has only to evoke the mother's voice for the daughter, prisoner of an absence permanently inscribed in her desires, to resist no longer.

She sings, like tumbling into the arms of a loving mother; she sings, like having fun, like drinking, like loving. The waltz is trivial, a little silly; the Devil and the mother join in with their nonexistent ghost voices. But the little song rises above them, dominating its parental shadows with a voice finally set free. Every flight soars higher and higher, bringing the moment of her death closer and closer. She falls, stifled by her song, dead of nothing, dead of the speed and drunkenness of a wild song; dead of nothing except song itself.

The two living men, the father and his son-in-law, run to her side—where the devil had they been, abandoning the young girl to her despair? Tail ends of voice trailing off to the soft accompaniment of cellos . . . scraps of song, "a song of love, crazy and sad" . . . that is the end. But what did she sing, just before dying? "It is my mother . . ." was her dying sigh. Yes, it is the mother, always, hidden under these masks of men, the giant, absent mother who eats dead daughters and devours their voice, so that the sons in drag have revenge on all women. It is just an entertainment, you see, the most successful, the most sumptuous, the easiest—the most beautiful show.

The hysteric at her midnight hour

> See see how I can fly
> Spin and rise
> Rise wingless, wingless
> Climb into the sky
> The way you fall . . .

They do fly. Great, absent-bodied birds, they fly away without the wings of Icarus, without feathers stuck by fragile wax to their shoulders; they fly away on the wings of song, and fall back to earth, like Icarus, burned from within. Mythical androgynes, with the sound that comes from their bodies they collect all the fantasies of sons seeking mothers and of abandoned daughters. This crazy, sad song of love is theirs. And Offenbach's innocent melodies, in their miraculous, simple freshness, connect with the very essence of myth. Behind the sublime voices and tortured bodies, the parental history, the eternal story of the hysterics plays out.

Frau Rosalie H. wanted to become a singer. But at the age of twenty-three she lost her voice. There was a lump in her throat; she was strangling. An analysis of her vocal cords revealed no anomaly, no constriction. She went to see the good doctor who took such fine care of hysterics. The good doctor, who had not yet become Sigmund Freud (it would take a few more years), hypnotized her. Frau Rosalie then remembered her childhood. An orphan, she had been raised in the home of her aunt, who was brutalized by a violent uncle, who was "obviously sick" and a womanizer. The mean uncle suffered from rheumatism; he wanted Rosalie to rub his back. And the scene—that terrible scene of all hysterics—followed the inevitable scenario.

"He was in bed, when, suddenly, throwing off the covers, he stood up and tried to grab her and throw her down." Just by remembering this man standing before her, whose powerful erection the good doctor suggests without saying, Frau Rosalie regained her voice. For the scene to be perfect, we must add, as did Doctor Freud, the information that he later tacked on to all his studies of hysterics. "Here, once again, it was the father and not the uncle," Freud wrote when he had become famous enough to dare speak the truth. So this is the voice's source: paternal violation—the secret fantasy that gave Maria Malibran all her voice, that made the sweet Antonia die, and that forever drives the imaginary figure of the prima donna. A timid, absent mother who has disappeared; a powerful, possessive father.

A bed, nighttime, a man standing, a muffled cry . . . and a woman who, following the repetitive modulations of her imperious body, sings, or can no longer sing; a raised voice, or one that falls gently away, a voice brought up by a silent blow. Choked with fear: Manuel Garcia was an analyst father, a brute of a father who played at strangling Desdemona to bring to life the voice of his daughter, the prima donna.

A bed, nighttime, a man standing, a violent cry . . . "Genti, servi, al traditore! . . ." Come, my men, my servants, after the traitor! . . . A woman wearing a nightgown, her hair down, emerges from her room to publicly denounce a rapist. She bandies passionate insults with him. She calls him a scoundrel; he calls her a madwoman. Madwomen. He is always surrounded by them. He, of all opera characters, has provoked the most commentary, and is the most ambiguous. And he, of all the fortunate or unfortunate phallocrats we are to meet throughout the operas, is the one who is the Rapist. This is Don Giovanni; no longer entirely "Don Juan."

The story: Leporello, the valet of Don Giovanni, a Spanish noble, keeps watch while his master breaks into the bedroom of a young girl, Donna Anna. Since he manages to be caught leaving the room, the young girl's father challenges him to a duel; Don Giovanni kills him. The young girl, who does not know her violator, swears she will have vengeance, with the aid of an innocuous fiancé, Don Ottavio, who tags along behind her like a puppy dog. Unscathed, Don Giovanni goes his way. Plagued by a woman whom he has abandoned, Donna Elvira, he assigns Leporello the task of getting rid of her, and hurries off to new conquests. The next will be a peasant woman, Zerlina, whom he seduces during a party celebrating her wedding to young Masetto. Elvira, Ottavio, and Anna conspire against the debaucher. During a splendid celebration that he organizes for the peasant couple, with the firm intention of finally seducing the bride, the three characters unmask themselves and threaten Don Giovanni with vengeance from heaven. This is not long in coming. Don Giovanni, as a joke, has invited the funeral statue of Donna Anna's father, the commander, to dinner with him. And the statue answers the invitation. Before the eyes of Elvira, begging her seducer to repent, and the terrified Leporello, the statue talks with Don Giovanni. Finally, it takes him by the hand and drags him off to Hell. Now that they are rid of Don Giovanni, all the characters get over him, and each of them seems to regain his or her tranquil existence, as if nothing had happened.[14]

So, there are three women surrounding the seducer. Three women represent the biography of seduction: the one already seduced, the past, the abandoned Elvira; the violating seduction, the present, Donna Anna; and the seduction to come, Zerlina, Don Giovanni's future. But each seduction has an element of rape. How do we know? By tracing the route taken by little Zerlina. Seduced, she gives her hand, and her body begins to let itself go. Twice the "bird in hand"[15] goes along with the intoxicating words and subtle music. When Don Giovanni finally manages to drag her into a separate room and starts doing things, there is a scream. The same scream that Donna Anna cried out in the darkness; the same scream that Frau Rosalie, hampered by the terrible figure of a father with an erection, cannot utter. Yes, at the end of the charming seduction is rape, its underlying violence. A brutal Don Giovanni, presses with all his weight, as inexpert in love as he is gifted in leading up to it. Zerlina cries out, with all the might of her deception, and the rape is a flop. Because, do you see what a strange story this is? This much sung character, this Don Giovanni who is so fascinating for generations of men with anxious peckers, is a pathetic man who does not get what he wants. Perhaps, perhaps this indeed is secretly what this opera is after.

There are so many theoretical fantasies invested in the image of Don Juan—and especially in Mozart's *Don Giovanni*—it would be difficult to expose them all, like taking slightly dirty adhesive off a messy cut. Let us give it a hard pull.

All these women around him are hysterics. Entrapped by a figure, a cloak, a hat, all are ready to give in to a mannequin passing himself off as Don Giovanni. Donna Elvira, who knew Don Giovanni's body and his voice, therefore lets herself be led off for a quick embrace by Leporello whose master has momentarily loaned him his cape and his hat. The real signifiers of Don Giovanni are empty clothes. There is nothing else. This is how hysteria functions. It is good for seducing, good for identifying, good for locating oneself with empty images, in order to reach the moment when she shies away and screams. In the stories of hysterics, the rape never takes place. All that is clear is that there is fear, threat, and the great, shadowy silhouette waiting in the dark.

So Freud, after having listened patiently and with tremulous passion to thousands of stories of hysterics raped by thousands of fathers, was siezed by great doubt. History was shaking on its foundations, and the founding father of the illustrious psychoanalytic science found himself confronted by an impossible dilemma. Either all the fathers were rapists or all the daughters were damned liars. He did not think too long about it; he worked too much by divine inspiration. And, because he sided with fathers, he decided that the sin lay with the daughters.

Now we have lying hysterics. They are touched by a lie whose significance is united with the most Christian of metaphysics. They bear the curse of the sorceresses, and of my mother Eve whom I can never thank enough for her boldness. OK: we lie. Maybe Donna Anna was never the object of an attempted rape; no doubt Don Giovanni went to her room to talk politics, because it seems he represents the revolution also. Maybe Zerlina cries over nothing. No doubt they are victims of their fantasies. Maybe all the evidence always given by cops about the obvious desires of raped women is true too. Musicologists see things no differently: both Henri Barrault and Pierre Jean Jouve, see the women surrounding Don Giovanni, and above all Donna Anna, as desiring rape.[16]

Let us tug a little harder on the adhesive tape. Yes, I know, when you pull slowly it hurts more. But this is important: inside Don Giovanni's cloak is hidden the fantasy of almost every man in love with opera. So, step by step, OK? Faced with these madwomen who are enamoured of rape, women who are ready (this is true) to rip the rapist's body into shreds like tearing bacchants, Don Giovanni is also a liar. The mannequin cheats with everyone. It goes without saying that he cheats with women; that is why one goes to hear *Don Giovanni*. He cheats with God; and the hypocrite philosophers' bellowing trumpets strike up a loud tune about rebellion against the social order. The simple fact remains: Don Giovanni lies to everyone. He is even flanked by a valet whose job it is to reinforce the lie and substantiate the myth. The catalog song sketches a seducer capable of having seduced "*mille e tre*" females. A thousand and three women: it is the superfluous detail, the three women tacked on, that alerts you to the lie and its mischief. Lie is shared all around; and Don Giovanni goes beyond the mythical difference between the sexes to join his feminine accomplices, by a subtle ellipse. He is hysterical like them.

The only ones who will say he is homosexual are those still unaware of the existence of bisexuality. Don Giovanni's homosexuality is scarcely more important than the powerful homosexuality binding the three seduced women and transforming them into avenging Christians. But Don Giovanni's hysteria is the emptiness of soul behind the cape and cloak, the marvelous and sublime put on that grips anyone in his presence, the comedian's paradox. A phantom of a man, a masquerade as perfect as that of the prima donna; and, like the prima donna, Don Giovanni escapes from his original sex to place all the ancient fantasies firmly within himself. The prima donna, costumed as a woman, is not a woman; Don Giovanni, decked out in masculine effects, is not a man.

Man and Woman: the opposition slips away, fugitive, captive, passing endlessly from one to the other.

In Mozart's opera, hysterics of both sexes are in collusion—the inspired man risking his ambiguous hide because he tried too hard to be incorporated in feminine fantasy, and the madwomen surrounding him, who in fact, have his hide. Don Giovanni is not far from Orpheus, torn apart by the violent bacchants intent upon their secrets and intent upon this man who was both too close to them and too far from them; because he too desires this. Freud reckoned only on the great primitive scene between father and daughters; he had not thought of the complex and tender scene that is played out, in *Don Giovanni* between a son and the daughters.

For who are the men surrounding him? A valet—less than nothing, a human double, a genuine soul, outside of the masters' circus where he is looked on as a sham. A puppet fiancé, a flimsy tenor, good only to huff and puff behind an Anna who is raging, whose fury he cannot calm, who will send him to wait in a corner while she goes into a convent to regain her breath and the memory of her cry in the night. And a father. A father who is weak and conquered at first, who is presented on stage only to show a quick and perfect death; but a father brought back to life in the dreadful figure of a stone statue, a father who swings from singularity to the universal. At first he is the father deprived of Donna Anna alone, then he becomes the father of all, but especially of Don Giovanni. And the final scene where the two voices respond to each other is the exact equivalent of the seduction scene between father and daughter: a father, standing, in the darkness, and the cry of the foundering hysteric. But this time the hysteric is a man. And everything changes as a result. No one sees the female part of Don Giovanni. His revolt is interpreted as something that only men are supposed to do: a sacrilegious and profaning act with an exalted idea.

I am much more seduced by a Don Giovanni shot through with panic yet standing up to everyone to fill as best he can his manly rags, than by the brave, raping hero who has been so praised. It is time to smash this idol and restore it to a truth, which, although no longer Mozart's truth nor that of the eighteenth century, is ours. If women are the only hysterics, the first lie, championed by Freud following so many others, will always pursue us. If men can be hysterics, we will share equally in the fantasy, the masquerade, the imaginary that is intersected by sexes escaping into each other, and we will no longer be mad or damned. We, as women, will be mad together with this cotton hero, and we will surround him with the tenderness he deserves. Then perhaps he will get back something more than the phallus he wears desperately with the guile of defeat — his missing sex.

At least one man would have understood something about all this — Louis Aragon writing *La Mise à mort*. A writer, who is as like him as a brother, is in love with a prima donna whose life he espouses. She has a stage name for others, a doubly foreign name where the mythical North mingles with Edgar Allan Poe's shadows: Ingeborg d'Usher. But he wants to call her other names he has found for her: Fern, Dawn, Madame, and finally, Murmur. Murmur . . . a very low voice, whispering in the ear, the opposite of the voice that opens out and sings. This obsessive caution will not keep the writer from utter defeat. When she sings, he is lost. When she sings, he is nothing anymore, despite his own celebrity. "She sings and I have stopped existing in order merely to follow. . . . What it is — is a flame like a bottle of perfume spilling, it is a happiness finally, more felt because of some ineffable absence, it is boundless unhappiness that contains itself only to grow." How well he knows! He suffers so from this that he becomes jealous of himself. To the point of not being able to meet his own eyes in a mirror, because Murmur's song is a spinning mirror that breaks all images and disconcerts the subject. And when he has pushed jealousy of himself to its farthest limits, he shatters the mirror and his reflection in a definitive act of madness. Oh ghost of Stilla. . . . But the story is reversed. The epoch when phantom prima donnas haunted the mirrors of their worshipers is past; in Aragon's prophetic novel, the prima donna is unscathed for the first time. And it is the man who is shattered, a crumbled reflection, undone, finally hysterical, attaining a masculine truth repressed by centuries of phallocracy.

The writer said of her, of the beloved prima donna: "This is always a woman who has reached her midnight hour." Isn't it the truth. Men are at their midday, the daylight hour when all the shadows are clear, when confusion is impossible; they live according to organized work time, the calm, social time where paths are marked. In the opera women do not sleep at night. They weep, they rebel, they wander, they pray, they kill if necessary: they act. Midnight, for them, is the hour of the eternal sabbat, their hour. It will cost them their lives. Othello, having scarcely awakened from murder will contemplate Desdemona's dead body at dawn; at sunrise Butterfly will seek the ancestral dagger to plunge into her abdomen. And life takes a turn, the mirror of song veers around, on the stage of the opera the usual values are toppling. Night opera, midnight women, tomorrow will be a day like any other, but tonight . . .

The quick feet of passion

It is a warm night and peaceful stars dot the sky when Floria Tosca stabs the chief of the Roman police. She is the most straightforward of all opera's heroines, the most the prima donna. It is her "real" profession in the Rome of 1800 where the drama unfolds. She sings in churches, in palaces, and on the stage. With her culminates the myth of the prima donna finding its perfect fulfillment. The story turns her life into a stage production, as if the stage were tailor-made for her. She will make opera within opera from the death of others; and with her own death, she will make singing's most symbolic gesture. Floria Tosca hurls herself from the top of the ramparts of Castel Sant'angelo: "Look look how I can fly . . .".

The story: Floria Tosca, the celebrated singer, has a young, revolutionary painter, Mario Caravadossi, for her lover. When the opera opens he is in a Roman church working on a portrait of the weeping Magdalen. He is alone but more or less surrounded by the sacristan who brings him food and cleans his brushes. A man, a fugitive, comes to find refuge in the church and asks Mario to help him. It is the former consul of Rome, Angelotti, who has just escaped from the Castel Sant'angelo. Rome in this period is under the protectorate of a queen and under the dictatorial rule of the chief of police, the fearful Scarpia, who hounds republicans. Mario hides Angelotti in a chapel, gives him lunch, helps him escape, and offers to hide him in his own house. But Tosca comes to visit her lover. She notes, jealously, that the Magdalen is the portrait of a penitent woman who comes often to pray in this church: a blond woman with blue eyes, the marquesa Attavanti. She does not know that the marquesa is Angelotti's sister and that, although she does indeed come often, it is to leave women's clothing in the chapel for her brother to use as a disguise in escaping. She makes a scene with Mario, orders him to give his Magdalen dark eyes, and then plans to meet him that very evening in their little house. There is the sound of a cannon. Angelotti's escape has been discovered . . . unless, perhaps it is to announce the victory of the royal troops over Bonaparte. Enter Scarpia. He announces that there has in fact, been a victory, and that a Te Deum is to be sung that very evening by Tosca in thanksgiving. But Scarpia discovers signs of Angelotti's flight: a fan he left behind, the basket of food that has disappeared. Tosca returns to the church to tell her lover

*she will not be able to meet him, and Scarpia rouses her jealousy, playing with
the fan that bears the marquesa's coat of arms. Tosca runs off; Scarpia has her
followed, certain that Angelotti will be wherever she is to meet her Mario.*

*In the second act, Scarpia is waiting. Mario has been arrested; Tosca is sing-
ing on a lower floor of the Farnese Palace beneath Scarpia's apartments. Mario
enters in chains. Scarpia questions him while, in the distance, Tosca's voice can
be heard singing. When she has finished, she too is summoned by Scarpia, who
has long desired her and is going to have her now, two ways, mixing police and
eroticism. Mario will be tortured in the next room while Tosca listens and little
by little gives in. She reveals Angelotti's hiding place to Scarpia. But a messenger comes to announce that the victory being celebrated is really a defeat (it is
Marengo). Mario loudly sings a republican profession of faith. So his death is
certain. Tosca tries to buy Scarpia with money. But he wants something else,
Tosca's body. She gives in under duress. At the moment when Scarpia throws himself upon her in an embrace, she stabs him with a table knife and takes the safe-
conduct that he had written for her and Mario, the promise of a fake execution,
making it possible for Mario to escape.*

*In the prison at Castel Sant'angelo, Mario calmly awaits his death. He is writ-
ing a last farewell to Tosca when she appears, bringing hope. They are saved.
All they have left to do is submit to a masquerade of execution. Tosca accompanies Mario to the firing squad. She watches the actions of the soldiers, the guns
being prepared, and after the shots when everyone has left, runs to Mario to tell
him he can get up and run away. But Scarpia deceived Tosca. The execution was
real; Mario is dead. At that very moment Scarpia's death is discovered and the
soldiers arrive to arrest Tosca, who leaps into the void.*[17]

Tosca, vertigo. The vertigo of a voice experiencing the events of opera within
an opera. A solitary woman's voice, driven, sped up, pressed by men. Tosca, or
jealousy and song in a mad race on the quick feet of passion. She never stops
running, entering, exiting, panting, pressed. And when by chance she is not on
the stage, her prima donna's voice fills the space outside, and suddenly everything is paralyzed, tenderly, as if for a moment she suspended the political drama
and the schemes of the men around her.

In the great church of Sant Andrea della Valle, the sun enters through clear
windows, lighting up the bright chapels and the religious paintings. Caravadossi
lolls around, the sacristan hovers about him, everything is cheerful. The violence of the world of politics is veiled and latent, suddenly appearing in the person
of Angelotti, the hounded fugitive. This is a man's world where there is no place
for the prima donna. The two men, Angelotti and Mario, talk to each other in
low, quick voices, until . . .

Until the voice is heard. Outside, behind the heavy doors of the church, the
voice calls, three times, more and more urgently. She calls, and everything stops.

She calls, and everything is quiet. Accompanied by very long *pizzicatti*, she enters quickly, as she always does. Her arms are full of flowers; she is innocence itself. The text states that she enters *"con una spezia di violenza."* With a sort of violence. From her very first words she is suspicious. Why had Mario locked himself in? Who was he speaking to? Lovingly, he lies, "To you." It takes three phrases before she regains the musical tenderness that went along with her flowers and her sweetness. Then, without thinking, in a pose where the gestures of the prima donna ennoble those of the stubborn little Roman woman whom she never ceases to be, she offers the flowers to the Madonna and kneels devoutly. Pause, pose, place the flowers, the voice is calm. Not for long. She starts right up again. Voraciously jealous, capable of anger because the sketch of a Magdalen promises to have blue eyes, and hers are dark, she fights affectionately. Do not forget that Angelotti, hidden in the chapel during all this banter, is dying of anxiety while he waits to escape. But Tosca does not know; Tosca knows nothing.

All she wants is Mario, the signifier of her impatience. She spends the entire opera calling him. From outside, when she comes into the church. From inside, when he is in Scarpia's torture chamber. She calls him from everywhere. When she comes back after Angelotti has fled and Scarpia has arrived right on his heels, she calls him again. That is when Scarpia, the hunter, baits Tosca, his falcon. With a single note he unwinds the thread to set his amorous trap. Mario's absence and the marquesa de Attavanti's fan—that is all it takes to send Tosca flying, pouncing on the lure. But before she goes, she weeps, and never is the music more powerful and tormented than at that moment when the loving accents of a love duet that has already died are echoing. The voice wavers, falters. So, she is to fall.

A warm, peaceful night. A night of celebration for the Roman monarchy. Through open windows, Scarpia hears instruments playing a gavotte. He has Rome in the palm of his hand. He rules the queen and the society. While he interrogates Mario, Tosca's voice suddenly rises above the others. And Mario, who held up against the questioning so well, softens: "La sua voce . . .". Her voice, her voice that is coming from another world, from the brilliant, despotic world whose harsh, dark face Mario is experiencing. The carefree voice professionally pursues its tune. . . .Tosca still does not know. Scarpia orders the windows shut. No more voice. And the light charm that held the two men in suspense, like a promise of tenderness, breaks off.

She enters. She calls. Once again her first word is "Mario!" He is there, a prisoner, hidden in a secret torture chamber. This is the role of her life as prima donna. A period of torture, a period of calm. A period of torture, and the open doors let the men's voices through, Mario screaming in pain, Scarpia questioning. A period of calm, the doors close, and the broken prima donna confesses, without singing any more. This is no longer the voice, these are spoken words.

How does she manage to come back to life so quickly? She is usually in such a hurry. How does she manage the time for a long, intimate breath, at the very moment when every exit is barred? Nonetheless, she must choose in that instant between bed with Scarpia, or Mario's death. And the voice relives her whole history, in the famous aria *"Vissi d'arte."*

"Vissi": I lived. *"Vissi d'arte, vissi d'amore"*: I lived for art, I lived for love. Just as in those privileged moments in analysis that are known in psychoanalytic jargon as "insights," in the twinkling of an eye, everything is understood. Everyday life no longer exists. Speed is of no use anymore, and voice can take its time. Under threat it lolls around, it takes a stroll through life. Until the man's desire, the desire of this all-powerful police officer makes itself clearly heard and calls her back to reality: "You are too beautiful, Tosca, and too much in love . . ."

Then she becomes the Diva again. The role of her life—she did not know— or else she always knew it—was this dramatic situation demanding that she give her body to save her lover. Her actions follow one another clearly, as in a stage production. She will say yes to Scarpia, demand a safe-conduct for Mario and herself, take the knife from the table where supper awaits, hide the weapon behind her back, wait for Scarpia to make his move, and then—strike—with all her force, as in the theater. She screams. And finally, in this long scream that is mingled with Scarpia's death cries, she says who she really is: "I am Tosca." That is to say, the prima donna. A chief of police is less powerful than a woman of the stage when she acts out the truth of her own life.

Still she will be slow as she leaves the room, and the music with her is even slower, as if it wanted to keep restraining the mad race that death stopped. She takes her time. According to tradition Sarah Bernhardt was the first to establish the coded gestures of Tosca: taking from the mantle the two lit candelabra, placing them on either side of Scarpia's body, detaching the great black crucifix from the wall, placing it piously on the police officer's chest, and contemplating her work. Her production. The action completed, after the crime and the real bloodletting—do not forget, it is the real blood of a role, it is fictional blood, an opera—Tosca moves to the other side of theater and acts on her own behalf. Scarpia is no longer merely dead, he is ready to meet God; that is what she wanted. During this protracted time, she has been something other than this fluttering woman, pursued by jealousy and by men. She is about to set off again on her mad dash; she still does not know everything.

All is calm in the Roman dawn. Calm as in a painting by Corot. The bells mean the rebirth of mornings with their order, and the joy of waking unthreatened. There is nothing more peaceful than this morning that breaks. Tosca's kisses, the stars slowly disappearing (the same stars that glittered in the darkness of the Farnese palace), all mingle in the purest farewell. Mario could die thus, effortlessly, if this running, breathless madwoman did not arrive so hurriedly.

When she comes on stage, the rhythm has a broken beat. Quickly she tells Mario everything: how she has killed Scarpia, how she has taken the safe-conduct, how he is to feign death, how they are going to escape. And she prepares him to play his role. Like a game of cops and robbers where she has succeeded in tricking the cop. And they perform the play. There, on this ancient platform, at the feet of the Christian dragon, they rehearse death. Mario thinks it is funny: *"Come la Tosca in teatro . . ."*. Yes, like Tosca, on the stage, he has to pretend, play dead. *"Non ridi . . ."*. Do not laugh, she says, this is a serious play. Completely unsuspecting, Mario, chuckling to himself, climbs toward the scaffold, and Tosca directs the production. But she does not know that the game has been fixed.

"Come e lunga l'attesa!" What a long wait! Oh impatient woman, who has never been able to wait! Oh hasty woman, this rushing, nonetheless, is what must fulfill your innermost impulse. . . . Mario dies, astonished, lost in the crazy laughter of his game, an apprentice comedian trapped in real theater. Tosca's voice directs what she believes is still an unmoving but living body.

"Do not move, wait some more, now move . . .". But the body, more dead than alive, returns unanswering silence to the prima donna. Tosca calls Mario again. Then she throws herself on him. Perhaps she does not understand; she repeats the uncomprehending words. *"Finire cosi, finire cosi . . ."*. To end like that.

On the cover of the score, and on the poster on the wall that I am looking at, she bends down. Her white dress is open on a very white neck, and she soberly places a crucifix on the dead policeman's corpse. Brown clouds form a blurred shadow around her. She is the one to decide, in spite of everything.

She decides on the candelabra, the crucifix, the pose. *Cosi*, she stages Scarpia's murder, *cosi*, she flies to Castel Sant'angelo, *cosi*, like that. Mario, too, asked her advice, so he would look real when he pretended to die. *"Non, ridi."* *"—Cosi?—Cosi."*

And now, now that she is alone and can no longer call him, the man who was her life, it is with a sort of violence—*"con una spezie di violenza"*—that she dashes to the parapet of Castel Sant'angelo. With the utmost force, the ultimate force, she hurls her voice into her own midnight. Gathering speed, finally, she gives in to the vertigo and finishes what she has never ceased to do from the beginning of the opera, except in that miraculous moment when she relived her life simply as one of art and of love. It is then, *cosi*, that she, Floria Tosca, leaps into the void, the prima donna.

Cosi fan tutte, under men's pressures.

Chapter 2
Dead Women

*In which we see a young Japanese lady waiting for nightingale
season; in which a daughter of Egypt allows herself to think all
by herself; in which an Irish witch poisons a motherless child.*

Think back, in the meshes of your musical memory, of just the opera notices, of
the images these little outline forms have left in the back of your mind. How
many bodies wearing the veil of darkness, how many criminal and consumptive
women wearing white shifts stained with blood, how many wrapped in tears and
murders? How many drooping heads, how many voices rising to the "crisis"
point where they faint away, imitating the last breath in a strange parody of death
throes, the high-pitched voice breathing its utmost opposite—expiring? Remember Butterfly, wrapped in a long red obi, she stabs herself and tears come to your
eyes; Violetta falls, Mimi is silenced, simply, and you are full of emotion. But
then other sounds, other lights interfere with your psychological illusions and dis-
mantle your emotions. All around you people are applauding; they stand and Butterfly is revived in the night lights. She is not a Japanese woman; she is plump,
she can laugh, and she is alive. Where are you coming from; what is it you are
leaving? Wake up, follow the rules, hit your two hands against each other; shout,
if you dare, the word bravo, which is also used for the "torero" who fights well.
And especially, do not think about the Nambikwara ethnologist (who will never
exist). With a profound sympathy that, thank goodness, we have no conception
of, he would watch from another world these people who are still hitting—their
hands now, for lack of anything else, before a woman who has just mimed her
death.

Think of the posters—the old posters published by Ricordi. This one for example. Completely blue, edged with a black line that vaguely recalls the preciosity
of some exotic box. A child, dressed completely in white, plays in a light so

golden that it merges with the chrysanthemum petals flying everywhere in the air. He is blindfolded and pigeon-toed. In his hand he holds a tiny, foolish American flag, full of stars. Far, far away from him, at the exact opposite edge of the space, the Japanese woman crawls toward him on all fours, arms outstretched. There is a white scarf fluttering inexplicably around her neck. On the ground there are lots of scattered flowers. The doors bang. No one is there; the house is empty. The two have been left alone for this ultimate encounter. The child plays at not being able to look at this familiar flag. The mother plays at pretending to play in front of her child, who does not know, and nothing, absolutely nothing indicates that in the folds of her kimono, plunged right into her abdomen, there is a dagger, and that this woman is dying. Nothing? Yes, one thing. In the turquoise background of the poster, and surrounding the date 1904, there is a mythical name. From Puccini's Italy at the dawn of the century right down to the rebellious Japan that killed the Occident within itself, this name has stood for the death of the geisha: *Madama Butterfly.*

The story: Pinkerton is a young American officer whose boat is anchored for a few months in Nagasaki Bay, near the turn of the century. For lack of anything better to do, he plays at marrying a very young girl, named Butterfly, who is fifteen years old and has had to work as a geisha ever since her father, a high official of the Nippon Empire, committed suicide on the orders of the Emperor. Cio-Cio-San (her real name) believes in this marriage; and when Pinkerton goes away, home to America, she waits for him, despite everyone's jeers. One day, the consul of the United States, who is a rather nice man, comes to tell her that her "husband" will not return. But to convince him, of who knows what, she shows him Pinkerton's son, whose existence no one except the servant suspected. Disturbed, the consul informs Pinkerton, who, back in Nagasaki with his ship, decides to take the boy home with him. The handsome sailor has brought his wife this time, the real one, an elegant American woman; and Butterfly finally understands. She gives him the child, but first, in front of the little boy, whom the servant has sent in to distract her from her sorrow, she stabs herself, just as her father killed himself, with the ritual knife, in the sight of her ancestral gods.[18]

What would someone, not knowing the story of the little geisha and how she died, see in the picture on the turquoise poster? A woman on all fours who seems to suffer physically, but—who knows, maybe she just has to go away? A child playing. The poster only hints at the deadly act, yet it incorporates an obvious depiction of death. This parading of death is the bait. You will not know why Butterfly crawls around like this in front of the blindfolded child unless you follow the musical story of the little Japanese woman, from the beginning. As for the death itself, you see it in the scarf—strangulation, something tight around the neck, like Isadora Duncan's long, strangling scarf. . . . But Butterfly dies by her own hand, a death she has prepared. All the women in opera die a death prepared for them by a slow plot, woven by furtive, fleeting heros, up to their glorious moment: a sung death. To fully understand, one must return to the source, to the curtain-raising, where, in words that are often trivial, the death is foreshadowed.

Butterfly's dagger, for example. It is not just any dagger. You see it the moment she arrives on the stage, dressed for the false wedding that only she believes is real. In the small bags she carries are little statues of gods, something to fill a pipe, a few cosmetics to whiten her face, and finally, the dagger, which she hides. It is the one her father used to commit "hara-kiri," as we call it. You do not know why it is flashed in the marriage scene; but there will have been some curse surrounding her, and in the midst of the fickle, butterflylike gaiety that sends Puccini's music fluttering, the threat of a future repetition will have been present. If you saw the poster, you will certainly know how this dagger will be used. . . . And signs of death are sprinkled throughout the opera, infinitesimal signs, infinitely interwoven with songs of love. Like the excruciating dialogue with her straw-and-whisky husband on their wedding night. "What a strange habit western men have, pinning the butterflies they catch to wooden boards!" exclaims the little girl. (She is barely fifteen, all you barrels of flesh who dare fill Butterfly's kimono. . . .) And Pinkerton, what do you think he will say? That there is some truth to it. That after all, you impale the butterflies to keep them from flying away. Puccini knows how to make a tenor voice spread its wings. Pinkerton holds Butterfly in his arms as he says these words to her. They sing a love duet, and you listen, carried away with delight. . . . Thus the American man foretells the dagger that will fix Butterfly, the butterfly-woman, an anatomical illustration, to the board of the white Occident.

Whenever I read over the words of opera libretti, at a distance from the music that arouses it the way the sexual member enraptures a body and brings it to life, I am astonished at their brutality, their blinding clarity. Pinkerton is a young macho whose language is crude: San Antonio, the dirty-talking commissioner, would have behaved in the same way. The female butterfly is impaled, and the opera draws out the metaphor to its most simplistic application: first a man's sexual member, then a dagger in the body. Butterfly dies the death of a Japanese woman, for love of an American.

Bit by bit, as she waits for the man whose return she expects when the robins come back (because he said he would), the story clarifies and tightens; as is often the case with Puccini's operas, what is melodious and simple is the free, unadorned plot. Butterfly has only a night and a day to live. All night long she has stood motionless, waiting. All night long her son and her servant, Suzuki, have slept by her side. When Butterfly's final wait begins, everything is bright and alive. The curtain rises on the final act, and the sailors of Nagasaki sing in the distance where the lights are still burning in the port. A morning like any other; the final act of an opera. The peace the wakening morning is sublime; however, there is nothing that could better signify death for anyone who has followed the web of song emprisoning the woman.

Butterfly's house is very high, on a hill that is hard to reach; when the white men climb it, they are out of breath. Suzuki and Butterfly stand motionless; Butterfly is so tired from her night's vigil, so unaware, that her servant can lead her to her room far from where she took her post to watch and wait. Butterfly's voice grows distant, reaches us from outside; the music gets slower and slower. Majestic and interrupted, the music alternates choked sighs with knowing whispers — the white men are plotting, while Butterfly sleeps during the dawn of her last day. And the music lifts into a great, sad waltz for the trio in which Suzuki, the consul, and Lieutenant Pinkerton come together; yes, he has come back — to recover his son from this forsaken woman.

All around her they plot. When she begins to suspect, the music panics, trapped. The tenor Pinkerton is given the sweet, lyrical developments — harps, arpeggios, slow melodies — as if Puccini wanted to signify the musical luxury this unchastened hero can afford, he who has a whole lifetime for remorse. For Butterfly there are silences, and breathlessness. It is true that she is going to die. She murmurs two questions: "Is he still alive?" He meaning Pinkerton. She has not yet seen him. "He is not coming back?" Long silences, voices that suddenly break.

How distant now the happy melodies! The butterfly is enclosed in an immense musical calm. Too much light, too much springtime — and those orange petals on the yellow ground of the turquoise poster. . . . Let the child play. All is calm, one might imagine that Butterfly wants to be alone to pray — just to pray.

But the music sounds the alarm; it is violent and explosive within a distinct and ritual rhythm. Mystical harmonies appear, along with resonant gongs. Memory becomes clearer; ancestral religion suddenly haunts the nearly empty stage where Butterfly barely moves. It is only the abrupt and chance appearance of the blond child that interrupts the unfolding of an undramatic, unsurprising ceremony. The child destined for a golden exile is the one who tears from Butterfly her rising voice, the tremendous heights, the superb cries finally set free, right up to the moment of decrescendo when she falls at last. She stabbed herself beneath her robes long before this, but no one could see. Not even the child, whom she has blindfolded, as if in play.

Not even the child. It is almost over. She pushes him gently toward the outside, away from the poster, away from the shadows where she has killed herself. On the picture that I look at while the music sings in my memory, who knows whether or not this outstretched arm is forcing him to leave, just before she falls, wrapped in this long bluish scarf that is fluttering for some unknown reason?

The gong strikes, its harmonics echo; she is dead now. One cannot help but believe it.

The music brings Pinkerton back to shore, in a final movement, like a bottle thrown up on the foam of a breaking wave, bitterly. There is always a man at the conclusion.

A man on the shore, where the foam is dirty.

Dead women, dead so often. There are those who die disemboweled, like Lulu at the sacrificial knife of Jack the Ripper, in a cruddy attic of smoggy London; there are those who die for having embodied too well the false identity of a marionette-woman or for having simply affirmed that they are not there where the men are looking for them. . . . Those who die of nothing, just like that—of fear, or fright, or sadness, or anxiety. Those who die poisoned, gently; those who are choked; those who fold in on themselves peacefully. Violent deaths, lyrical deaths, gentle deaths, talkative or silent deaths. . . . You could easily draw up a list of them. In other times, in serious structuralist conclaves—in days now known as bygone—you would have been entitled to a clean blackboard, just to classify them all, these dead women, according to the instrument of their death or the guilty party.

Nine by knife, two of them suicides; three by fire; two who jump; two consumptives; three who drown; three poisoned; two of fright; and a few unclassifiable, thank god for them, dying without anyone knowing why or how. Still, that is just the first sorting. And with my nice clean slate in my hands, I examine all those dream names in their pigeonholes, like butterflies spread out on boards. All that is left is to write their names above them: Violetta, Mimi, Gilda, Norma, Brunhilde, Senta, Antonia, Marfa. . . . The frightened, pathetic exercise of taxonomic intelligence, reassuring itself by filling its sensible little categories. But no matter how hard I laugh, there is always this constant: death by a man. Whether they do it themselves, like Butterfly, or are stabbed, like Carmen, the provenance of the knife, or the choking hand, or the fading breath is a man, and the result is fatal.

Plain and simple, just like real life. Like all pictures this one only brings out something obvious—something that was present in reality; that is how life is. Was this detour in capital letters necessary, or this display of music in all its magnificent splendor, just to lay low centuries of oppression and domesticity? So what is this pleasure in opera; what is perverse about it? And this durability (whereas the form has been dead for nearly half a century)—what is it linked to? What awarenesses dimmed by beauty and the sublime come to stand in the darkness of the hall and watch the infinitely repetitive spectacle of a woman who dies, murdered?

Faremen

The most feminist, the most stubborn of these dead women is Carmen the Gypsy, Carmen the damned.

Just the same, this woman who says no will die too. This woman who makes decisions all alone, while all around her the men keep busy with their little schemes as brigands and soldiers. She is the very pure, very free, Carmen. My best friend, my favorite.

I have always heard permanent ridicule heaped on this opera; no music has been more mockingly misappropriated. Toreadors, blaring music, and a gaudy Spain. . . . They always forget the death. When mockery becomes involved I get uneasy; something in me wants to understand. Wherever laughter takes hold, some unrecognized truth is lying low; surely we have not been reading Freud all this time just to forget his lessons. But *Carmen*'s music, ridiculed by the North, in the south of France has become the symbolic and ritual theme for bullfight entrances, for *paseos* where, dressed in silk and gold, the still-intact toreros parade. This is one of opera's inspired and unconscious transferences: music devoted to a woman convokes virile heroes. And the heroes are just as brilliant and combative as Carmen, playing with the lure and the animal with horns as if they were daggers.

Carmen, whose music is the echo of living it up for generations of children who were taken to the races; Carmen, in the moment of her death, represents the one and only freedom to choose, decision, provocation. She is the image, foreseen and doomed, of a woman who refuses masculine yokes and who must pay for it with her life.

The story: Carmen works in a cigarette factory in Seville where only women work, guarded by soldiers. Every day the men are waiting for them when they get off. Following a brawl among the women in which she was involved, Carmen, the most sought after by the men, finds herself charged for having refused to justify herself to the captain. To keep out of prison, Carmen seduces the corporal who is supposed to take her there: Don José, who is really a nice, quiet fellow, engaged to sweet Micaela, whom it seems he is in love with. But for love, José lets Carmen get away and finds himself in her place in prison. When he gets out, Carmen, touched by his gesture, persuades him to desert, especially since he has just fought with his own captain—over Carmen's beautiful eyes. The smugglers Carmen now works with could use another strapping young man like Don José. She gets what she wants: José deserts and follows her. But she quickly tires of him and falls in love with a matador, Escamillo, who is also mad about her. In the mountains where the smugglers move their illicit merchandise, two visitors appear on the same night: Escamillo, who is looking for Carmen and seems to be expected by her, and Micaela, who comes to tell José that his mother is dying. Crazy with anger, but obliged to go, telling her that they will meet again, José leaves Carmen. Later, José tracks Carmen down at the gates of the arena where Escamillo is fighting the bull. He begs her to leave with him, and since she will have no more of him and says so plainly, and there is nothing to be done about it, he stabs her and lets himself be arrested. That's it.[19]

Holiday in Seville. The bright white arenas of Maestranza are joyous; decorations painted in golden yellow trace baroque arabesques on the walls; the tall red doors with their black nails are wide open, and so are the black iron gates, enclosing the amphitheater with a necklace of openwork. There is buying and selling: cakes, cigarettes. It is noisy and jostling, a humming, harmless festival. Often, in opera, the premises of death unfold this way, at the height of joy, on a peaceful morning or in the glow of dawn or sunset. As if this death were preparing itself with the tender care with which one dresses a young girl, a child, a bride; as if you were opening a freshly made bed to sleep in it. And ears begin to listen attentively, hearts prepare a space inside for registering the divine performance for what is always the first and always the last time . . .

Once upon a time—this is a true story—there was a poor old woman who loved opera to death, and who probably was not rich enough to afford herself the luxury of a whole production. Consequently, throughout her entire oldladyhood, the women who ushered saw her arrive just before the curtain went up on the final act; she took advantage of the seats that were left empty, and explained in embarrassment, "I come for the death."

Holiday in Seville. Caught in the crowd, Carmen is all dressed up like a lady— Carmen the Gypsy. Therefore, somewhat whore, somewhat Jewess, somewhat Arab, entirely illegal, always on the margins of life. Wearing the cheap flounces used by Bizet, Meilhac, and Halévy to confine their representation of woman, Carmen is no more a Gypsy than Butterfly is a Japanese woman. All we have are images comparable to those tourist dolls we bring back from our trips, limited stereotypes of women whom we have not met although we searched in vain in the places where our cultivated hearts dreamed they would be: in the alleys, in the temples, in the palaces, on the garden steps. Look at a Carmen doll: she wears a Sevillan comb on her chignon, her jewelry of filigreed gold jingles, the fringes of her shawl move like serpents, and there are flounces everywhere. . . . That is no Gypsy. But through this French music, borne on words written by the two most famous French librettists of Offenbach's time,[20] adapted from a story by a French writer who was an amateur of the exotic[21], the whole extinct history of a wandering people comes to light. Try to hear through all the lace the distorted echo of truth. Carmen, like Esmeralda a daughter of Egypt, is the musical heiress of the vast spaces traveled by the Gypsy people: India, where the word *Manush* comes from, then Egypt and the Maghreb, all the way to Spain. And everywhere they went, they were subjected to the unerasable marks of juridical and murderous exclusion.

When I first mentioned Carmen, she was working in a cigarette factory, which is the lowest level of proletariat in Seville. Even there she was unable to find her place, because wherever she is, as a Gypsy, there is no fixed place for Carmen. In fifteenth-century Spain, the Gypsies were deprived of the right to practice any of the professions compatible with a nomadic life: horse-trading, blacksmithing, basketry, all were prohibited. In the eighteenth century the recalcitrant were branded with a red-hot iron and condemned to death. . . . Carmen works free as a bird; wandering professions—illegal and clandestine—would suit her better. So you can understand why she sings for all she is worth about freedom. The freedom to travel, *faremen* in the Rom dialect, is the freedom to exist. A sedentary nomad no longer exists, and Carmen fights for the right to live.

How she ended up behind bars I really do not know. Some of the women said she hit first, others defended her, and because after all she is only a Gypsy, the captain locked her up. It is of no importance with women like that. "These people who usually have no home or fixed residence, and who exercise or pretend to exercise some wandering trade. Their women seem very beautiful under their filthy rags; they tell fortunes, and are all robbers or thieves. . . . Woe to the region they pass through and especially those where they stay! Vegetables from the gardens, chickens from the barnyard, a wallet forgotten on a table by a door or window, a calf or horse at pasture—for them it is all for the taking. They live on our land as if it were a conquered territory." No, this is not in the libretto; but it is the good solid compost it springs from, the good old French stock: the text is by someone named Reville, and you will find it in a report to the House in 1908.[22]

I clearly remember that she seemed not at all surprised at being locked up. She even seemed to expect it, singing dreamily instead of answering the captain's questions, talking about love when he talked to her about justice. . . . And, in a corner, José, the only one who was not looking at her, mended his equipment, poor dear. Because he paid no attention to her, she threw the flower she was wearing in her hair at his head—the way knights used to throw down a glove. The Gypsy's first transgression: she takes the initiative in lovemaking. The rest will follow; seduction, escape, endless song, freedom.

Bitch. That is what the right-thinkers of the world call her. But what does she do? She acts like a man, that is all. And when she sings, already imprisoned in the ropes binding her arms, the words capture the bird-man in flight, just as Mozart's Don Giovanni catches his pretty misses. She has been forbidden to speak, so she sings. A song with a double meaning, whose words say she is available. Her lover can go to the devil, she has sent him packing, and here it is the weekend, the time for leisure and strolling along, making love. . . . José has only one thing to say: "Be quiet! I told you not to talk to me." They all say that.

So Carmen stands up and sweetly sings the rebellious words: "I am not talking to you, I am singing for myself, and I am thinking: it is not forbidden to
think."

This is what all women say. But yes, it is forbidden for women to think in this
stifling Europe where they are just barely beginning to take off. And singing for
oneself when one is the prisoner of a young corporal is making eyes at him.
Thinking is seducing.

Escaped—mysteriously set free—we find her in this gypsyish, nocturnal place
where she and her people spend their time. It is the tavern of her friend Lilas
Pastias, in the shadow of the ramparts. Nobody is doing anything there; they wait.
And Carmen sings the marvelous song in which the French words somehow take
on a Gypsy ring. Listen to these astonishing words: "*Les tringles des sistres
tintaient.*" The sistrum's rods were jingling. . . . Can you hear them, these
instruments from Egypt, these metal rattles jingling like sistra? And do you know
what, according to Plutarch, is the archaic origin of this music? Osiris (Plutarch
says Jupiter because he tended to get all the gods mixed up), one day found he
was unable to walk: his two thighs, his two legs were joined together, like the
legs of a mummy dried with natron. "He was ashamed and kept to himself; but
Isis cut them for him and split them apart so then she could tell him to go ahead
and walk straight." Ever since that time, in the festivals of Isis the goddess of
generation, sistra are shaken and their rods jingle. See how Carmen becomes a
sacred priestess. . . . For, Plutarch continues, "things have to shake and never
stop moving, and nearly come alive, and collapse, as if they were going to sleep
and languishing . . .". There, in Lilas Pastias's tavern where the soldiers are
half-asleep, drunk on manzanilla, Carmen shakes, wakes, sings like the sistra;
that is what is called a stirring woman. Her function is certainly to disrupt.

"The rods on the sistra jingled with a metallic brilliance, and at the sound of
this strange music the Zingarella stood up." And, in the golden mouth of Carmen
the Egyptian, the Gypsy hall all lit up in the open air, —nomadic fires in the forest,
a dazzling glow in the night—becomes a celebration of nocturnal Isis. In Christian mythology it has become an essential part of the ritual. Remember the Easter
legend that says when the bells go to Rome the belltowers are quiet. Silent, voice-
less, the great Christian instruments are in mourning. It is Good Friday; Christ is
dead. Then, in place of the bells, instruments of darkness ring out—rattles and
sistra, little night sounds.

Darkness is Carmen's light. In daylight she is threatened. Leaving the great
majestic building that is the tobacco factory in Seville, or in front of the arena,
Carmen is prey to social pressure, whose appointed representative is José. But
in the tavern, at nightfall, by candlelight, or at night, in the mountains with the
smugglers, Carmen is queen and out of danger. The opera is constructed on alter-
nations: by day Carmen in prison; by night Carmen triumphant and Don José the

deserter for her sake. By night she is in command; in the brilliant sun of the bull-fights she dies.

Now we see her at the gates of the arena, where she will not enter. You could say she asked for it. By diverting Don José first from his duty as jailer, then from his duty as a soldier, by proposing simultaneously desertion and freedom, she gets him into a position where he can no longer do without her. By deciding to do without him, by preferring a refined and famous toreador, one wearing a uniform of gold like the dragoon's uniform José used to wear, she signs her own sentence. Take away the mantillas, the golden colors, the cigars—take away Egypt and the memory of Isis—and the tale you will hear is about any woman at all. José follows her in the crowd. Everything is peaceful when José surprises her and prevents her from passing. He prevents; he is a man. He ties her up; he loves her; he shackles her. Now the crowd is somewhere else, inside the arena, in this other universe of spectacle whose sound surrounds the separated lovers. The drama will be played out in a space between two theaters: the opera theater and the fictional amphitheater. Thousands of faces. Between the two theaters lies an empty space, the forsaken passages of the arena, the place one passes through. A place just right for dying; a place, however, with nothing tragic about it, just a vast hallway with stairs, cloakrooms, and cushions for sale. Between Carmen, brilliant in her holiday dress, and José, who is as dark as the wall, between these two the Gypsy's death is decided.

She says no. No again. No! She does not want him, does not love him any-more. He is bleating and he is dangerous, he repeats over and over: "There is still time. . . . There is time to save yourself and to save me with you." Ah, here is the naked truth: what has to be saved is the man's image, damaged by pure and simple jealousy, that can bring on all the deaths in the world. Then, since nothing can convince this man that she has decided to break with him, she commits the sacred and stubborn act that condemns her to death. Haughty, vio-lent, a goddess in her freedom, she pulls the ring he gave her from her finger and flings it in his face. The dagger plunges. The body slumps. "So, damned woman!" José shouted as he killed her. Damned always and eternally.

She knew of her death beforehand. During the restless night of smugglers car-rying bundles through the mountains, a scene of foreboding took place. The three women traveling with the smugglers were reading cards. Another archaic action. For most people it is an action that is a little ridiculous and a little disturbing, something one plays at while carefully defending oneself with a fragile rational-ism, one so fragile, so tenuous. . . . But for a Gypsy it is truth speaking. When Carmen draws near the cards, the music becomes strong and resolute. "Hurry up" she commands. The death cards come up. "Death, I saw it, him first, me next, for both of us, death." There is nothing more troubling than this dark, low-pitched song, immensely slow and religious, with the rhythm of some inmost, penetrating course. "It is useless, the cards are sincere, they never lie." It is said.

By taking superstition seriously, as an interpretation of reality, Carmen the fortuneteller is united with the great prophetesses, with the energy of seers, and the legendary prescience of sorceresses. Dying because you must die, you might as well choose the stakes, and the moment. Carmen is the somber and revolutionary proclamation of a woman who chooses to die before a man decides it for her.

The sound of the fight rises from the humming arena. Suddenly Carmen is dead. I remember her dancing and singing quietly; I remember her loving, perhaps for the first time, and her truly tender words spoken emotionally to the bullfighter she fancies. Maybe this was her chance. But there she is on the ground, a dagger in her body. The man is still there, senseless. The police are the only ones who will come out to attend to them. The crowd is busy somewhere else. And Carmen has died alone, her only spectators her murderer, you, us, me.

But on her prima donna's body, while the curtain lowers, a veiled shadow rises. The one who was Mother, who, after Osiris died, gave birth to the posthumous Horus, the one who smiles on the high temple walls and in the depths of secret tombs, the one who opened Osiris's legs, the one who still seeks the scattered pieces of her spouse's body—the Great Isis gives the rebellious Gypsy life with her ancient breath. "Egypt, Egypt! Your great motionless gods have shoulders whitened by birds' droppings, and the wind blowing on the desert stirs the ashes of your dead."[23]

The possum and the lost child

The next scene takes place on windswept moors. Or on the empty set of a deserted stage. The nearby sea clouds the air with its roar. There is already a dead man there, stretched out full length. The group surrounding him is overcome; and on his body lies a woman, perhaps she has fainted, perhaps she is dead . . . Tristan and Isolde. Of all the deaths in opera this is the most famous; this is the one that gave its name to a form of lyrical death—*Liebestod*, love-death. Isolde, tearing herself from Tristan's body, fills all of space with her endless song, a sea of music, infinite—until it reaches the death of the voice, the death of the woman, the absolute triumph of musical harmony. It is also the easiest death and the most deceptive; the worst death women's hearts are offered.

The story: Tristan is sent by his uncle and suzerain, King Marke, to bring back an Irish woman, Isolde, whom Tristan captured after a mortal combat with Isolde's fiancé, Morholt. On the boat back to Brittany, the two protagonists find they love each other, all the more because they are sure they are going to die, and, that being the case, there is nothing to prevent their declaring their love to one another. But, whether by good or bad fortune, the death philter that Isolde meant to give Tristan is in reality a love philter substituted by the servant

Brangane: a perfectly useless potion since they are already in love. When the boat lands, Tristan and Isolde are wrapped in each other's arms. King Marke boards the boat just when they are forcibly separated by Brangane and Kurwenal, Tristan's squire. They reunite that night to sing the impossible and desired meeting, their union in love. Brangane warns them in vain: day breaks and King Marke arrives, informed by his vassal Melot. In desperation Tristan throws himself on Melot's sword, mortally wounding himself. In the final act he lies dying in his country, Kareol, watched over by his squire. Isolde is long in coming but finally arrives. Tristan tears off his bandages and dies in her arms. King Marke appears with Brangane, who has told him everything, to be grieving spectators, while Isolde who has no physical wound dies of love on Tristan's body.[24]

Yes, Isolde has an easy death. From the beginning everything leads to it, as if the two lovers were like two marionnettes worked by some invisible shadow puppeteer on parallel bars, on a track where they are never to be united. An easy death, because it has been baptized "love-death," and because it makes the idea of death trite, then familiar, desirable, tamed. *Liebestod*: not far at all from *Liebelei*, the sad, sweet love of the Viennese shopgirl. Cabbage soup, jam tarts, superficial sentiments, and Schnitzler's ghost writing romantic stories *mezzo voce* in the Vienna of decadence. Isolde, the sublimated shopgirl. This is the original mould of all those picture romances where, in some mythical storeroom eternally haunted by old castoffs, "love and death, death and love" intersect. In opera to love is to wish to die; it is to count our steps in the sandy path leading to death, for the sake of our collective joy. And in *Tristan and Isolde*, whose plot is reduced to its simplest form, this is perfectly demonstrated.

A boat at sea, whose purpose is never to reach the shore. A deck is the scene of their first love; all around are sailors, ropes, the steady work of those who hoist, and furl, and scrub, and steer the course. No solitude for them in the space full of people; held prisoners by the sea. The sailors, like all crowds who sing in chorus, know everything. It is a sailor's voice that begins the opera: "The wind blows and blows. . . . Oh sorrowful misfortune! Ireland's daughter, loving and wild . . .". There we have it—the misfortune: Isolde's wildness.

Tristan has traveled far away to get her, according to the kinship rules requiring a man to marry a woman from somewhere other than his home. The marriage entails an exchange of material goods, but the exchange of material goods controls the marriage. This is all normal. Tristan, as custom would have it, is related to King Marke for whom he is seeking this faraway wife: he is his nephew, even his "son" because Marke brought him up in his home. A man goes in search of a wife for an uncle or a father; this is all normal. And the dramatic events leading up to Isolde's being carried off are normal also: battle with Morholt, the jousting that is like the one central to French history, between Olivier and Roland, resulting in Roland's marriage to the beautiful Aude. All royal marriages are clinched after wars, as if these wars had no other function than to bring about the union in one bed of two children raised in different places. Tristan is definitely a well brought up young man, and Isolde is a nice young girl who has been taught, as tradition would have it, the use of herbs, potions, and philters. That is how Tristan found her. Dying from a wound, he had been placed on a skiff with his harp; his arms and a cover protected him from the wind and spray. A boat takes him to Isolde: a boat takes them both away; later, a boat will bring him Isolde once again. None of that is written in Wagner's libretto, because he catches the soaring lovers on the wing, when the story has already begun. The lovers' origins, their intersecting memories, are buried in some preopera; but the opera inherits them.

If this story is one of a royal marriage that obeys the old Celtic laws, as well as the later laws of courtly love grafted by Gottfried de Strasbourg onto the myth, what are the reasons for the fatal love? And what misfortune carries the wild daughter of Ireland along with it? Can we go together—in a dream flash—into the amazonian forests where strange demiurgelike animals and badly brought up women disturb men's order?[25] We will find Isolde there, in an unexpected figure; we will encounter the eternal conflict between men and women, depicted in their archaic purity by peoples who have no knowledge of history, nor of industry, and who probably do not even exist anymore. Culture there belongs to men; nature in her unpredictability remains tied up with women: cataclysms, endless rain, illness, earthquakes and that mysterious phenomenon, women's periods—this all stems from disorder, perceived as such by the men, even if it is a matter of some powerful, original order that they are always trying to control. But nature and culture, that powerful opposition, keep no such distance between them; intermediary universes arrange themselves to fill in the distance, cross over the spaces, and arrive at a precarious balance, metastable, dangerous, and necessary. Consequently, in the mythic universe, intermediate characters make their appearance, all bearing the marks of ambivalence: neither good nor bad, they simultaneously partake of the greatest danger and the most helpful and beneficial effects.

Among these characters you will find a formidable feminine character—a bad mother who abandons her small child on a tree branch while she gathers dead fish from the river. You have to know that they fish there by using a poison to paralyze the fish, killing them without destroying their edibility. Also, you should know that this bad mother is herself the daughter of a fearsome grandmother, guilty of having poisoned her own son by squatting over his face while he was asleep and letting out stinking farts on his nose to make him sick. No, I am not forgetting Isolde; yes, I am still trying to find her. Be patient a little longer; she is lurking behind the great fever trees.

This bad mother is closely akin to two other intermediary characters. First, the rainbow. Our unworthy mother goes off after the fish and eats them so voraciously that she swells, swells, and bursts like a frog. And all the sicknesses, which were not yet in existence, come out of her exploded body. Remember that Tristan was sick and cared for by Isolde: we shall have to keep this in mind. After all the sicknesses are born, the woman is cut into two parts and transformed into a rainbow. The rainbow is simultaneously the bearer of good things—it announces the rainy season—and the cause of every cataclysm. The Indians claim that it is the cause of human illness, the rainbow, the ultimate figure of the mother who abandoned her child to devour the river fish so fast. But no, in the end, I am not forgetting Isolde! She is hidden in the bends of the rainbow.

To find her, we have to dig in the bag of myths, this inexhaustible supply, for the second character related to the bad mother. Both opposite and identical: a very good mother, who feeds and is kind, but a stinking mother. It is the sarigue, a South American opossum, a pretty little animal that looks like a skunk or a polecat and that stinks. Sickness, stink, poison . . . all that is feminine. Sickness comes from woman's body; and the odor of women—*odor di femine* sang the tantalized, hysterical seducer—always stinks. The Indians tell that when the animals made vaginas for the women, who were still without them, the armadillo was extremely careful to rub these new orifices with a bit of rotten nut. So vaginas will smell like they ought to smell: bad. As for the fish-poison, it comes, the Indians say, from feminine filth: good, because it makes eating possible, and because it attracts sexual desires, and bad because it is dangerous enough to kill. Women are poisoners. Now we can see our Isolde through the twining liana in the trees.

The rainbow is another being endowed with an interesting peculiarity: it is chromatic. Its gradation of color is through tiny differences. Just as, in musical chromatics, sounds are organized in a logic of small intervals. Here then is how the rainbow and women are related: they are chromatic beings, that is to say, ambivalent intermediaries between the order of nature and that of culture. And here, finally, is our Isolde: like the possum, like the bad mother, she is a chromatic being. A poisoner, she is as much the dispenser of life—with her beneficial herbs and the love potion—as the dispenser of death, with the evil philtre that she has in store for Tristan. She is good and bad, by virtue of her mythical capacities: "Oh sorrowful misfortune! Ireland's daughter, loving and wild . . .". There will be too much proximity between Isolde and Tristan, because they will be committing incest, and because, through his kinship with Marke and the workings of marriage, Tristan will be Isolde's nephew, nearly her son. . . .They are crossing over the limits of men's order.

But it so happens that chromatism, this art of small intervals, is the law of musical composition in the *Liebestod* and in all of Wagner's opera. And chromatism, whether that of the rainbow or of music, is always associated with affliction, with suffering, with mourning and death. That is as true for the Indians as for Rousseau, who writes in the *Dictionnaire de musique*: "The chromatic genre is wonderful for expressing pain and affliction; its intensified sounds tear the soul as they rise. It is no less powerful when it descends; then one thinks one is hearing real moans.'' Chromatism is too intermediate; its rises, its descents, its imperceptible sliding are profoundly seductive. This, then, explains Isolde's character: her profound seduction, her ambivalence as an Irish sorceress, her capacity to provide good and evil, and the impossibility men have of controlling the powers that she embodies—odors that are both stinking and attractive, potions that are murderous or beneficial, a deadly love, poison troubling the soul. Hence the charm of Wagner's music is even more linked to death than its chromatism implies, and only a woman can be its afflicted heroine, the sorceress from Ireland, equipped with the powerful magic of distance, and ''stinking'' of that very same feminine sexual stink that seduces Tristan the moment they meet. How could anyone think Isolde was a woman who did not wash?

And Tristan? Just perfect for being seduced. Sickly and puny in the old, original text, he is always ill, as if he had some mysterious infection that never went away. Love is to be his last infection. To make sure he will die of it this time, in Wagner's opera he rips the bandages from his infected wound. Tristan treats himself to an episode of unequivocal madness; ''mad Tristan''; mimicking insanity joins all the marginal characters of the Middle Ages, the lepers, idiots, plague victims, the ones stricken with curses. For all these ills there is one blatant cause: Tristan's very name suggests a birth costing his mother her life. Motherless child, he will be the sad child, tristful Tristan, for whom any life is impossible.

The coming together of nurturing mother, bighearted possum, and the child weaned from birth, solves the problem. And something that might develop as an ordinary story, in which a nephew goes to find a foreign wife for his royal uncle, turns into this magnificent myth, these heartrending strains that for centuries have marked the horizon of our imaginary as lovers. Every man is Tristan, the tristful knight, willing himself motherless, seeking the generous breast of a childless woman capable of poisoning him with love; every woman is Isolde, odorous and seductive, above all chromatic, dedicated to small intervals, small movements even in death. Even in death: Isolde dies as only a woman can die, by small intervals.

A boat at sea. On the deck facing each other are the possum and the lost child. She, the poisoner, offers him what she thinks is a death philter. He takes it passionately, with some presentiment of the other poison poured for him, and he drinks it. She drinks in turn—I am no longer in Indian America—and both are lost.

It remains to be proven to the whole world that all true love is deadly. Adultery is not enough; because, changing the medieval myth in which King Marke makes up his mind to condemn the lovers to death (burning Tristan alive and sending Isolde to live with the lepers) Wagner makes King Marke a magnanimous old man. However often they may meet at night by torchlight, however much they sing their own deaths, when King Marke surprises them he does not condemn, he laments. It was all for naught. That is the turning point of the opera. Tristan decides to force the fate that wants nothing to do with him. He flings himself on Melot's sword and is impaled.

There is nothing now that could prevent their death. The last part of the story brings out the suicidal truth. Tristan sends for Isolde, who, finally, after a long, a very long wait, eventually comes. On the moor where Tristan is dying, overcome by the infection that eats away at him, a shepherd is to signal the white-sailed boat's arrival. For a long time the shepherd's flute sings only of the empty sea; and then the music turns joyful: there she is. Tristan pulls off his bandages so his blood will run out to meet his beloved. Not him, he does not count anymore; but his blood, the only vigor left him, this vital flow, is thus sent out toward the original poisoner, as if in return for something owed her. Tristan dies in the arms of Isolde. Tristan dies alone: Isolde does not die in the same instant. We wrongly retain the image of the two dying one death. Tristan gets there ahead of Isolde. She will just barely have time, coming to her senses when everyone thinks she is already dead, to get up again and sing the famous, rotten love-death. It is a confused discourse in which death, the sea, waves, light, and heaven produce an apotheosis for her that is mystical and musical, in which it is her turn to die alone, despite the final chord when the chromatics are resolved in the only major key in the opera. Their deaths are separate, competitive, divided. That is the outcome of passion and its disappointing result.

Yes, an easy love-death, and our hearts, all sticky with the sublime and with music, always follow it with feeling. But beyond the chromatic chords that make this love-death be an immense rising toward a resolution that is exclusively musical, the mythical and dramatic structure tells of death in separation, lovers who fail, the poverty of a love founded on the poisoning of a sick child by a witch who is too beautiful. Be that as it may. To make generations of romantics weep, record covers, posters, symbols, and stage productions will vie with one another in repeating the image of the embracing couple and their separate graves joined by the same rose tree. The ultimate joining between those who should not have joined; just as the rainbow joins heaven and earth, nature and culture, man and woman, the lovers' rose tree rises from one tomb and, forming something like a curved arch, thrusts itself into the other. This is their only real reunion: natural, definitive, and symbolic.

Three women in opera die three deaths: by Japanese dagger, by Spanish knife, and by love. Three women: three foreigners. Isolde from Ireland, a foreigner on Breton soil; Carmen, a foreigner on Spanish soil, who has come from all over the world via Africa and Egypt; Butterfly, a foreigner to the Occident, but who makes herself a foreigner in her own country by marrying a man whose name — not of her land — she openly claims. Butterfly, whose Japanese name is masked in Italian by the English signifier for an insect, regains her country at the same time she dies a Japanese death. Carmen the Gypsy rediscovers her origins by accepting the destiny fixed for her by cards and by fate. Isolde, the Irish woman, finds her proper identity with great difficulty, through the song that finishes her and that finally belongs to her and to her alone; but it is a song of death.

You will see: opera heroines will often be foreigners. That is what catches them in a social system that is unable to tolerate their presence for fear of repudiating itself. This is how opera reveals its peculiar function: to seduce like possums, by means of aesthetic pleasure, and to show, by means of music's seduction (making one forget the essential), how women die—without anyone thinking, as long as the marvelous voice is singing, to wonder why. You will see: their foreignness is not always geographical; it appears in a detail, a profession, an age no longer said to be womanly. But always, by some means or other, they cross over a rigorous, invisible line, the line that makes them unbearable; so they will have to be punished. They struggle for a long time, for several hours of music, an infinitely long time, in the labyrinth of plots, stories, myths, leading them, although it is already late, to the supreme outcome where everyone knew they would have to end up.

A great, silent room, where a young mother lies peacefully in bed. Next to her, a cradle and a baby, a little girl. The sheets are perfectly clean and everything is quiet. A doctor and a grandfather watch over her. When the curtain rises, the only sign that there is anything strange is that the husband is absent. But he enters now and tries to make his young wife tell him: What secret? What torture? She has forgotten everything. But yes, she had been faithful; but yes, she loved that young man, was he not her brother-in-law, was that not normal? She does not even know that she has given birth to a little girl; they show her the baby. How little she is. . . . The man beside her insists desperately, but she is already too far away, wounded with a wound other than that of childbirth alone.

The birth of her daughter is joined with her death agony. But, like a counterpoint to all this sung violence, Mélisande; the woman comes from elsewhere, dies in silence. All around her bustle the husband, the doctor, the grandfather, men who speak and stir about, living and useless. Not one of them could see that she is in the process of dying, that she dies . . .that she is dead. The servant-women are the ones who know; they fall to their knees. And the doctor certifies: "The women are right," while something like the memory of a bell tolls. They were right to see and to know, while all these men noticed nothing. Dead in silence, so quickly, said the men. But yes, silent, just as she had always been. Deceitful and innocent. Dead without warning, in defiance of the rules of opera and belcanto. Her last breath is not a song; her death is not even staged, unless it is by those old women who stand for a truth of the people that goes beyond a public, who report a life departed and the refusal of drama. You did not hear her die: Mélisande, or the thwarted outcome of a heroine of silence and fear.[26]

Chapter 3
Family Affairs,
or the *Parents Terribles*

In which we see a prostitute follow the Way of the Cross; in which a Spanish Emperor saves his grandson from the stake and his daughter-in-law from despair; in which a father and a mother quarrel about the education of their pubescent daughter.

Waltzes. Slow waltzes, loving or sad—even the cadence is stifling; brilliant, breathless waltzes, propelled by hidden legs rushing across waxed floors. Trivial, vulgar, rotten waltzes. This is Paris around mid-century, in places full of foliage, furs and black suits. The men look like undertakers, the women are half-naked. This opera heroine is called the *Traviata*; in Italian that means the reprobate. It is the exemplary history of a woman crushed by the bourgeois family, exemplary because the entire history of opera pivots around things at stake in the family. There is a common law, there are fathers to defend and apply it, and there are rebels.

Violetta Valéry, known as the reprobate, finds she rebels without even trying. If she gives in to the harsh familial law imposed on her by a bourgeois father, it will be to follow a way of the cross where *passion* develops to its final end. Every family contains within its history and its dealings required rites of passage; boys, to a greater or lesser degree, either submit to them or go away. But the girls who are constrained have no choice other than excess. Violetta, outside the family, has no other solution for escaping the evil ways into which life has led her than the deadly rite of sacrifice. And these waltzes, their quick or slow propulsion, endlessly wavering the way one falters before falling dizzily, create something like a flickering light where glances, cries, and words sparkle and go out.

Who whirls like this in a three-beat rhythm, in a heart passing from one to the other, in alternating current, from arm to arm? The *Traviata's* way of the cross is not made up of sorrowful stations on a straight, uphill road. She spins from waltz to waltz, scarcely settling, like a tired bird, long enough to catch her unhealthy breath. All around her, members of the family judge, execute, and lay down the law. She dances, she drinks. But the champagne she swallows has none of the grandiose vainglory of Don Giovanni's goblet; her steps are numbered and her lifetime. She waltzes her sorrow and her days; she embodies the dancer in the secret schemes of the seated bourgeoisie, who adorn her, dress her, undress her, and prostitute her.

The story: Violetta Valéry lives in the luxury of kept women. During a brilliant evening at her home — or rather at the home of the man whose property she is — she suddenly gasps for breath. Her frivolous friends do not know she is "consumptive." Alfredo Germont, a young man of a good provençal family, notices. He loves Violetta and offers his love to her, although she has never wanted to experience that pleasure. At first she refuses him, vaguely sensing some danger. But in the second act we find her spinning out love's sweet dream with Alfredo in a little house near Paris, where the open air is curing her of her illness. Everything would be fine if Alfredo's father did not turn up suddenly to threaten them, convinced that Violetta is squandering the family fortune. He does notice, with some confusion, that Violetta is selling furniture to keep up the house. Be that as it may; by means of blackmail he manages to induce Violetta to leave Alfredo. The motive is obvious: Alfredo's sister must marry and the family cannot put up with a lack of respectability in one of its sons. Violetta, giving Alfredo no explanation, returns to her former life. Alfredo pursues her and humiliates her, provoking a scandal. In the final act, Violetta is dying, alone and impoverished. But she awaits Alfredo's visit. He comes, followed by his papa, who has forgiven her. They all make plans for the future. . . . It is too late. Violetta spits out her life in a song of resurrection.[27]

Where should Violetta be placed in social comedy? No category really fits her. Prostitute? Not enough streetwalking. Demimondaine? Not lively enough for that. Both outside the straight and narrow path of marriage, and outside the evil paths where nothing is serious, Violetta is nowhere. She is a good girl, with none of Carmen's radical foreignness, and a lost girl, not one of the family. She is intermediate; a reprobate is what she is. One who would have been able; one possessing those mysterious, innate qualities of soul that the bourgeoisie recognizes among its own kind: a certain sense of duty, a generosity with money, an acute sense of kinship, and an indefinable air of the homebody making this heroine of prostitution seem like a housewife who has strayed into kitchens that are cooking up evil. But there you have it, she is "fallen."

Where does she come from? No one could say. Like her sister in *Mystères de Paris*, a novel whose basic mysticism Frederick Engels was able to detect — like Fleur-de-Marie, Violetta has fallen in the gutter by mistake and is marked, perhaps, by a corrupted childhood. She will lose her life, coughing in muddy, slippery places. She is sucked into unmarked swamps, interstices that are neither bourgeois, nor workingclass, nor noble. Places of circulation where women get stuck in the mud; ones they will never get out of. The family's son can take a spin there, he will get out just fine, having seen life; but the woman never gets out. These are the bourgeoisie's exclusive harems. Because she wanted to leave, Violetta must pay the required price, her life itself.

These are corrupt places. In the original, written as a novel by the younger Alexandre Dumas, the young man has the casket enclosing the body of Marguerite, the lady of the Camellias, opened after a year. He is repaid with nauseating odors but cannot bear to smell them. The woman's body is there, ravaged, undone, defeated materially. She has arrived at that ultimate decomposition for which prostitution is the metaphor. But reread old Engels. Do you know what he says in *Origins of the Family, Private Property and the State*? The real family — the one you know so well — has not always existed. There were group families, the initial communities, different matriarchies; scholars have cast that theory aside now, but the origins of family are not very important. Engels's notion of the bourgeois family was this: it is fiercely monogamous and tempered by adultery and prostitution. The tenacity with which it insists on monogamy, the fact that there can no longer be more than one wife, is to guarantee the exclusive transmission of private property. That is the up side; the down side is prostitution, money that circulates without ever settling down, and women one does not marry because they are in the wrong class: there are mothers, who beget heirs, and then there are all those others who guarantee nothing — nuns, whores, actresses, maids, Gypsies, those little heroines whom opera transforms for an evening into phony, temporary queens. Prostitution decays, it is rot; but it is terrific manure to fertilize bourgeois lands. The romantic hero, contemplating his lady's runny sockets and the place where her breasts used to be, is looking at the metaphor of a social body; he looks at its excrement and its wastes. And he goes away to cry somewhere safe.

And always those waltzes sweeping my heart away with them . . . so I forget the wicked plot. Take a look. Violetta has left the demimonde. It is unimportant, just a woman whose existence is evil who has decided to let herself be loved. Who could guess that she has crossed the line of demarcation between one world and another, between a good life and a bad one? She is to learn quickly that she is in foreign soil. Nonetheless, she lives there peacefully, in a country house. It might be in the valley of the Bièvre River or of the Chevreuse. It is the rustic world of second homes. Violetta and Alfredo live as if they were on Robinson Crusoe's deserted isle. Then the father turns up. He comes and speaks down to her with the bluntness of the property owner. This woman is eating up the wealth of his family. What is really at stake suddenly comes out; up to now all you have heard are words of love. But love is nothing, it is a dangerous myth and Violetta knew that beforehand. Behind these remedies of the heart lies money. Cash, land, possessions. But Alfredo, that nice young man, is a little, well mannered pimp. Violetta is selling her own possessions, reversing the prostitution. Do you think the father of the family takes offense at this? Not at all. Reassured, he takes a breath and advances his attack. Violetta shows him the bills: a fantastic move in a sentimental opera. She shows him the papers recording the sales. She knows moneyed men well. But it is not enough.

Father Germont rubs his hands together. He has to negotiate and quickly. This phenomenal scene is a business transaction. You think it is a touching duet between a wounded father and a suffering woman? Then listen to the words, see the truth. The father of the family is marrying off Alfredo's sister. The noble feelings he concedes to the prostitute are of no interest to him. Except in one way: it is how he will be able to trap her. That is where the ignominy begins. Listen to him describe, with tender, peaceful music, the little pure, and virginal girl in the sunshine of Provence where she is ready for a reliable husband. If the son of the family keeps up his mischief it is good-bye to the marriage, good-bye to the increased patrimony. She, the other, is pure as an angel; Violetta resists not a second. Not a grumble. All right, she will go away for a while, since it is necessary. But no. Germont wants everything, right away. Complete abandonment, a real sacrifice.

Ah, the little invalid, how she argues! She sings spasmodic gasps, she cries out her love in the syncopation of music that skips beats, she utters her broken cries, to tell him that she is being asked to give up her entire life. Yes, that is what he wants. The father of the family hammers out his stubborn intentions in solid phrases, and she defends herself before him with sighs that would move stones and break hearts. The lily-white image of the other woman, the pure one, hangs there to trap the lost woman. Then, to extract the bargain from her, the father describes the future to her. She is young, beautiful, and loved. But later? She will never be the wife. And Violetta, while the other one reels off words without a pause, keeps on murmuring: "E vero . . .". It is true. She will never enter the family. And it is at this moment that she gives up; her melody becomes sublime, now she surpasses herself. If she can no longer be the whore, and cannot be the wife, she still can take on the role of nun.

Sacrifice; the word worked. In her captive memory there are other words that have sung out recently: "the exquisite cross of love." Alfred sang this to persuade her to renounce the rapid, dead end, sensual pleasures of prostitution. "The cross," said the son. "Sacrifice," says the father. The moment of fulfillment has come. There are only the nails left to drive into the woman's tender palms.

Violetta dreams of virtue. To become an angel of purity, like the unknown young girl arranging bouquets of flowers and embroidering, she must become a whore again, and lose Alfredo. Is bourgeois morality strong enough for this? The father has proved that her salvation lies in her loss. And, while Violetta's tears flow in a duet that has become a love duet, the father treats himself to the deli-

cious luxury of pity. "*Piangi, misera!*" Weep, poor woman. They are in each
other's arms, the father holding up the prostitute. But, by a slippage of images
and roles, now that the deal is clinched and the father has won, she has become
like his daughter. There is one sole condition: that the other daughter know her
sacrifice. That Violetta be spoken of in this way. That she exist in the family, a
lost phantom who guarantees with her gutter the happiness of another woman.
She is strangely integrated now. She is the loose woman, pleasure's daughter,
then the chosen woman, the adopted daughter. Violetta will soon be dead.

The trap is religious. When Fleur-de-Marie goes to see the priest, trusting in
him, he does not absolve her. Every stain is final.—Is that what the Gospel
says?—The prostituted woman, even if she was raped, has nothing to hope for
on this earth. "You must give up any hope of erasing this distressing chapter
from your life, but you must put your hope in the infinite mercy of God. For
you, poor child, there are tears here below, remorse and expiation; but one day,
above, there will be pardon and eternal bliss!" Fleur-de-Marie and Violetta bear
the same stigmata. The distressing chapter. It is no great leap from syphilis to
consumption: two bodily corruptions inherited by those who are not part of the
family. It is their only inheritance; it ensures the other's reproduction, the real
inheritance, contracts, signatures, properties. Germont turns Violetta into a saint;
he is no dummy. He turns a material inheritance, that he was afraid of losing,
into a spiritual inheritance.

"*E vero.*" It's true, Violetta murmurs, stricken with the evidence when the
father describes her old age to her. He hits the woman in her heart. By promis-
ing her wrinkles and physical decline if she lives, he is offering her sacrifice, in
fact, a beautiful death. Now is that not that glorious?

La Traviata was a failure at first; the Italian bourgeoisie had little appreciation
for the harshness, even when tempered by music, of a production where they
had to face up to all this. Verdi was living at the time in a common law marriage, outside the limits; *La Traviata* was set in the eighteenth century, no doubt
just because it seemed prudent. But no one was fooled by that. The failure was
not permanent. Today, when the family is completing one stage of its history,
with decline on the way, the bourgeois once again are moved by the prostitute's
crucifixion. And they let themselves be carried away by the rhythm of the
waltzes.

In the improbable event that the wonderful melodic proliferation has performed its essential function and distanced you from monetary issues, the act
between the conclusion of the deal and Violetta's death will be a harsh reminder.
Everyone is there, in a gambling hall; they are playing for big stakes, throwing
away, squandering. In vengeance—poor dear, he is suffering!—Alfredo publicly
throws the notes, with which he thinks to repay his debt, all over his former lover.
Like father like son; young Germont takes after someone. They have a sense of
honor in that family. Violetta is covered with bank notes the way Christ was cov-

ered with spit. . . . She is already in the throes of death, richly dressed; but soon, deprived of her means of making money—her body—all she can do is to sink gradually into poverty.

Nothing is lacking in this mystical fable. Nothing, not even resurrection. At the moment when everything comes back to life, when, with the damsel properly married, the father and son come back, haunted by vague remorse, Violetta thinks she is reviving and says so. Outside the Carnival parade goes by in the distance, the procession of the Boeuf Gras, the fatted calf. Horses pull immense cardboard lyres, and enormous puppets with huge heads waddle their way along the Great Boulevards. It is an anonymous festival under all this confetti. But she is no longer listening, she is concentrating on her suffocating lungs, oblivious to her former life departing with each breath. And yet, she says: "It is strange . . .". Indeed it is strange. On her feet, freed from the deadly weight of her decayed lungs, Violetta finally breathes freely. She revives. No. She falls, dead.

Because you had better not fool around with the family. One can still get by with using mystical arms to camouflage questions of inheritance, but imagine for a bit that she really survives. . . . It would start all over again. Violetta's resurrection must shortly precede her physical death. Now, this is really a good deal. The undertakers can cry in peace; she will have a tomb sculptured in stone, with an angel on top crying chiseled tears; and Alfredo will marry—Violetta demanded he do so. He will be able to show her portrait to his young wife. Having to show a wife the face of a dead woman is not a lot to pay for a marriage. Taken over by the tenacious desire to enter the family at all costs, she has only this pitiful means at her disposal. She can have herself told and shown, she can become a saint whose legend will be passed on to the children when they are big enough. The legend of the reprobate. Reprobate, she says, baptizing herself in a sensational sound that is suddenly full of the church.

But we heard her, alive. In the first act she really sang: she is incapable of sexual heights; she is frigid; she does not know how. But a man in love with her appears and there she is, the reprobate. It is Alfredo who diverts her from the safe track where champagne made her head spin. He prostitutes her with love itself. Love, the dirty trick! Every crime in opera is committed in its name! As a final memory, among a thousand echos of waltzes, keep that one rare moment when nothing dances anymore. Listen to the frantic cry she pulls from the depth of her guts to exclaim to Alfredo that she loves him, when she has already decided to leave him. She throws herself on him, she stammers, she splutters: "Ah, my Alfredo, ah . . .". A song without words, a pure cry that is all alarm, the real farewell to a body that she has just decided to kill.

A little French princess

A cloister. Dark. There are golden gates; the light barely passes inside these walls in this barren land. A royal tomb on a scale befitting the ghost it contains. The presence of Emperor Charles V sweeps from the other side of death to fill the entire space. Before this tomb (where it is almost night even though it is full daylight outside) Elisabeth de Valois waits alone.

The story: Fontainebleau, just before the signing of the treaty of Cateau-Cambrésis that ended the war between Spain and France. In the forest Princess Elisabeth meets a Spanish envoy who shows her the portrait of the man for whom she is destined, Prince Carlos of Spain, son of Philip II. A heavenly surprise: the envoy and Don Carlos are one and the same. They fall in love, they are going to marry, and in the distance cannon shots and shouting signal the signing of the treaty. But it is not to be Carlos who marries Elisabeth, it is his father, King Philip himself; that is the decision of the diplomats. Putting an end to a love barely begun, and now impossible.

Things go badly between Carlos and his suspicious father. A justified suspicion: the young man supports the rebels of Flanders, hoping that his father will turn their management over to him. Such hopes are a waste of time and effort: the king listens to no one. He barely, distantly, listens to the Count of Posa, Carlos's friend, who describes to him the "deadly peace" sweeping over his empire. And even though he listens, he cannot truly be friends with him. The lovers see each other, chastely, despite the protocol forbidding it. What is more, the Princess Eboli, an attendant to Elisabeth the queen, jealously discovers their secret and denounces them to the king. Anger. Vengeance. The king decides, and the Grand Inquisitor agrees, to send his son to the stake. The Count of Posa vainly sacrifices his life in an attempt to divert the royal wrath, which is reinforced by an obvious will for political elimination. Carlos and Elisabeth meet one last time before the tomb of Charles V, where they are surprised by Philip II and the Grand Inquisitor. But, at the very moment when the soldiers of the Inquisition are about to sieze the young man, Charles V, or a monk who looks like him, rises from the tomb; he draws Carlos to him, and before the stupefied onlookers who are fixed to the spot, the grandfather and the grandson are engulfed in the shadows. A pretty gloomy story.[28]

Apparently, this is an opera of men. Yes, the central hero is a young man, Don Carlo, whose name Verdi and his librettists, Méry and du Locle, picked up in Schiller. Carlos is the rebel, sacrificed youth, and republican ideas projected onto Philip II's Spain; Carlos is unhappy love, the absolute victim of his father. . . . Surrounding him is a clan of men in conflict: his father, Philip II, his ghostly grandfather, Charles V, the Grand Inquisitor—all on the same royal side. Facing them stand Posa, his dearest friend, and the republicans of Flanders. The whole bunch at war, one camp against the other, with violent confrontations. They betray, they plot, they curse, they whisper. The opera is dominated by masculine tonalities; three bass voices where it is hard to establish any hierarchy among the burgraves. One is the holder of royal power, Philip II, a gloomy and solitary prince, a wild boar in his private wallow, the Escorial Palace. The other holds him in the palm of his hand. This is the Inquisitor, blind but backed by two little monks, impotent but omnipotent in State decisions. When these two are allied against Philip's own son, Church and State come together to destroy him; they disappear when confronted with the third power, the third bass: the monastic ghost of Charles V. It is hard to imagine darker royal deeds in the struggle for supreme paternity: The real father, the spiritual father, and the grandfather are quarreling over a son. Three generations of paternal power give *Don Carlo* the dark radiance of a monarchical opera, in which no woman has a place.

Confronting them, freedom is baritone. The envoys from Flanders and Posa, the mediator, caught between his friendship for Carlos and his respect for the king, are baritones. The tenor is the masculine victim, verging on femininity in his weakness and privation. And finally the woman, the little princess. Ghosts, blindmen, make up an entire, enclosed, and terrible world where Elisabeth of Valois, who is now Queen of Spain, struggles like a fly in a trap. The fleeting image of her father Henry II of France is in the air, it passes briefly in the courtly telling of a great tournament to be held there, with the king among the combatants. And blinded, the king lost his life in the royal tournament. Then pass the ghosts of Henry II's wives and the struggles (in which the little princess must have already found herself involved) between Catherine de Medicis and Diane de Poitiers, the true and false queens. And she, a true queen, is a foreigner exchanged like a war prize after a battle. Isolated and constrained like that other figure who resembles her: the beautiful queen in *Ruy Blas*.

How many of these women feel this nostalgia for the land of their birth, are marked with the seal of misfortune, are deported? Their original desire, their sadness, their violence, their necessary lie are not communicable in the country where they are living. From this inner exile is born the sweet lament that enhances Carmen's charm when she sings and dances, Violetta's cries when she decides to die of love, Mélisande's silence, and Butterfly's suicidal purity. The return to their country can be accomplished only in death, suffering, or betrayal.

Never will they see it again. Never will they return. Like the soul exiled in flesh, they become something like madwomen, distraught metaphysical dancers on the high wire of impassioned voices. Sophia, Wisdom, has lost her wings for good. They are like this mythical woman, this mad prostitute, whom a charlatan of the hellenistic world, Simon the Magician, displayed in the troubled regions where Greek Platonism and Roman eagles were making a bad mix. He showed her at the fair, and, dazzled, the curious gawked at Wisdom herself, fallen. Her gaze vague, her body neglected, Sophia danced at the end of a chain to Simon's command, like Lulu commanded by her trainer. Exiled, and only half-women because of the weight of their symbolic role, these prima donnas, commanded by conductors with their batons, sing for us gawkers. And we take them as the figure of women's unhappiness; and like the passersby in Alexandria, in Pergamon and Thebes, we revel in this spectacle that masks our reality. One day, however, Simon the Magician wanted to fly over the city's ramparts; but he was not a woman and he broke his neck. No one knows what became of the mad woman who accompanied him. She became a prima donna, her name is Carmen, Mélisande, Isolde or Elisabeth de Valois.

Excluded, everywhere in her kingdom she is excluded. Her only space is a royal palace; her only freedom the secret. When, she risks violating the protocol to receive Carlos, her only love, who is now her son-in-law, in secret, the king appears and immediately banishes the only Frenchwoman in her retinue. There is a song of this little French woman's nostalgia, with steady flutes phrasing her resignation. Excluded; from the heart of everyone around her, because the only heart she could rely on is forbidden her. She becomes a mere extra in the royal retinue, the sumptuous figure of a virgin set in heavy cloaks, when she has to be present at the autodafé and the martyrdom of the Jews, on the great square where Philip II has just had his son, Carlos, arrested. A lost voice in a vast choir, she is powerless and useless. Perhaps her only role is as a mysterious voice, not her own but one like it, falling out of the theater's limbo, when the Jews pass in procession to the stake.

She waits, alone in the deserted cloister, alone in defiance of the prohibitions, finally alone. This is her moment, this is her song. You saw her in the first act as the excited, young woman about to be married, then quickly disappointed by the change in husbands: she was promised Carlos, she gets his father, Philip. Then you saw her as the queen, constrained by her dignity, painfully resisting a forbidden love. Now she is to meet the young prince for a final farewell before he flees the dangerous paternal presence. But at this precise moment the constraints of kinship and court disappear. Now she does not weep, either about herself, or about the one she loves, or about her exile, or about her unhappiness. With a surprising foresight she addresses herself to the dead man in his tomb, to the one who understood the vanities of this world. She speaks to the ghost of that emperor Charles V who did not die as king but retreated into a convent to finish his days in a monk's habit. And so the symbolic link between a woman and a dead grandfather unfolds.

All the relationships were formed among men. The father and the son in a violent dialogue. The king and the Inquisitor in a dialogue of powers. The son and the friend in a dialogue of friendship and rebellion. The king and Posa in a dialogue of antagonism and respect. But, between Elisabeth and her royal husband there is no exchange; between Elisabeth and her lover there are violent, stolen words. There is no mother lurking about who could take on the tender function of mediator. And a perverse function is placed on Elisabeth's shoulders: she has to be Carlos's "mother." The *infante*'s real mother is dead. Elisabeth is his

"stepmother." They call each other *mia madre, mio figlio*. And if a name slips
out it is because the law has faded for just an instant before the quickly repressed
memory of their childhood love.

Incest lies in wait for them, and so does King Philip. Carlos was the fiancé.
In one glorious blast of a cannon, announcing the signing of a peace treaty, he
became the son. Her husband, the real one, this king Philip, lives too much in
the shadow of his dead father to be really a man. Ill acknowledged as king, he is
the shadow of a shadow, backed by a blind Inquisitor; there is not much to rejoice
about. The only thing that placates Philip is the foreshadowing of his death. His
wife does not love him—he knows she loves his son—and he must sleep alone.
He will sleep in his royal cloak in the tomb he is preparing for himself. That is
to be his truth. Philip II, the king who put Hieronymous Bosch's mad paintings
at the doorway to his bedroom, intending his own solitary mortification, is not
really alive. And because he is like someone already dead, crushed from birth
by the weight of his father, King Philip can do nothing against his son, even
though he has taken the woman his son loves.

This family is fatherless, despite all the characters who are father figures. Elisabeth, alone in the cloister, commits the missing act. She, the woman, speaks
to the only real father of this opera: a dead king. Consequently, he gives her,
from beyond the tomb, the power finally to assume the role of mother that she
had never accepted. At the moment when Elisabeth, sublimating her adolescent
passion, decides to act as a mother and renounces the role of lover assigned her
by her musical destiny, the opera finds its resolution. The conflicts were all locked
in place; the king and his son were at war with each other, one of them armed
with the Inquisition and the other with the revolt of Flanders. The king and his
wife were at war. There was no possible end to it.

But when Elisabeth's song is over, Charles V, beseeched and summoned by
this living woman, restores the story's missing link. This is the explanation for
the fabulous, mythical ending in which the ghost, rising from his tomb, King
and Inquisitor notwithstanding, swallows up the young *infante* in darkness. The
grandfather's ghost saves the grandson in the purest of symbolic gestures, simultaneously restoring to him the simulacrum of a mother.

In the luminous serenity of their lovers' farewell, just before the entrance of
the magical presence of the dead king, Elisabeth and Carlos met again for an
untroubled duet. How bright it was at Fontainebleau, in the thickets where they
fell in love, when all was clear and unthreatened! Between the innocent duet of
the first act and the sublimated duet of the last, much suffering will have passed
through the songs of these two young people. Elisabeth will spend the whole
opera changing generations, finally accepting her position as wife of a man she
almost had as a father-in-law. At the end of her long struggle, she no longer has
anything to lose; it is the story of her conversion from lover into mother.

But—outside this same cloister where the tomb awaited her; just now, when, as a young queen she rested a moment in the sun while her royal husband prayed inside—she cries out, as did Violetta just now, in a long winged moan inscribing the religious gesture that finishes the process. Carlos enters and sees her.

Against all protocol she sends her retinue away, and he embraces her, passionately, on the verge of incest. . . . The sky opens up, the world exists no more, laws are abolished . . .

She says no.

And when he has fled, the eternal cry, heavy with suffering, rises, the swift call rises, lifting toward the heights of the scale, only to plummet immediately in a long, dying chord, in a prayer. This is the rise and fall of Elisabeth de Valois, in a single musical phrase: rise, die, revive, descend, suffer, pray to God.

Why, at the moment of this sublime cry, does the vague memory of the real Elisabeth come to mind? The story Schiller wrote down is not imaginary. There was a real Don Carlos, a monstrous *infante* who was no doubt psychotic, cruel, and notorious for his fits of sadism. His stepmother cares for him tenderly, just as a very young girl, exiled in an enclosed world, might care for a mad child. In Hieronymous Bosch's paintings, which King Philip contemplated every evening, Paradise and the first family are side by side with Hell and the innocent Delights. That was kinship and its deformed legacies. The enormous weight of a dead emperor, a defeated Armada, and a rigid Spain that tortured Jews, inhabit the music of this opera driven mad by the constant crossbreeding of the political, the religious, and the family.

Elisabeth's first words, the first words of all, refer to this burden of history that will destroy her. Alone in the forest of Fontainebleau, the daughter, still in her native land, sits down; her young page tries to find out where they are because they are a little lost in this clearing. She says only: "*Ah, come stanca sono . . .*". Ah, I am so tired. There is a great distance between the fatigue of a young girl who has walked too far in her princess gown and the royal fatigue of the queen bent beneath the weight of a cloak of gold, whose weight is symbolic. Later, in the Spanish empire left by Charles V to an exhausted family, in the empire where the sun never set—so great was the extent of its territory, Elisabeth will follow the waning light; and, finally accepting to share the existence of that eternal son Philip II, she, the exiled one, will be the only real heir to the empire.

The flute, the little bells, and coloratura

The eighteenth century. The real dawn of the bourgeois family. The time when, between the poor peasant families losing numerous children in a lifetime and the noble families fixing each of theirs up with solid stations, the real solid family, endowed with few children, dedicated to a good, monogamous reproduction installs itself. A family even more dedicated to crushing women who step out of the docile line of wives and daughters. Let us leave Verdi and the blazing tempos of marches and waltzes. Here are Mozart and his heavenly ambiguities.

Perhaps you have already been told that *The Magic Flute* was a masonic opera, an initiation passage halfway between mystical fantasy and history. No doubt the three majestic chords in which Mozart unites history and the code of the secret society pursuing men's freedom have been painted in glowing colors for you. You will have heard the praises of Zarastro the Magus sung, along with the stirring progress of two innocent beings who pass through a series of enchanted ordeals at their own pace. Why not strip off the Egyptian claptrap? Let us forget the Syrian fluff, the animal skins, the triangular emblems, forget the blue sky, the moon, the sun, and the stars; let us leave the temple of Isis. In the characters' finely woven fabric, a different story becomes apparent, like on a curtain where a design appears at dusk that one had not seen before. Look at *The Magic Flute* "backlit" from beyond the symbolic and conventional signs, and you will be able to hear the violence of a family quarreling over a daughter.

The story: Tamino, prince of his estate and extremely innocent, battles in vain against a monster. At the moment when he succumbs, he is saved by three women. They are attendants to the Queen of the Night. To make up for having saved him, they take him to this sovereign, who is cloaked in all the marvels of the Darkness. She asks Tamino to bring back her daughter Pamina, who had been carried off by the Magus Zorastro, and she entrusts the young prince with a portrait of the princess, with whom he falls immediately in love. Tamino, accompanied by Papageno, the Queen's charming and timid birdcatcher, goes off to free the captive. She is, indeed, locked up by Zorastro, but for her own good. Bit by bit, Tamino sees that the Evil is not where he thought it was, and that the enemy is the queen. He agrees to undergo initiation by ordeal at the temple of Wisdom, enduring hunger, thirst, and especially silence in cruel situations. When Pamina sees, for example, that Tamino does not answer her anymore—she does not know he is constrained to silence—she tries to commit suicide. Three angels come to her aid. She rejoins Tamino and together they cross fire and water to arrive finally at Light. Zarastro abdicates in their favor; the Queen of the Night, who wanted to attempt an armed attack, is defeated. As for Papageno, who did not, however, overcome a single one of the obstacles, he finds that, despite his failures, he is provided with a wife of his own . . . Papagena. And the flute? It is a magical instrument, given to Tamino by the Queen of the Night to keep danger away. But it used to belong to Zarastro.[29]

A child battles a monster. It has to be perfectly obvious that the huge monster attacking Tamino is a cardboard monster. His red teeth, his fiery felt tongue breathe imaginary fire, and he rolls his shoebutton eyes, manipulated by an extra from inside the great green carcass. Two springs make the wings of this clawed dragon work. The child faints. Tamino is a little boy. Monsters are really scary. They are big, and they frighten you. And the painted wooden sword is powerless against the terrors of the game. Tamino dies of anxiety.

A little girl pretends to be locked up. She is the little princess in an unknown palace, and, just like in a dream, an ugly black man who rolls his shoebutton eyes is threatening to rape her. She cries very very loudly. A Monostatos touching you is very scary; luckily daddy is not far away and mummy is pretending she is on a trip. Pamina is just a kid. Tamino and Pamina are basically children playing prince and princess. A few details forewarn of the impending seriousness of the game. The little prince will not conquer the monster with his little sword, and the little princess senses that the fire she is playing with might well burn her. Adolescence is not far off; and with it the end of the childhood recounted by *The Magic Flute*.

Until the very end, Papageno, because he is half animal, will keep the unchastened nature of this first world, the world of children. A birdcatcher covered with feathers—is this man or bird? His obvious moral weaknesses are no cause for reproach. He is not of the elite. He is just a little bird, a kind of savage, good for manifesting everything about man that does not manage to rise above his domesticated condition. Cowardly (they call this cowardliness), clumsy, talkative, greedy, he is only good for reproduction. Proof? His one and only love duet, with Papagena, evokes the flock of children that are sure to result from this lineage. His future is called Papagena: just as in French a feminine ending is assigned to a sort of animal and *chien* (dog) becomes *chienne* (bitch), this little female has no identity of her own. She is nothing other than Papageno's female; hence, Papagen(a). They play daddy and mummy together. They are incapable of passing through the stages that should have led them to adulthood, to be grown-ups. They remain children . . .

Bless them. Papageno, the primitive stage of unabashed desires, Papageno, disobedience and innocent tricks, is also the poor man, the slave, the future proletarian, whose only wealth is his children. When this all begins, Tamino and Papageno are separated only by an underlying class difference, but they are two children who play. When it is all over, Tamino has become King, adult, serious, and responsible; only Papageno has been able to retain his childhood. One more step, and he will play at smashing his childhood friend's face in. That will come later.

When Tamino and Pamina, who have only seen each other by the intermediary of a portrait and kind words, meet for the first time, they rush to each other. "It is him!" "It is her!" they cry, and wrapped in each other's arms they stick together, the way children do in their most affectionate gestures, their arms squeezing so hard you cannot breathe. They are going to play at love; they have not yet discovered the distance, the suffering, the mourning, and the desolation. That comes soon. The parents—the terrible parents—are going to see to their apprenticeship. They will separate them—the way they themselves are already separated in hatred. They will reunite them afterward, but in the little Pamina's charm there appears something like an echo of suffering; she already knows. And Tamino, from now on the possessor of the power he has inherited from his royal tutor Zorastro, bears himself with a dangerous gravity. He has become a man; he has undergone the ordeals. They have lost their childhood, they have grown up. And never again will they be able to rejoin Papageno and Papagena.

Leaving childhood, to go where? In *The Magic Flute* there are no reunited parents; rather, there is a radical divorce between the mother, the world of women, and the father, king in the world of men. These two, the Queen of the Night and Zarastro, no doubt loved each other once, as Tamino and Pamina love each other today. But they are separated by the insurmountable distance separating Night from Day and the Moon from the blazing Sun. The first world, once childhood is left behind, is the women's world, occupied by the Queen and the three women who attend her. Three useless vixens, species feminine. And the wonderful Queen with the coloratura passages that make this role absolutely perilous for any prima donna.

The Queen of the Night is the only one who expresses herself in a part that is technically unbearable, intenable tessitura. It is an intransmissible language. Whatever she says, whether it is sad or violent, the words she sings do not come across. She speaks a language that terrifies and seduces, but do we have any idea at all what she is saying? She speaks not at all to reason. She does not make sense; she sings purely affective language far beyond the words stringing out the signified. Coloratura is repetition stretched out on a flashy melody, in a register where the voice can do no more than emit—meaningless syllables, note after note. A madwoman, cut off from everyone else, the Queen of the Night has no other language than her fearsome and beautiful song. Black, dressed in silver, nocturnal, the queen sings, and everything is in this song. For the frightened children who recognize in her the great, mad song of the Mother suffering, she sings their babbling language, hard to recognize, transformed into rage and tenderness. This is a losing song; it is femininity's song.

The winning world is the other one, the father's, the men's world. And that is what it says. I am not making it up, sweetheart, that is what it says. When Tamino, who has grown up a bit, arrives at the doors of the temple, men's voices refuse to let him in, first one door, then another; the third finally opens for him. First lesson: a mother's arms are always open, but not the doors to knowledge. It is good to experience men's rejection. So that the initiate who speaks to him finds a lost boy, ready to hear: he has been afraid, he has been cold; he listens to a man for the first time. What does this man tell him? Things are not what they appear; the world is illusion, and reality is hard to discover. Who told Tamino that Zarastro was a bad man, a tyrant? The Queen of the Night. But is she not a woman? And a woman—that is something that talks a lot and knows nothing

. . . . The text says that plain as day. A mean story. The boy does not resist the version of the facts the initiate presents him, not even for a minute. He changes sides immediately; he accepts the argument about feminine chatter without desiring even a hint of proof. And this is how a young man, still too soft to be done with dragon fantasies, moves into his real place, after having been lost by mistake (while unconscious) in the great arms of the Mother with a superhuman voice.

Well, so, women chatter. Little Pamina gets to find out more about this. She meets Tamino, who is in love with her, while he is subjected to the ordeal of silence. And she cannot bear his incomprehensible silence. Immediately she *interprets*. He does not love her anymore, that is certain. Pamina the chatterer does not understand the harsh law of silence — and why should she understand it? Tell me. Why should she know? And how not go crazy over it? It is enough to make one die of grief. No one subjects Pamina to the ordeal. If she meets her prince, it is not so that she herself can undergo the ordeal of suffering; it is so that she can act as the instrument for the man's ordeal. Women are not subjected to ordeal; it is not worth it. Pamina, in hysterics, gives in to the Mother's voice inside herself and unleashes capacities for grief that Tamino does not have. To save her, "they" have posted children there. Real children — angels — whose voices have not yet developed, a little screechy and out of tune, shaky and unsure. That is what it takes to bring her back to reality and to decide not to kill herself. Between maternal madness and paternal enigma — who said Zarastro was good? — the little girl does not know. She does not need to know; all she has to do is suffer.

Zarastro the ineffable is highly respectable. What? Here is a good and fair man who spreads good wherever he goes, a man acclaimed by the people, a man who is finally wise enough to abdicate when the young couple reaches maturity. What are you saying? He kidnapped a daughter from her mother? You are joking I suppose; you know perfectly well that that is necessary and that girls would be unable to remain in the maternal world. And the relationship between mother and daughter, broken off completely? Suppose we talk about something else . . . about the necessity for education, the magnificent ideas expressed by Mozart — more justice, more light — let us look at Goethe — That's it! Suppose we talk about Goethe's death, about *mehr Licht*, about those wonderful humanist ideas, in short, about the French Revolution . . .

My voice trails off in embarrassed mumblings. Nothing I can do gets through this skin toughened by centuries of repression. The queen is lost, the voice is crushed beneath the stones of the temple; mine is too. Women's undoing is ensured. And thousands of initiates tell me in a single grumbling voice that Pamina the girl-child pulls through best of all, that the Mother is evil. The children of *The Magic Flute* learn enough about their parents' divorce to make them

lose heart. Zarastro and the Queen of the Night: a real couple, full of hate, argu-
ing over their baby girl.

"Strength is the victor, rewarding an eternal crown to beauty and to wisdom."
These are the last words of the opera. Bravo strength; bravo manhood's new hair,
priests; bravo wisdom, police for Reason. . . . Tamino valiantly keeps going his
own sweet way; ah, what a good young man, how well he resists in the company
of the little animal Papageno who devours the fruits, the water, and the wine
offered by mysteriously disguised creatures. . . . For him the inheritance. For
Pamina suffering and going along with him. Also for Pamina the enigmatic deed.
Such a deed will pass on to Tamino the magic flute inherited from Zarastro,
passed on to the Queen of the Night; and now, from woman to man, it falls into
the hands of the boy to help him cross fiery and watery hells. The flute started
with a man—Zarastro carved it from an oak one stormy night—and comes back
to a man; women just pass it on. Their weak hands hold onto nothing. If there is
an opera that clearly shows, with all its verbal and musical power, the crushing
symbolics of men over women, it is *The Magic Flute*. Divine Mozart? This is
he. The ideals of fraternity and liberty? The very same. There are a few holes in
the exalted cloth of our pious humanism.

Two miraculous moments escape the misogynous consciousness of their creator. When Pamina, all alone, is shut up in Zarastro's palace, and emprisoned in
her anguish, Papageno breaks in and recognizes her. The two children embrace
each other madly in complete disregard of the laws they will learn later. Papageno the servant, and Pamina the princess sing a duet whose tenderness tells of
the innocence of two hearts ready to fall in love. Ready to fall in love: they sing
that man and woman are complementary, that love exists, that there is happiness, such happiness! . . . It does not last. Neither of them falls in love with the
other. To each his/her own; they are not to talk to each other again.

Later. Pamina has found her own; Papageno is still waiting for his. Pamina
loves Tamino, who loves her too; their wrenches are for later, when Pamina has
become a mother and will have her turn to lose her own daughter. . . . Nothing
has been put off longer and nothing is purer than the moment when they finally
come together. From the heart of darkness rises the voice of the young girl. She
is calling: "O my Tamino, what happiness . . .". As for him, he does what he
can. He replies, echoing: "Pamina, my Pamina, what happiness . . .". But, like
the first happiness, this cannot last. For Pamina, chattering Pamina, daughter of
her mother, there will be future children, flowers, happiness, but only happiness. For Tamino, who has become a man, there will be justice and new dragons, which, you can be sure, he will defeat with no difficulty this time. He gets
the flute, the strength, the violence and the right.

You do not like my story? You prefer *The Magic Flute* of your childhood and
the birdcatcher's lighthearted laughter while he looks for his bird? . . . Yes. But
men's education suppresses its own violences, and I have never yet seen my

heart's version of the *Flute*. In it the good priests with majestic voices would do what they really do; they would shove Pamina forcibly into the cubbyhole where Zarastro locks her up, they would beat up the Queen of the Night, they would kick Papageno, the truth at last. . . . The complicity between the young boy and the men could be read, clear as day, as well as the oppression they impose heavily on the little birdcatcher, and the dishonor of the women whom they subjugate. The music would be no less divine; but it would then serve a more just cause. And the children who play together would no longer suffer so many irreparable wrenchings between their fearsome parents. Night would no longer be violent, Day would no longer be brutal. It would be another world, which does not yet exist.

We would need another Mozart, one who did not eternally seek vengeance for having been, as a child, a learned birdcatcher, trained to catch harpsichord-birds; a Mozart who . . . but I am delirious, jubilantly. For a long time to come it will be under the sign of *The Magic Flute* that the defeat and undoing of the queen and the end of Night is carried out.

We are in Mycenae, crouched lions overhead. The sun blazes; inside the palace it is cool. It is the time she goes to mourn her father, and the cries she hurls at heaven to conjure up the murdered king frightens the servant populace. She shouts loudly enough to shake walls. . . . She comes at you with her nails. She is so terrifying, this daughter mourning her father, that she makes her mother Clytemnestra, the criminal, dream. But is she, Clytemnestra, really a murderer, she who thought to avenge the murder of her daughter Iphigenia by killing Agamemnon? From crime to crime, from father to daughter, then again from mother to daughter, the family history is perpetuated. It can come to an end later only through the intervention of men and the invention of law. In opera space-time women cry. The women, the survivors, fight one another, each one the bearer of a man: Clytemnestra carries within herself a second husband, Aegisthus the coward; Electra carries her father, Agamemnon, and her brother, Orestes. When Orestes shows up he is instrumental, her agent for matricide. Women's voices shout at death, shout beneath the walls. They die, both of them: Clytemnestra by Orestes's knife and Electra of pleasure. The mother, dead, in the long history of a feminine law, will have been the final incarnation of the mythical matriarchy; with her the historic undoing and defeat of femininity begins. The victorious woman, the one who defends the father's power, will, with her vengeance, have betrayed the cause of women.

The last couple remains. Little Chrysothemis, the passive sister; and Orestes, who goes mad, pursued by black, hissing, serpentine goddesses, Furies, the Erinnyes. The walls of Mycenae ring with the two women's cries of death and hatred. The fight between men and women is even more deadly when a woman makes herself the instrument of men's vengeance against their peers. And it is more permanently deadly when the fight pits a daughter against her mother. That, said Giraudoux, when the crimes have been committed, is what is called dawn. But the dawn rising over Mycenae is the dawn of our repression.[30]

Chapter 4
The Girls Who Leap into Space

*In which we see a mother make jam and a girl write a letter
to no one in particular; in which a feminine Pierrot cannot
light her candle and dies of cold; in which some betrayed
fiancées dream they are hallucinating; in which we discover
Kierkegaard and a clumsy Don Juan.*

For a girl infinity is as natural as the idea that all love must be happy.
Everywhere a girl turns she finds infinity surrounding her, and she is
able to jump into it; her leaping is feminine and not masculine. Men
usually are so clumsy! To jump they speed up, they have to get ready
way ahead of time, they calculate the distance visually, they start off a
few times but get scared and go back. Finally they jump and fall inside.
A girl jumps differently. . . . Her jump is a gliding flight. And when
she reaches the other side she finds that, instead of being exhausted by
the effort, she is more beautiful than ever, even more full of soul, she
throws a kiss to those of us who remained behind. Young, newborn,
like a flower growing from mountain roots, she sways over the abyss
until we are almost dizzy.

Ah, Søren Kierkegaard, how you loved girls. . . . What countless hymns you
wrote to these girls who jump with fantastic energy and then fall into unspeakable suffering! What countless sad songs to the heroines of seduction, whose
destroyed innocence is all that interests you. Only girls like Zerlina, Marguerite,
Donna Elvira, Marie Beaumarchais—and Antigone as well, whom you thought
had a sort of incestuous secret so you could love her more dearly. Søren Kierkegaard, showman of she-bears and dashed women, philosophical acrobat, how
you loved girls!

Opera is full of girls like this, but they were not enough for you, so you made
up a tale for yourself, something halfway between novel and libretto. In this tale,
the hero, one of your doubles, makes one of these feminine flowers, in whom

78

this vital energy is rising, love him. She becomes engaged to him, yet he convinces her to break it off and to follow him in a love unsullied by any social tie. Cordelia, whom you named after a girl famous for being sacrificed, does everything he wants. She jumps; she jumps again, keeps jumping until the final leap. Oh, you do veil it with modest names. She fucks. And your hero ditches her. A sorry story. The music of the text, the music you say is the "privileged medium of sensuality," makes the shabbiness of this little scenario count among your philosophical acts of revenge. Seduced, Cordelia is worthless. She has jumped when she should not have jumped any more. Scarcely born, she dies immediately. *Le Journal du séducteur* is the name of the tale.

Preserves

Silver birches, warm twilight; it is summer on the Russian plain. This is certainly the only opera that starts with preserves. This jam. . . . How could anyone imagine it is the key to *Eugen Onegin*? At the front of the stage, it is warm and pleasant; night is coming soon; they have to hurry but not too fast; Mme Larina and the nurse are stirring the marmelade in copper pots. In the distance, beyond these women who are already old, there are two girls singing. A pipe and a nightingale, they sing simply at the edge of night. They sing a peaceful song of sorrow and tenderness. And the two melancholy old women remember; once Mme Larina sang like that, they both recall it well. She loved Richardson so much, she was young. . . . Engaged to a man she did not love, in love with another, this former girl, so elegant, now grown old, remembers a tune from her youth through the melodies of her own daughters. She was called "Céline." And then the marriage and the husband, and then . . . she was revolted, then she got used to it. No more sentiment, no more elegance, no more romantic books. Instead "woolen vests and quilted hats." Serfs come to bring her the first wheat harvested, and Mme Larina's nostalgia and her preserve-making come to an end with a philosophy comprised in a single sentence. Her words are firm and muted in counterpoint with the songs of the two girls: "Habit is a gift from heaven that takes the place of happiness for us."

Eugen Onegin, or how girls repeat their mothers' history.

The story: Tatiana and Olga are the two daughters of a rather well-to-do landowner, Mme Larina. Olga is almost engaged to a young poet, Lenski. He has just come to visit, accompanied by Eugene, a dandy, glamorously equipped with all the latest city styles. Lenski pays court to Olga, Tatiana and Eugene talk. Tatiana has fallen in love at first sight. That night she writes him a long, passionate letter. But the next day, Eugene receives the letter coolly, somewhat mockingly. Later, there is a party at the Larine's. Olga dances with Lenski, Tatiana with Eugene. Just to make the gossips who are cackling about him seem ridicu-

lous, and because he is bored to death, Eugene pays court to Olga. Tragedy erupts: Lenski challenges his friend to a duel and Eugene's first pistol shot kills the poet. Years later, we find Eugene Onegin in Petersburg. He is more and more bored. A gorgeous woman comes in, the most stunning of all: it is Princess Gremine—Tatiana. Prince Gremine is a friend of Onegin's but it is Onegin's turn to fall madly in love. He surprises Tatiana at home and declares his passion in vain. He is too late and Tatiana will remain faithful to her husband. Nostalgia is no longer what it was, and yet it is what it never ceased being.[31]

Eugen Onegin is not a dramatic opera. Nothing happens in it—well, almost nothing. There is a girl, a youthful love, a duel, a taste for the pleasure of repetition, an immense sadness—nothing, I call it. Onegin is a very small young man, rather obnoxious, insignificant. Pushkin gives him a cowlick in a derisive little sketch. And then we've heard often enough that this work by Pushkin, whose position in Russian is so essential, is impossible to translate in any language. This is a long, untranslatable poem about the Russian bourgeoisie, the jam it made, what it read and the little heartbreaks that disturb temporarily—only temporarily—women's and men's souls. It took Tchaikovski, never more inspired than in his operas, to succeed in describing the birches, the quilted hats, the brilliant waltzes of the court and the rustic polkas of a society that looked to Europe for everything. This watered-down romanticism, this humble stew of Sturm und Drang, this sweetness everywhere is barely interrupted by a few, great, passionate developments: the suffering of the poet Lenski, his fleeting death, and the last sobs of a dandy who, you can be sure, will feed his ennui with this hopeless love.

But there is Tatiana. Rising above all else, moving as ardently through the spaces of the country house as through those of the brilliant St. Petersburg, there is the girl and the seduction. From the moment she lifts her sad voice in the duet sung in the familiar twilight, there enters a passionate serenity, a swan's wing, a despondancy, a fragility, still somehow resistant, that are not to be belied. Listen to the contrasting representations of her. Listen to how the girl gets caught in a trap she does not know about. Here she is in love with a dandy, like her mother. Does she know that? It is not necessary: the unconscious works without a word's being said, through silences. And, like Mme Larina, she marries someone else; like her, she gets used to it. At least enough—"wool vests and quilted hats"—to reject Onegin's love. An old memory from her youth, one so long awaited, one she loved still. This is the story of a reasonable woman; not really the makings of a "good" opera libretto.

But yes. Hear how the drama is muffled and the suffering crushed beneath peace and family life. Onegin is a seducer. He makes eyes at Tatiana from boredom, eyes enough to make her take the plunge with the letter she wrote him. It is also boredom that makes him decide to pay court to Olga . . . a real seducer, as

Søren Kierkegaard understood it. He is a "little guy" of no substance, there only to arouse, arousing emotion and disappointment, disseminating chaos. All for nothing. There is only one loss of life — opera requires that there be at least one death. The kind and futile Lenski, sacrificed figure of the poet who is dear to Pushkin, dies. Pushkin ends up identifying with him and dying of it.

But the living Tatiana is a woman poet. It falls to her, in a world in which her mother and her nurse are old, to embody youth. Youth broken in two by male seduction. Tatiana's youth — broken, forsaken, defeated, undone. But not her beauty, at least; when she makes her entrance as the princess Gremine, wearing a crimson beret that goes straight to Onegin's heart — the things things depend on! — Tatiana has become a woman. And a faithful wife. This is a cruel tale and more lifelike than many others on the opera stage. Emerging from the violent emotions of Verdi, Puccini, and Bellini, I was bored to death the first time I saw *Eugen Onegin*. I remember mentioning this boredom to Pierre Macherey, a Marxist theoretician with very sound ideas and feelings about opera. But his reply was: "You'll see. . . . It is an opera that talks about the loves of youth. It comes back to you later." It was true. Later, after-the-fact — when my youthful loves had been smashed as well, memories, tones of voice return. As if it were our own adolescence and our own dreams coming back.

Tatiana is in her room. Gently now, the violins sing as if their hearts would break. Gently, softly: the nurse is still there, come to tuck her little girl in. The little girl has grown up with no warning. She questions the nurse: Were you ever in love? Well, no, no one talked about love in those days. And the nurse tells her story. It is a story showing brutally — but still so sweetly, how peaceful it is in this girlish room — the huge and radical class difference. At thirteen the nurse's marriage was arranged by her parents and a matchmaker; her father gave her his blessing, they braided her hair beautifully, and then suddenly she was in another family. The nurse sings words that are simple and truthful. But Tatiana hears nothing because she suffers so. She says she is in love. The nurse, who has no idea what she is talking about, thinks she is sick and goes to find some holy water. And the music has a double line: for Tatiana there is the periodic, romantic soaring, and for the nurse there is the regular, traditional rhythm of a lament that knows only of passing time and getting used to things. This old peasant woman will have to be made to leave the room, in order for bourgeois "passion" finally to burst out.

Tatiana is alone, in her white nightgown. The cellos hesitate as she does, they envelop her and begin the long, very long phrase carrying the girl by slowly rising scales to the heights of love's passion. Punctuated by peaceful flutes and sweet oboes, the letter is written while Tatiana sings to the rhythm of her pen racing on the page. Fate has ordained, him, God, us, a dream, an angel, or a devil . . . disjointed words, words balanced on the music, words of love for no one, for a phantom love. Absent in body, full of the nothing characteristic of this opera, full of the emptiness of youthful passions and their empty violence, Tatiana writes a letter. Girls write letters.

Often, letters are written during operas. But they are meant to make sense, to produce some intrigue, to move characters in the direction of some action that will advance the libretto. There are letters of rendezvous, grateful letters from a heroine who has lost her family, the false letters of a traitor. You will not see them written because only their meaning is important. But with Tatiana it is something else: she writes—that is the action. She writes—that is the intrigue and the heart of the matter. That brief moment, the few minutes of singing alone represent a whole long night of love: her one and only night of love. Her real winged leap, her "soaring flight." On the other side of night we find her newborn, like a flower that grew from mountain roots.

A good one to deceive. Ready for the act of seduction itself. Oh, I have read you over and over again, Søren, I understand perfectly well what you write so complacently. No, seduction is not only the act of making oneself be loved when one does not love; it is, above all, making the one who loves you know that you do not love—breaking her flight, clipping her wings, making her bend her neck. It is making the girl bear this disappointment within herself, mistrustful ever after. It is dawn. The nurse returns, Tatiana is more beautiful than ever, a little pale; the nurse is worried. Tatiana gives her the letter the way one jumps off into space. Who has never thrown a letter into an irreversible hole, with a beating heart and spirit agape at a point of no return?

When Eugene Onegin, paternalistic enough to be insulting, speaks to Tatiana from the heights of his great age, telling her, in fact, that a girl can perfectly well substitute other dreams for her dreams, her only reply is: "What shame!" . . . It is all over already. The rest—the ball, the duel, the waltzes at the court in St. Petersburg—are only the ups and downs that confirm it. Everything has been staked.

Once again, the girl will be paid homage. This time by an old man, an eccentric Frenchman, M. Triquet, who is a very charming neighbor. With a lovesong straight from the mythical France that, in Russia, stands for charm and affairs of the heart, he tells Tatiana of his old man's adoration. It is just a simple ballad. The couplets are idiotic and the puns stupid. But Tatiana reigns as queen then at this provincial ball, where she is adored by an old Frenchman and scorned by the other. When Onegin, in this other ball where she wears a beret of scarlet velvet, considers her worthy of him at last, time and the unerasable mark made by the seduction will have taken their toll; the discrepancy is all that remains. She loved him, he did not love her; he loves her, she is no longer free. The curtain falls on youthful loves; the girl is gone. The time to make preserves has come.

A moonlike Pierrot

One can also die of youth—of too much flame wasted when everywhere is cold, when no stove is hot enough to warm what is inside and life slips away quietly, without warning. You can die like that, on tiptoe, while all around you everything swirls and whirls. This time there are no parents around. In *La Bohème* all the characters are desperately young. No one is evil; it is the opera of innocence. A woman loses her life in it, of course. But it is as if there were no responsibility, as if nothing happened other than this great cold, freezing them all, which one of them, a woman, cannot withstand. Very young people bustle all around this girl dying nicely on an old mattress. Powerless, fickle, and serious at the same time, they surround the dying girl with their presents, their tenderness, and their incapacity to master a too harsh reality. More than any other opera, Puccini's *La Bohème* confronts the girl with the infinity she seeks, with an invisible purity at play in the extravagant exhilaration of irresponsible celebrations, in a charming casualness where each one knows from the outset that he can lose and accepts this without even thinking to protest. *La Bohème*, is natural death. Christian tragedy is radically absent and the heart is forever cleansed of what is tragic about love. This is the naked, new skin of a child's sorrow just before it turns over a new leaf and shrinks away.

The story: Rodolfo, Marcel, Schaunard, and Colline are friends. They live together in great poverty, making do, conning their landlord when it is time to pay him the rent, and helping each other out in a romantic Paris. It is a bohemian existence. One night—Christmas Eve—it is cold outdoors and scarcely warm in the friends' room. Rodolfo is alone when Mimi, a young girl who is a neighbor, knocks on the door. She has no more matches; her candle is out. Rodolfo sees that she is coughing and is cold, and he keeps her there with him, where they talk and fall in love. And, since it is Christmas, they go out with the others to celebrate in Paris. Marcello has a flirtatious, charming, and crazy girlfriend, Musetta; but he is mad at her, because she has dropped him for Alcindoro de Mittoneaux, who is older and richer than Marcello. Lovers' quarrels, childrens' parades. Rodolfo buys Mimi a pink bonnet to seal their love. But two months later it is February and getting colder and colder. Mimi goes to see Marcello and Musetta in their tiny room where they are still sulking at each other. Mimi is worried and unhappy because Rodolfo is jealous, encouraging her to leave, wanting nothing to do with her anymore. She sees him coming. She hides behind a tree and finds out the truth: Rodolfo does want her to leave him. But it is because she is seriously ill and he has no money to pay for her care. She reveals her presence and, with great emotion, Rodolfo and Mimi decide to spend at least the winter together. Later, Rodolfo and Marcello are alone; they speak of Musetta and Mimi, now wealthily installed. But Musetta appears, completely distraught; she arrives moments before the dying Mimi, who is returning to Rodolfo. It is late, too late; Musetta looks for a muff and Colline goes off to sell her coat to pay the doctor, all in vain. Mimi is getting ready to die and all the while Rodolfo sees nothing. She dies; he does not see.[32]

Christmas Eve, elsewhere, in the houses of the rich, everything is ready for the midnight feast. Mimi knocks on the door like *mon ami Pierrot*. The girl takes after Pierrot with her ingenuous grace, her pale innocence, and the simplicity with which she announces, in a melody so well known that one's heart must make an effort to rediscover it: *Mi chiamamo Mimi*. Her name is Mimi. There she is. Her candle is gone and it is dark, she is afraid. Come in, neighbor, it is no warmer here than at your place, but there will be two of us. It is a lonely, sad night for two hearts that fall in love. Mimi—Pierrot has put out her candle and now she manages to make a second mistake. She leaves her key at the young man's place, she comes back. And he, the rascal—they are five-year-olds who like lollipops and playing tricks—hides the key that he has found.

Her candle goes out. It is dark but the fear is gone; there is all the wonder of a long duet in which sweet, spiraling harpsongs and serene melodies tenderly embrace. How do they exist? Like children. He is a poet, that says it all. She does not do anything; she waters her flowers at the window, she embroiders silk and satin for other people, that is all. She loves everything. She breathes roses, petal by petal, and the world is beautiful, innocent, and pure, like Pierrot's heart. What is more, she does not know how she got the name Mimi, because her real name is Lucia, Light. And that is what she has just lost, the light.

They are very young, hardly more than children. They play at love, having both just discovered this awesome electric train, this wonderful toy. They are able to be no longer afraid of the dark. Each one will be the other's illusory protection, a great, generous breast where the milk of human kindness flows. And, when she has lost her petals at the end of her flowerlike life, Mimi will return to her friend in search of arms that will hold her, the touch of a hand, the vast calm of a death where she is not alone any more. It is not sad, it is not fun. It is childhood and its misunderstood heartbreak.

But little Light has far different resources than those of the nice poet. She and she alone clearly accepts her fatal illness; she and she alone decides about her dying. Like Tatiana she jumps, she takes flight, returning to collapse gently, delicate and strong, brave despite her fear of the dark and this endless cold creeping over her. Infinity for Mimi is warmth. In *La Bohème* all the action is between cold and warmth. Mimi's hands are cold; Rodolfo, irresistibly, wants to warm them.

It all takes place in the intense winter cold, when Mimi, at the gates of Hell, goes to find help in the snow and the rare passersby are wrapped so warmly. The houses are shut up tight; you can see the light inside through the bright windows. But the young people are outdoors. This tubercular girl sings her love in the snow and tries to ignore it, leaping over winter as if she leaps beyond the void. Staying with Rodolfo, when all he can offer is the heat of his own body, is playing with death. But that is what she decides to do. After winter comes the time for flowers. . . . When she dies she is cold all over. Winter has won. All around her the others are bearing up, perfectly healthy. Only she . . . Pierrot the girlfriend, plays one last time with her shopgirl trinkets; a pink bonnet that Rodolfo had pressed to his heart, a muff. Pierrot is dying; but Pierrot is not an unhappy man with a sorrowful brow.

Pierrot is a girl.

The roles are reversed. Pierrot is the girl and Colombine the poet. Rodolfo, a lightweight—sensitive, impotent, and innocent—Rodolfo-Colombine leads Mimi to her destruction. In the opera, just like in psychoanalysis, everything counts; and, just like in an analysis, the important part of the signifier is said in passing, lightly, at the beginning, and nothing points to its being the crux of the drama. Like in an analysis, when the end approaches the signifier lying in wait reappears, sounding an alarm in the spectator's watchful unconscious. Benumbed by the music his heart, although in the dark, gets the message and is moved by it unawares. Butterfly's surprise that anyone would pin butterflies to a board; Prince Tamino's fainting; or Carmen's first words: "When will I love you? Well, I do not know . . .". And in *La Bohème*, a few words said to each other, words of no importance, with no aria, no quotation marks.

Mimi and Rodolfo have gone out in each other's arms, bound to one another for better or for worse in the only winter they will have. They are in the street, in the midst of the Christmas crowd, near the Cafe Momus sparkling with light and warmth. A group of happy friends is there, and when the poet introduces Mimi to them, he composes a sort of impromptu elegy to describe this girl and his budding love. "This is Mimi, a happy girl-flower; she complements the bohemian world—it is the poet and she the poetry. And while flowers spring from the poet's mind, the flowers of springtime come from Mimi's fingers." A well-turned phrase indeed, a melodious and felicitous compliment; night is so beautiful for young love! But the truth lies in Colline's and Schaunard's mocking remarks: the rhetoric was not bad but hardly better quality than a runner-up. Truth blows over like a cool breeze; Rodolfo's love is rhetoric.

There is no rhetoric that does not describe fate; and Mimi's fate is written in Rodolfo's words. She is poetry: already no longer a woman she will never be one. A girl doomed to her flowers, she is to have no other existence. She is trapped in the poet's images. As Muse and inspiration she joins the troop of girls sacrificed by the seducer so he can live in a suspended time: a moment of poetry, yet another, one last day of winter, yet another, and life stops. Then only Rodolfo will wake up, and he saw nothing. He did not do it on purpose.

They are surrounded by a crowd, by life, by joy that is a little violent, and the crush of evening parties. Children everywhere; indulgent parents, it is a kids' Saturnalia. Parpignol, who sells flowers and sweets, pushes his cart around. They buy wooden horses and trumpets and the pink bonnet for Mimi, the one she so longed for. They eat, they spend; they no longer live in frigid poverty.

Another bright and beautiful girl is singing. Musetta is as lively as Mimi is sickly, as solid as the other is delicate, as pigheaded as the other is sweet. She is one of the few women in all of Puccini's works who does not die of dependence. I love her, with her taunting lowcut dresses, her provocative velvets, the tricks she admits to, and her lousy temper. Musetta sets herself there, perched up high, something to be reckoned with, scathing; the first thing one hears is her laughter. She sets herself up with glass in hand and sings very loudly to provoke her lover, Marcello. And the old fogey who came with her is scared to death: "*Parla piano . . .*". How far will this crazy she-devil go?

She sings. She is queen. Musetta's waltz avenges generations of women. "When I walk alone through the streets, people stop to see me and look at my beauty from head to toe." From head to toe. . . . The image of a woman comes up, one who is a little fat and very blond, a Lola-Lola sheathed in black, a scandalous Lulu, bringing death, they say, to anyone who begins to love her. Musetta stands up for herself, and if, in this adolescent opera, she is unable to develop a monadic position as femme fatale, it is because childhood is still too close at hand. Musetta tries her hand at freedom. "And then I savor what their eyes are asking when they make eyes at me; they show they know what charm there is inside me. The scent of desire surrounds me and makes me happy! . . . And you who know, you who remember, you suffer. . . . How could you escape?" It all waltzes and twirls in a generous, and superficial, drunken rhythm. Musetta is just a bit tipsy. She feels great in her beautiful, brand-new dress, and she too goes ahead and takes the girl's leap, provocatively, making them all watch her jump into infinity. Actually, there is something the matter with her foot, it hurts. (Art in its infancy; the infancy of wiles). The old fogey leans over to look at the bruised foot and goes off to find a shoemaker . . . and barefoot Musetta falls into her Marcello's arms.

This shoeless foot is also the opera. This little hint of happy existence in a place where the completely expected death is going to play itself out; this lunatic cavorting from note to note in a torrential rhythm; this whiff of operetta, when we know tragedy is just around the corner, since that is what we came for—that is opera. Opera—"a mixture of genres," and triviality inscribed at the very heart of what is noble. This is how death approaches, through the joyful raindrops of real gaiety. Moments of sweetness, moments of peace, lightning flashes of mischief and happiness that are preserved, the infinite grace of a joy dispensed by opera, which is nonetheless created for the representation of suffering. Moments of peace: the opera lets the heart take a breath. *La Bohème* moves from sadness to gaiety, from medical students' jokes to powerful emotion, from youth living its happiest days to a hint of the agony of approaching age. Musetta has won back her lover; she lives. Close beside her, her delicate, elegiac double looks on with innocent astonishment. There is a good division of roles: the gay one, the sad one; the living, the dying; the foolish, the wise. Virgins from the Gospel.

The real end concerns Mimi alone. At the moment of death she does not complain. She does not even have Violetta's tiny rebellion, her violent lament over dying so young, so young . . . no. Everything she sings is as gentle as a caress. The men around her attend to "the necessities." They sell things, they try to find a tonic; nobody is fooled but you certainly have to pretend, keep busy . . . stage it. Mimi is gasping for breath when the seductive spiral, which Rodolfo sang to keep her in the dark, returns. She coughs, she leaves; already she is not there anymore. But life's ritornello keeps on; Puccini never misses a chance to emphasize the ordinariness of death. It is an everyday affair when someone dies.

There is the last spiral, all wrapped back on itself; already the notes are unable to climb to the top of the scale, already the voice is singing a single infinite repetition. . . . Only the bronze gong sounds the chords of Mimi's death knell. Rodolfo thinks she is asleep: *E tranquilla.* And, tranquil himself, because she is sleeping, he closes the curtains. He sees nothing except, after a few minutes, he notices that everyone is looking at him. Then and then alone, having let the death of the one who sang to him so tenderly of love go by, he can wail his big man's sorrow. How good it feels to be sorry for the living body of the dead prima donna, how alive one is . . . Musetta's muff, useless on the icy hands of the dead girl, summarizes *La Bohème* and the foolish confidence. *La Bohème* and the wasted life; *La Bohème*, the wine drunk, the stove warmed, the shawl dropping, the plate breaking, and Musetta's bare foot; *La Bohème*, the snow that hurts, the cough that will not go away, the crazy arguments, and Mimi's pink bonnet. *La Bohème*, or winter's cold and Christmas Eve.

The song of lunatic women

When the thread draws taut, when it stretches the whole length of anguish, and when it breaks, releasing the tension and discharging its affect, the girl flies so far, so far that it drives her crazy. A frantic, abandoned madwoman, her body displayed before an audience glued to their seats, she sings words that make sense only to her. That is called delirium, an "unreading." It could be called "dechant," a descant, a disillusionment, "unsinging"; because it is a disenchantment, a descant driving these innocent girls, caught in others' webs, mad. "Every girl is an Ariadne in relation to her heart's labyrinth. She holds the string that makes it possible to find oneself when one is inside, but she does not know how to use it herself." Yes.

Yes, Kierkegaard lets his dismal, deceitful seducer say this. The seducer holds the spool of thread, guides the girl, lights the successive rooms, and lets go of the thread: then the web remains but her orientation has been lost. That is when Elvira in *I Puritani* and Lucia in *Lucia di Lammermoor* lose what is called "reason." Yet, while their coloratura passages frolic in the intoxicated happiness of song, their words are still there, along with their sense, which they have not lost. Only memory, all too present in a family that no longer wishes to or is able to see it, is lost, and they are the living perpetuation of this memory. They no longer know what to do with reality, but the thread is there; they cling to it, throw it out in melodies, like Cordelia, the Kierkegaardian seducer's imaginary fiancée who throws away their two engagement rings and cries out "Vive l'amour"! A cry of distress? No, crazy affirmation: "Vive l'amour" madly cry those quashed girls, the madwomen of opera. Pretty feebleminded everyone says. But no, they are hardheaded, bent on holding on to their desire even when everything gets in the way. The madwomen who sing are stubborn and determined in their song, and their intertwining voices scale the walls of reason, reaching higher than what is sensible, far higher than reality.

The story: Lucia di Lammermoor is a Scottish Juliette. The trite struggle between families is fought out on her body. Lucia-Juliette loves Romeo-Edgar, an evil brother swaps one ring for another, treachery is everywhere. Lucia finds herself married to the brother she does not love. Snap. The thread breaks. Lucia, on her wedding night, stabs her brand-new husband. She comes down the great staircase, her wedding gown all stained with blood. Here is this crazy bride who has just killed her husband. The lost fiancé, who she thinks betrayed her, who thinks she betrayed him, is not far away; but for her he is right in front of her. The foolish virgin's wise reason hallucinates her desire: Edgar, finally Edgar, is with her. She is in her nightgown, it is their wedding night; forgotten are the murdered husband and the bloodstains. She dies. Later, so does Edgar, but it is less important.[33]

When the drama really begins, it is in the midst of a brilliant celebration, with lively dances and a crowd of guests. Everything skips along in time, moving at a brisk, slightly clumsy tempo. There is all the fake gaiety of a noble wedding. Suddenly a bass voice foreshadows the silence of a whispered terror; Lucia has killed her husband upstairs, during the party. An irresponsible act. Nobody mentions murder. Madness is there, focusing the crowd in a fascinated gaze. (In Charcot's amphitheater they craned their necks and their eyes bugged out, all the better to see the master and the woman spread out, gone wild; to see her breasts bared by madness, her disheveled hair, her lifeless arms dangling, and her faraway gaze, closed in and asleep. The hysteric turns her body over to anyone who wants to see it, she is somewhere else, in the infinite space of the expansiveness she longs for. She sleeps. And Charcot discusses her.) The messenger describes her as if he had seen her; his compassion sets the act in a scene of craziness, and no one makes a move. Is the staircase empty? What is going on up there? A dead body, a legal rapist murdered, trails of blood; her hand did not shake, it was direct. Silence still.

Here she comes. She is coming down; how she does it is important. Like a bride on the steps of the church, like Cécile Sorel on the great staircase at the operetta, like a queen, she descends toward her subjects, whom she does not see. Sweet and gentle, she is sleepwalking; she wanders step by step, note by note. A flute tenderly guides her feet, accompanying her melody, looking after her. *Adagio*. Lucia heads toward the meeting she expects. She has awaited this moment so long. It is all just the way she wanted it, happy, reunited. The love-song exchanged beside a spring comes back to her like the sign of her happiness.

Snap: it is not true anymore. Lucia wavers. For just a second she almost lost Ariadne's thread. But it did not break, the voice seeks it out, way up high, and finally finds it again, this thread guiding her dreams. Her dreams are lifelike. If she looked around her, if she saw this crowd staring at her, if she regained consciousness, all would be lost.

Then, in a miraculous leap, Lucia flies toward Edgar, welcomes him, speaks to him, loves him, embraces in her empty arms an absent, hallucinated lover. Passion comes to life, the loving voice sings more steadily. Here is the sublime duet where the partner is missing; the phantom duet. It is a slow, sweet waltz, happy and tender. Lucia waltzes with her empty love. "Alfin son tua" she tells him. Finally, finally, I am yours, and you are mine. . . . "Alfin sei mio." . . . They way they hoped it would be! But it is over, the tears, the misery, and the loss of love.

Everything is fine. She experiences the desire of this man whose presence her song creates so powerfully, but all around her a horrified murmur nullifies her dream reality. Lucia, madly in love, continues to waltz; the flute follows, and takes hold of her in its embrace, the spectral substitute for her absent Edgar. Lucia's voice converses with the flute's replies and echoes; Lucia is alone no more, she will never be alone again. The voice rises, loses the words, sings itself out and finally rests, then it takes off again in a lively movement that is almost childish. Lucia dances with her desires: listen how joyful, airy, and peaceful it is. Who says anything about unhappiness? Madwomen's voices sing the most perfect happiness, agreeing with Rousseau's philosophical truth: "My most perfect happiness was in dream."

Pensively, the bloody dreamer, the murderess, rediscovers song's childhood and its desiring freedom. There is no clamor able to reach her from her surroundings. Each time the still motionless witnesses intervene in chorus she takes off again—higher, higher, and fainter each time. Off into the shadows of the unhappy world; she dismisses those who are separated from her forever, those who do not comprehend how perfectly complete is her joy. The curtain falls on Lucia's jubilation, set free and rising still.

Jean Chantavoine's commentary on this: "Essentially, in Lucia's 'madness aria' an adagio of great melodic charm and a sort of waltz succeed each other. The waltz is less felicitous, but its absurdity is justified by the errors of a demented woman who discovers in horror itself a subject of joy." Hurrah for Chantavoine, well-named in French, "Oatsinger." . . . Indeed it is "a sort of waltz"; and yes, Oatsinger, she is a "demented woman," a young madwoman, but she is happy. And she is not deceiving herself. At *Hernani*'s premiere, the young lions backing Victor Hugo[34] called out to the classic bald heads gleaming in the lights: "Knees! To the guillotine!"

Chantavoine, the author of *Petit Guide de l'auditeur de musique, cent opéras célèbres* in librairie Plon's collection "le Bon Plaisir," 1948, is a knee. And knees, meant to bend before reality, know nothing of the resources of girls' madness, nor of their joyous music.

In the final act all that is left of Lucia is her tomb.

Elvira and Amina

All Bellini's work is moved by broken unions. There is a sudden moment of fragility, when the space to be jumped is too vast, when the chasm of rupture opens beneath the woman's feet, and there sings the slow rhythm, the distraught fiancées' mad lament. There amble violins and the broad measures of a heart whose beat has slowed, in a very peaceful dream where grief is simply told. Cigarette smoke marks the way taken in luminous spaces and vanishes. This is how slowly your heart beats when you are asleep; this is the sleeping heart of dreaming sleepwalkers who cross worm-eaten footbridges with adorable steps and surmount obstacles with the song of the unconscious.

The story: Elvira, daughter of a puritan, must marry Sir Richard Forth, but she loves Lord Talbot who is on the Stuart's side. At this period in seventeenth-century England, the puritan supporters of Cromwell and the cavalier supporters of monarchy were at war. Despite the discord, Elvira's father agrees to her marriage with Lord Talbot. But Talbot, the monarchist, for political reasons helps the wife of Charles Stuart, Queen Henrietta of France, escape disguised in Elvira's bridal veil. Elvira believes she has been abandoned and goes mad. Only Cromwell's victory, giving amnesty to all political prisoners, saves Talbot from death following his arrest. Elvira regains her sanity and marries Talbot as originally planned.[35]

Elvira, who has gone mad because she has lost her fiancé, moves with a slow, grand pace, nocturnal and ceremonious as the Racinian beauties who have just been raped in their sleep by some unknown tyrant. Her lament stirs the heart; her mistaken images are visually haunting; and the rhythm of her daring and hesitant step beats in my breast, as if, stricken by a fatal dizziness, I am about to fall. Unrecognizable words and faces are reeling. *"O rendetemi la speme, o lasciatemi morir."*

Those are her first words. Give me back my hope, or let me die. *Lasciatemi morir. . . .* The primordial song of the abandoned nymph, endowed by Monteverdi with an almost imperceptible melody, accompanied by scales descending toward a darker and darker whirlpool. Then, like Donizetti in *Lucia de Lammermoor*, Bellini suddenly breaks the slow pace of delirium to launch the woman into the outrageous joy of wild, uncalled for, vertiginous notes. Little sparkling trumpets sound the joyful onslaught of fantasies. Elvira, like Lucia, passes rashly into the magical order of her desires. And what do madwomen find in their delirium? The marriage that eludes them.

Amina, a young peasant woman, in an innocent Switzerland that Rousseau would have recognized, is Bellini's *Somnambule*, the sleepwalker.

The story: Amina must marry Elvino, all is for the best in the best of worlds; but Lisa, the village innkeeper, is very much in love with Elvino. Then the local lord returns; and in the middle of the night Amina goes into his room and is found there asleep. She is a sleepwalker, but only the lord understands the strange illness. Elvino does not believe in her innocence and suddenly prefers Lisa. The lord tries to explain Amina's ailment to everybody, but no one believes him. At that moment the girl appears, in the midst of a sleepwalking attack; sound asleep she crosses a little bridge that collapses after she crosses. Elvino had reclaimed his ring but now he slips it onto her finger again, and she awakens a bride.[36]

Asleep, she enters the room of a man who is not her fiancé; and she dreams of him in this other's arms. There will be a heavy price to pay. She will have to risk her life. Just when the fiancé, who believes he has been betrayed, is about to marry someone else, the sleepwalking girl appears, through a window overhanging a mill. Far below lie the stream and the huge wheel that endlessly, rhythmically, keeps milling wheat.

And sleeping, Amina walks; and almost falls, on the rotten plank that gives. The only thing protecting her is sleep. A somnolent prophetess, she tells the truth in her sleep to the man she loves, whom she has lost in a dream. An originating scene: churning water, the original, living, dangerous force; the absolute danger of emptiness and death; the unconscious and the magical sleep of a threatened virgin. And, just as they were present to witness Lucia's bloody madness, there are others everywhere, always others to witness. The women talk to them without knowing who they are; Lucia and Amina sing as if they were blind, their utterances stolen from desire and thrown in the distorted face of whoever caused the break. The heart, inseparable from its action, still washes through the girl's rhythmical body.

Will they remember all this later? Will they remember those gratuitous moments when, more than any other time, they were beyond constraints, outside of the system, dreaming their mystical marriage at the top of their sweet voices? At the sleepwalker's feet the water roars, and she sings; men mill around Elvira, and she sings. The marvelous and only way out of human plots: join the inspired sibyl on her three-legged stool; show everyone the feminine underside, its victory and its vistas; and so take off like Michelet's sorceress flying away into ethereal heights on the great black ram, while the lord and his serfs hound her with pikes and fangs.

Running away, running amok, dawdling along for all to see, in regions where no one can join her. The music holds back, as if, by accompanying her too quickly and loudly it could throw the sleepwalker off balance and disrupt the delirious utterance. Time no longer exists, the time of plots. This is the endless duration of the unconscious drive—the body that does not tremble, the sure footsteps on decaying boards, voices confidently fixed on scales of inhuman scale. They will win. Risking all for all this way, when they awake they will find an emotional audience of the men who had abandoned them. But the ordeal was necessary; they had to cross the bridge, confront phantoms, and display their ecstatic bodies and distraught voices to everyone. Opera exacts this payment; it is the only one for which it will turn loose its prey. Even then Bellini is all tenderness for the women he creates; even then his music wraps them attentively in vigilance, weaving biological rhythms around them so the body can get its bearings.

Heliotropes

Despite the boredom of enjoying, from its earliest youthful days, a portion of the respectability that is the privilege of old age, marriage will always be a respectable institution. In contrast, engagement is a truly human invention, and consequently is so self-important and ludicrous that a girl in her whirlwind passion carries on regardless, both conscious of this self-importance and feeling her soul's energy circulating throughout her being like some superior blood. (Søren Kierkegaard)

I cling tightly to this perplexing spool of thread that has me stumped, this thread twisted so tightly that it is hard for my fingers to undo it at all. The thread of conjugal union, what kinship has at stake: opera represents it on stage in an endless procession of bound couples and couples whose bonds are weak or coming undone, who spin like marionettes under the silent authority of an audience watching the spectacle of marriages coming apart, being repaired, ending, and being annulled. A man takes a wife, he is engaged to her; a man, because he has some political duty, or because some other woman appears on the scene, breaks it off. And there, all alone, is the fiancée, the crucified prostitute, the isolated princess. A man breaks the thread society wound, and the thread rises, light as gossamer, to catch in the branches of the highest trees. The woman goes mad, madly abandoned, free at last in the present time of voice. But the thread needs only to turn into a spider's web, or to return to a vegetable existence; the girl needs only to turn into a bird, for the spool to find the lost end again and rewind the Law. Brides—twice brides, once in their mad wedding dream and again in a recovered reality.

"What is important now is to lead her so that, in her bold flight, she loses sight of the marriage, and more generally of the solid ground of reality."

While this great, vital pulsation drives them, these women will show everyone primeval femininity and its powers of control. Not too much is needed: fiancés, arms outstretched, are at the end of the bridge to welcome the unfaithful fiancée—the one unfaithful to reality.

But when the girl has jumped, when the bridge has been crossed, when the seduction completes its murderous process, Soren's seducer loses interest. "She has been deflowered, and these are no longer times when the sorrow of a forsaken girl transforms her into a heliotrope." Heliotrope, the flower that turns toward the sun, keeping the mark of the radiant phallus even in metamorphosis; heliotrope, the flower without freedom, incapable of holding its head up, obedient to its master's direction, to the orientation and timing dictated by the daystar. Heliotrope, a flower without night, a flower without madness and desire, a flower in eternal submission. Madwomen are not like that. Women seduced are. The madwomen, crossing over the bridge, have been able to get outside seduction and turn it back on the seducer. Corresponding to the image of the heliotrope is a flower that never fades: the everlasting.

The fall of Don Juan

Once again the cursed shadow passes, the opera of operas, the supreme alibi. Mandolin and cape, gauntlets and champagne in procession. The statue come alive goes by, along with legions of reproaches. Don Giovanni's ghost is passing.

Alas. The desire to write chokes me now. So often admired, so often written, so often invoked, this Don Giovanni, comma, by Mozart, comma, you know, comma, the most-beautiful-opera on the masculine scale. All the words of teachers and seniors come back to me; they awarded *Don Giovanni* the prize for excellence among operas. They disgusted me. They took away the flavor of "*La ci darem la mano*," and I no longer even like to sing it. Ah, men, how much you love Don Giovanni! And no, I just cannot. But the seducer of Kierkegaard's *Journal* hands me a tiny golden key, which lets me out of my refusal. "If I was a God," he says, after having "deflowered" Cordelia, "If I was a God, I would do what Neptune did for a nymph, I would transform her *into a man*."[37]

Who will give me back the Don Juan of my youth, the pure, blind love, imprisoned in fantasies my men have? As a girl I could not resist. Sometimes Zerlina, sometimes Donna Anna, sometimes Elvira, I gave in while defending myself, "*vorrei e no vorrei*," I want to and I do not want to; I sought vengeance impressively, for a trifle, fantasizing the supreme offense of rape that is always on the horizon of a girl's imaginary; I had a mystical forgiveness, pursuing the beloved with charitable parables. And Don Juan, for his part, did just fine, thank you.

I remember one day at the Opera. The stage was immense and it was red; the characters in this sublime farce seemed minuscule and dwarfed by the space. Don Juan, gesturing grandly with his cape, caught his foot in a guitar, and came crashing down, ludicrously, head over heels, down the huge staircase on which he was delivering his famous serenade. Doubtless my memory amplifies the incredible noise. Doubtless the audience barely breathed a sound then, the way they do when an acrobat misses the trapeze; they concentrate on forgetting the accident, they blot it out. But this is the image of Don Juan my ears remember: the seducer betrayed by balance, the awkwardness of an actor stricken with dizziness or fear, the myth that loses countenance for a thunderbolt second, and shows its underside. Don Juan's ass rolling down the stairs: all the champagne seductions and lavish splendors of this rebel hero are gone. No, Don Juan is not to haunt my musical universe. Ah, one should never swear not to drink the water from this fountain ever again. . . . But, at least for now, the time it will take to write and read this book — we don't have to worry. Others have described already and, until the world changes will continue to describe, the imposing glamor of the man who stands up to God, to death, to women, and is swallowed up in hell to ease the conscience of a jubilant social body. I know all that; but I am not forgetting the fixation men have on *Don Giovanni*, I am not forgetting the eroticism of Pierre Jean Jouve, that great heroine killer and opera lover. No. Like Carmen: no. . . .

Yes, once, just once, listen to the intoxication of success, the slight dizziness from victory and force. Because this time it takes place in the American West by pioneer candlelight, because the pistol sometimes drowns out the voice, and because there is a sheriff in it, a real one. It is an opera willing to laugh. Its very title, so moving in Italian — *la Fanciulla del West*, where the lovely, winged word *fanciulla* unites the girl with her family affiliation by a diminutive — in French translation always sounds vulgar: *la Fille du Far West*, a Western call girl. And the pure, young girl, valiant Minnie, sounds like a whore. Yes, she is a bar keeper in the far West. There is a seductive gangleader, a mean sheriff in love, a brave pioneer woman. . . . It could be a horse opera.[38]

But look beyond the movie screen where the steely blue gaze and phallocratic chins of American heroes parade in your memory. Listen with your innermost heart. Look: she is playing cards with her lover. She almost shouts when she lays her cards on the table. Then she grabs her wounded lover by the waist and, in a sublime gesture, while the music writhes in pain, she drags him to the hideout. But above all, oh, above all, she does it when she has won the hand — three aces and two of a kind — finally, we have the flawless exception, and happiness dearly won. They go, the bandit and the girl, off into the rising sun, and the sky resounds with the cheers that go with them.

Is it because this opera is like the too close and too violent myth of swaggering films in which mothers and whores escort weary heroes? Is it because it shows a woman out to win her love, a woman who wins painlessly, without defeat, without coming undone? This opera is not particularly popular. It would take the greatest sensibility to women's defeated soul to manage to succeed with this masterpiece. It would take someone most intimately accustomed to feminine pain to love a heroine to the point of transforming her into a tender and victorious warrior woman. It would take, oh, role reversal, Giacomo Puccini and Mimi's revenge. Minnie, the girl, is the rising sun; contrasted to her nocturnal sisters, she is the day that does not close on an act of mourning. Opera lovers do not like this antiheroine. She is made for tomorrow. Tomorrow she will set out, lit by the brilliance of her victory.

One more marriage. Two very young couples radiating happiness. It is time for a toast. Each of them raises his or her glass to the health of the beloved. Nothing around them exists anymore and the transparent music wraps them in light. The sun of Italy bathes them in all its brilliance; one girl is named for a bird and one for a flower, their names are Dorabella and Fiordiligi. The two fiancés come from away; they are Turks, what could be more seductive? Their mustaches, their lavishly embroidered robes, their turbans, all make them ravishing foreigners, ravishers.[39]

Treachery. Fraudulence. Deception. The two fiancés slip away and come back in their "normal" clothes; each one, to test the love of the betrothed, is in disguise, they have changed places, each one courting another's fiancée. . . . The girls have surrendered to their desire. "Turn your head and there's another love . . .". And the wonderful happiness, the moment of the perfect toast, was a false marriage, with a false official, a false contract and false fiancés . . . It was all false. Except for the ephemeral happiness. Except for the real, fleeting desire between two couples who go back to their original state like good boys and girls. Each one regains his or her initial partner, but no one will be able to forget the harmony discovered and the suspended music that bloomed.

There will be a real marriage, but the brides and grooms will not be the same. Hands will vainly seek each other and not hold the dearest ones they held — now prisoners, close at hand. Hand games, mean games. . . . The title of this opera is dedicated to all women: *Cosi fan tutte*: all women are like that, say the men.

Chapter 5
Furies and Gods, or Wanings of the Moon

In which we see a cannibal princess yield to the omnipotence of the Male-Sun; in which a Gallic priestess stands up to Rome; in which a thirty-year-old woman grows old in a day; in which a sorceress answers none of the questions asked her.

Cannibal head and women's periods

Nighttime. It is a Chinese, faraway night in shades of blue. It is the night to execute the ones condemned to death; the legendary executioner raises his great, shining blade; the shadows are full of torches and lights. The crowd, alternating between delight and terror, rapturously watches the cruel spectacle, and immediately recoils from it. It is the dark of night when the goddess Moon appears, at the same time as silence.

The Cashinawa Indians, throughout the long Amazon valley populated with painted men and naked rivers, tell the story of the Moon's origin. "Long ago, there was no moon, or stars, or rainbow, and night was absolutely black. This situation was changed because of a girl who did not want to get married. Her name was Moon. Her mother, exasperated by her stubbornness, chased her out. The girl wandered tearfully for a long time, and when she wanted to go home, the old woman refused to let her in: "You can just sleep outside," she shouted. "That will teach you for not wanting to get married!" The girl ran around desperately, beating on the door and sobbing. The mother was so furious with all this carrying-on that she armed herself with a machete, let her daughter in, and cut off her head, which rolled on the ground. Then she threw her daughter's body in the river.

All night the girl's head rolled and moaned around the hut. After pondering her future, the girl's head decided to turn herself into a moon. "That way," she thought, "I will be seen only at a distance." She promised her mother that she would not hold a grudge if her mother would give her some balls of string. Holding one end in her teeth she had herself towed off into the heavens by a vulture. The decapitated girl's eyes became the stars and her blood the rainbow. From that day on women have bled once a month. When the blood clots, black children are born to them. If it is the sperm that clots, the children are born white.[40]

Turandot, Giacomo Puccini's final opera, tells of the last adventure of the free Moon. A girl who refuses to marry, a cruel mother, women's periods, their blood, and the decapitated head are reunited in that mysterious space traversing unconsciousnesses throughout the people of the world. Elsewhere, in the same Amazon valley, other tribes continue the girl's story: the moaning head rolls from door to door, chases men, jumps on their shoulders and hangs on, a ravenous cannibal. Elsewhere, in earliest Greece, Diana the huntress, the beloved Artemis, throws the sacrilegious Actaeon to her hunting dogs because he was guilty of having looked at her when she was naked, taking a bath. Transformed into a deer, the man who has become a beast succumbs to animal desire and dies of it. Elsewhere, in the modern America of our electrifying dreams, a woman has just written a treatise on conception, adopting for her own purposes the influences of the Moon on menstrual cycles. At nightfall, in absolute darkness, follow the secret rhythm bound to the silver crescent, to the shining and terrifying divinity who inhabits the night.

The story: Turandot, a Manchu princess, has sworn to marry no one unless there is a man who is able to solve three riddles that she alone can ask. The old emperor of China has accepted the girl's condition. When the opera begins, they are about to execute the prince of Persia, who has not found the answers. Hiding in the crowd is Prince Calaf, a Mongol whose army has just been defeated by the Chinese army. Led by a young, faithful slavegirl who has always been in love with him, Calaf rediscovers Timour, his old, blind father, living incognito. Calaf joins the Chinese crowd in cursing Turandot. But when she appears at the window, he falls in love with her, and, despite Liu's and Timour's entreaties, he strikes the gong that signals a new suitor entering the lists, announcing the next ordeal. The ordeals take place before the whole court and an agonized crowd. But Calaf solves the three riddles, after Turandot told him how she has reached such a point: a grandmother, who was once raped by a Mongol, appeared to her in a dream one day, and decreed a murderous law for the little girl: to seek vengeance. Despite Calaf's success, Turandot refuses to give in; the prince, whom no one knows, proposes a bargain. If she finds out his name, he will give her up. All night long Turandot searches for it, threatening death to anyone who will not help her. Dawn comes and still no one has discovered the name. The ministers have captured Timour and Liu and want to torture them to make them speak. To spare the old man from suffering, Liu sacrifices herself and says that she alone knows the secret. But to keep herself from talking, as soon as she begins to surrender to the torture, she stabs herself before the astonished Turandot. Overwhelmed, the princess yields to the prince's assaults, accepting his love and his hand. Dawn breaks.[41]

It is dark when the opera begins. The night is murmurous and stormy, crowded with people, with crying and shuddering. Ever since Turandot began her reign with its homicidal law, the legendary Peking no longer sleeps: the tragedy of executions takes place far from daylight. When the opera begins the stage is crowded with people; all the characters are there, and *she* is their only concern. We do not see her. But the night in Peking feels the great weight of her presence. We have to wait through a long period of popular outcry, we have to wait through the funeral procession taking the young prince of Persia to his death before the silent princess Turandot will appear. Magnificently beautiful and terrifying, this figure of the silent woman is stripped of song. But, even though she is silent, she does not remain completely immobile. She makes one precise gesture, just one: the "no" of a hand brought down, refusing grace to the prince who is going to die for her; although he cries out her name . . . Turandot. . . . The first figure of Turandot is the silence of death itself, the silence of a lifeless drive, the stifling of words, nipping cries of tenderness, feelings, and fears in the bud. In a Florentine convent, Fra Angelico painted a monk whose finger on his lips prescribes the law of silence for those dead to the world. This is how Turandot lives, withdrawn, absent, and inaccessible. This is how she seduces, attracting those who love the smell of mortal danger, the sublime and dangerous beauty she has. They will plunge into ordeal the way one dives into a stormy sea.

Look at the poster again, another by Ricordi, dated 1928; the poster of Butterfly, with the scarf and background turquoise, dated 1904. Tastes have changed. The elegant softness of scarves, à la Isadora Duncan, the scattered flowers have been succeeded by the stylized design of "modern style." Look at this huge face, gazing at us with slanted eyes, outlined in black, made up boyishly. An exotically shaped coiffure makes her look like a queen. There are two dragons on top of it, and their mouths, fraught with teeth, drip golden beads. Her mouth is closed in silence; her face is impassive. And just above her brow, there is a large red heart, upside down, as if it were a mystical sign. No doubt the poster's creator did not dare set it right side up, fearing it might be confused with the heart of the Virgin of the Seven Sorrows. Nonetheless, the symbol is there; and Turandot confronts us with this bleeding heart, upside down, weighing with all its splendor on her enigmatic gaze.

In this dreamworld where Gozzi was the first to set the plot of *Turandot*, western fantasies of lunar death and the dangerous virgin intersect with Italian fantasies that bring in their wake the mocking little world of *commedia dell'arte*. The companions of the princess are puppets and funambulists, and an oriental atmosphere, concealing survivals from Greek paganism and initiation mysteries, echoes in Puccini's opera. *Turandot* is a carnival tale of the sort E. T. A. Hoff-mann wrote: in *La Princess Brambilla*, during the wild celebration where the young people's intoxications are described, the princess appears to the story's young hero when he picks up a bottle. Out of the narrow neck of the bottle comes the head of the princess. It is just a head, emerging from an orifice, the way Turan-dot's moonlike head emerges — also the way the decapitated suitors' detached heads end up.

Heads chopped off, symbols of a deadly love, round heads like the nightstar when it shines, full. *Turandot* is continually played out between tragedy and a minor mime show. Mythic massacres and shamanistic voyages join there with the pirouettes of Harlequin, Pantalon, and Colombine, who are brought together in the three grotesque figures representing the princess's three ministers, Ping, Pang, and Pong. Their giggling, their assorted tricks, their cartoon appearance, big leather noses, feathered hats, twisted bodies, jerky gestures, signify a medi-ocre and touching humanity faced with the terrifying figure of a virgin beyond humanity, the Sphinx with golden claws, the living monster, in short — the Moon, the cannibal head.

On that night, when the silent princess appears on the balcony, there is no Moon shining in the sky; as in the Cashinawa myth, there is almost total dark-ness. And the crowd, worried by this absence, begs the Moon, the absent star. "Oh truncated, bloodless, gloomy head," they sing. "Oh weary lover of dead men, show your face. . . . Bodiless head, cannibal head, human face that devours," they continue. The invocation completed, the princess and the Moon appear simultaneously, both silent, cold, and shining. The Chinese crowd, a huge and unique population, tells the truth about the weary lover of dead men.

A truncated, bodiless head. I will return to the Cashinawa myth, if you do not mind. A girl refuses to marry and there is total darkness. The moon must be gen-erated: it will be the girl's head. A chopped off head in the Cashinawa myth; one chopped off head after plenty of others, in *Turandot*. In the Cashinawa myth, the head that has become the Moon will regulate the light in the sky; there is to be a day, there is to be a night, a daytime light and a nocturnal, feminine light. But this same movement will leave women affected by the initial rebellion. Because the girl refused to marry, the mythical consequence will be that women have to bleed every month, marked by the sign of fertility and necessary union. That will teach them. You have to keep them under control, these women who are so close to chaos and so incapable of submitting to the slow, regular rhythm that men want.

Badly brought up, these girls: either they refuse to wait or else they expect too much. One of them, the Girl-who-was-mad-for-honey, could not wait to eat the dangerous, intoxicating honey found in the hollow trunks of trees; she will suffer harsh consequences. Ah, she eats the honey in the forest without waiting for it to be collected and prudently prepared by the group, diluting the dangerous product into a slightly intoxicating drink at the proper time. Well, she will have a flesh-eating jaguar for a husband, who will devour her. Turandot, the other badly brought up girl, expects too much and refuses to marry. Well, her husband will be a Tartar. Women are never on time. Turandot reverses the order, refuses to bleed for a man, refuses fertility, keeps herself a virgin—which brings on the Moon and its procession of dangers. What the worried, murmuring crowd says in the Peking night implies the ferocious and loving battle between women and men.

A battle to the death, three grotesque and charming ministers sing it plainly, in black and white, in capering, falsetto voices. Three bearers of the truth, shielded by their status as clowns. Peuh, they say, peuh! What is Turandot? "A girl with a crown on her head and a cloak with tassels. . . . But if you undress her, there is flesh, raw flesh, something inedible!" Turandot is raw, the savage girl of nature who refuses to be "cooked." The ones who are cooked are the girls who accept being warmed over the burning fire of love and marriage. Turandot is cold, inedible. . . . Wonderful words that fly by like feathers in the breeze, gliding along the musical giggles of Ping, Pang and Pong with the truth about the cannibal struggle. Who will eat whom? The man who cooks the woman or the raw woman? The opera begins with a cannibal night. When the opera is over, day breaks at last over Peking, relieved of darkness. What has happened? Nothing. Just a woman who gives up and gets married.

We finally heard her, at the end of a long march by the mandarins and girls. Orders come from the princess; her rag of a father, with his voice of cotton fluff, obeys. Finally, Turandot's voice rises. Lofty, among the highest peaks of superhuman voices, imperially, she sings her own myth, her originating fantasy. A cry that is not hers. "In this royal palace, for thousands and thousands of years, a desperate cry rang out." Turandot flings this cry before her as if to shield herself; this cry is her very identity. However, it is the cry of another woman: a distant ancestor of Turandot's who ruled thousands and thousands of years ago and who was killed by an invading Mongol. Turandot is a woman possessed. "This cry took refuge in my soul." Ah. Once again here is the familiar hysteric from our childhoods, the woman who has no soul, the one who finds her own soul in that of others, in a lost past where the recalcitrant, the irrepressible, and the rebels from this endless war live on.

Milan, November 1978. When I tell this story before an audience, a very irritated young woman stands up and describes what she calls her "disgust." Turandot is just a nasty bitch, she says, and she is certainly lucky to find a guy willing to have her in the end. . . . How these stories trap you! How they latch onto your heart, there or somewhere else! How they cut you to the quick—in what unknown, innermost suffering?

This cry took refuge in my soul. A man appeared then, "a man like you," Turandot exclaims to Calaf, about whom she knows nothing except that he is a man. But the myth is implacable. And this stranger of the male sex who will get the better of the lunar Sphinx is of the same blood as the Mongol ancestor who raped the princess Lou-Ling. Because he is able to repeat history, he will solve the riddles. Because the possession of their two ancestors circulates from one to the other, from the conquered, anonymous Tartar to the bloody princess, Calaf will be able to devote himself to the ordeals without danger.

It is true that the riddles are transparent: Hope, who dies every day and comes back to life every night; Blood, "vivid glow of the setting sun," the blood spilling—from men in torture and war, and from women; and Turandot herself, ice that ignites. Night and day. Cold and hot. Couples are at the heart of the riddles. The feminine half of the couple, the one who refuses, asks a simple riddle that the other half will answer without trying, so easily, so masterfully, that he runs no risk in asking a riddle in turn: what is his name?

Inside the space of hazy memories, the Oedipus myth unfurls. But it is as if all its elements were scattered, each distributed to a different character, with the result that Oedipus is there, in echo, but broken in pieces. A female Sphinx: Turandot. A father who would have inherited both Laius's age and Tiresias's knowledge, thanks to his blindness. A stranger with no family, who conquers a queen. A curse on a city: Turandot's bloody law. Oedipus is a woman; Oedipus is a man. Our myths become confused like a reflection in water troubled by a tossed stone.

For, to cut the endless thread of the deadly repetition of Turandot's dream, some woman's blood is necessary. It will have to flow before the eyes of the princess to set an example for her. And this other Jocasta ia a simple slave, little Liu, the perfect victim. Heiress to the sacrificed women whom Puccini could make sing their hearts out, Liu stabs herself. Puccini stopped there—at the mournful procession singing the death of a woman to protect a man, in the presence of a woman who refuses her femininity.

That is the last scene he was able to write before he boarded the train carrying him to a throat operation from which he did not return. But as the train left, he lowered the window, and in a voice I imagine to have lost its resonance, because he was stricken with throat cancer, he whispered to Toscanini who had accompanied him: "Take good care of my dear princess, my beautiful Turandot." The evening of the first production, April 25, 1926, at la Scala in Milan, Toscanini rested his baton after Liu's death, and the curtain fell. That, no doubt, was the only real production of *Turandot*.

Franco Alfano ended the opera according to directions left by Puccini, who wanted to achieve in the final scene a love duet as beautiful as Tristan's. . . . Alas! It is quick and proper. Calaf takes possession of Turandot; we have had enough fun. And we watch him kiss her forcibly, in a crashing, orchestral, meaningful roar; watch him checkmate her, for good! Early flowers, choirs of girls, syrupy sentiment; Butterfly's devastated soul passes, like a regret, and an echo of sea subsiding . . .

"My glory is ended" moans Turandot. The male Sun rises, the Moon sets, the sovereign lord of Marriage and Daylight wins. It would take a Busby Berkeley or a Stanley Donen to bring the involuntary clowning, the botched truth of this grandiose finale back. Musical comedy would have to prevail over opera. Feathered legs and sequined figures would whirl around the happy couple, and Turandot, now free, surrounded by drum majorettes wearing peacock feathers, would descend a huge staircase while boys wearing little bells twirled their wooden swords in time . . .

"Take good care of my dear princess," was the hushed whisper of her old, dying lover. Like Carmen, only night is propitious to her mystery—the swarming, anxious night of the first act; the mad and troubled night of the final act. Thousands of Chinese people search for an unknown name, Prince Calaf hears this turmoil surrounding him and no one sleeps in the threatened city: "*Nessun dorma.*" Yes, Turandot rules at night, sleepless and loveless night, the wild, proud night of a sorceress.

Rome, sole object of my resentment

A chaste goddess, still young and wounded so soon, a chaste Moon, dear to the heart of an old man in love, who pursues in her the approach of the death he senses. "*Casta Diva.*" The lilt of these words in our memory is so strong that we have forgotten their meaning. Once again there is the Moon, the goddess of the prophetic furies, but the princess has grown old. She has become a druid priestess, in a Gaul dreamed up by Felice Romani and Bellini; a Gaul where romantic Italy fantasizes the fierce, feminine resistances surrounding its Eternal City. Vanquished she will be, but at least she will drag the Roman down with her. This is the threatened Moon Age, its maturing wane; this is *Norma*.

The story: Pollione, a Roman proconsul serving in Gallia, which is still scarcely under control, is obsessed with the Gallic priestesses. Long ago he had seduced the priestess Norma, secretly fathering two children by her, and now he is in love with the young Adalgisa who is vowed to the god Irminsul. Norma holds off the danger of war and latent rebellion by preaching peace, while Pollione is persuading Adalgisa to follow him to Rome and become his wife. Adalgisa admits everything to Norma; everything, even the name of her lover. The two women declare their anger, with Adalgisa taking the betrayed Norma's side. Norma is distraught and wants to kill her children; but, changing her mind, she asks Adalgisa to marry Pollione; plots, hesitations, plans. . . . Pollione is determined to carry Adalgisa off by force. Norma then strikes the sacred shield, calling the war-

riors to war; a sacrificial victim is required. Norma declares that a priestess has betrayed her vows and will be the victim. One last time she tries in vain to persuade Pollione to give up. But, as Pollione waits agonizingly for Adalgisa's name to be pronounced, Norma gives her own name to her compatriots. Moved by such nobility, Pollione feels his love revive and joins the mother of his children on the pyre. It is as fine as anything classical.[42]

Ah, if only one could write like Michelet writing *La Sorcière*. . . . If, like he, one could plunge into haunted memories where the story of a single, identical woman unrolls throughout the centuries. *La Sorcière* recounts the stages of feminine resistance born in the twilight of paganism, when the little Roman gods, the little gods of forest and hearth, had to draw back before the overpowering God of Christian monotheism. "A strong, hardy religion like Greek paganism begins with a sibyl and ends with a witch. The first, a beautiful virgin, rocked it in the light of day, captivated and glorified it. Later, in the darkness of the middle ages, a demeaned and sick religion was hidden in the heaths and forests by the sorceress, whose fearless pity fed it and kept it alive. Woman, thus, is the Mother of religions, the tender guardian and faithful nurse. The gods, like men, are born and die on her breast."

A wonderful text, shot through with discoveries daily corroborated by the sufferings of hysterics on the analyst's couch and by the astounding collections made by ethnologists who, staring wide-eyed and apalled at millennia of underestimated femininity, finally saw the light. These furies, these goddesses, these women with fearsome arms and inspired eyes, these Turandots and Normas collected the witch's inheritance in the nineteenth century. Behind the metal sheaths covering their grotesque nails—and the Far East always mirrors the colonial image of our Torture gardens and our napalm in Vietnam—these women are thinly disguised resistants to the enemy. Look at these foreign women, riding in golden carriages from distant lands where we have reduced the population to be no more than that—images. They are our feminine images set up as examples, all decked out in Gallic tatters, Chinese gowns, Irish tempers, and Gypsy craziness. Look at these recalcitrant women, bent on their own destruction, determined to leave their lives behind. Turandot resists the Mongol rapist, Norma resists Rome, Isolde resists Tristan, who enthralls her, Carmen the Gypsy resists all men. These women are all exotic: racist opera lights them like a trail of gunpowder, like a pack of matches with one strike burning all its fire. Resistant women, burned women: that was the fate of the Sorceress, and it is Norma's. Bellini's opera ends with a pyre.

But between Turandot and Norma, there is the passage transforming the young virgin into an old woman. This is how Michelet tells it: the child witch, born of no one on the deserted heaths, innocently busies herself in her empty house, while the first demon, the sprite, the cricket come to seduce her beside the cradle of her child. Wretchedness does the rest. The forsaken young woman, who asked the old spirit of Latin paganism for help, becomes mature and beautiful, full-blown in her radiant flesh and her green dress. Then, at the height of her radiance (now sacrilegious), the lord and his serfs nail her to her door with stakes, lifting her dress to show her naked butt as a sign of debauchery. Soon afterward we find her being hounded in the heart of the forest, where she has taken refuge in her realm.

In this domain she is the first doctor: she helps other women with their loves and the fruits of love, preparing philters to poison Tristan or to make him fall in love, giving abortions to the poor, and caring for the wretched. Right up until the day of that dreadful century, the hour that Descartes completed the *Discourse on Method*, the time of trials, the time when the inspired Michelet saved her life with the stroke of a pen, calling the great black goat to save her. And she flies off on its back, laughing her mad laugh. . . . This is the original story behind the furies of opera, who only echo this tacit epic.

And so the young Turandot, under the protection of night, asks help from the suppressed fears of her people and gets it. She makes them accept her terror throughout her virginity. And in her extreme youth and invulnerability, she resists, entrapping men where they are most solid: in their knowledge of riddles. Next thing you know, there she is, married. Just imagine that Norma is Turandot grown old. Like Turandot she yielded to an enemy's seductions: for the Chinese woman it was the Mongol conquerer; for the woman of Gaul it was the Roman. Man gave both the law that makes them be women and mothers; then comes the day when the husband and father betrays the woman, who has become undesirable. That is where Norma's story begins.

Just as Mme Larina sings the minor key that will be Tatiana's future old age in *Eugen Onegin*, in *Norma* two identical figures face each other, the young woman and the old, bound together by the same man, Pollione. Norma and Adalgisa are the past and the present of a single colonial love: the conquerer takes forcibly, seduces, and carries off; that is his pleasure, that is what moves him. Pasolini the Italian understood it, confiding the role of Medea to a Greek woman, Maria Callas; but Medea goes to the furthest reaches of sacred crime, killing her own children. This very action makes her closely akin to the Greek monsters, those unstable intermediaries between animals and gods, above and beyond human laws.

Norma is not Medea, not a goddess; Norma is only a woman. Completely hemmed in by endlessly involved betrayals, she ends up surrendering before rebelling. With all her heart she embodies defeated Gaul, ready to become Roman; and *Rome*, the terrible, magical word, is the embodiment of every oppression. Punic heroines, Carthaginian princesses prepared to die rather than be Roman women, the women of Numance, rebels against the rigid Imperial order, rise up in Norma. But Norma also prefigures the married vestals of Heliogabalus, as well as incestuous and murderous empresses. She even prefigures the diabolical popesses, still titillating cardinals in the Curia when the conclave is ready to elect a pope and they have to check one another to make sure that *"duos habet, et bene pendentes . . ."*. The sacred city has a long, long history. The space laid out there by Romulus demarcated once and for all a divine territory, where the unique god, overcoming centuries of polytheism, was easily installed in the midst of paganism. There all the multiple gods, ibis-headed monsters and light-giving women, found they were dispossessed of their powers. From then on there is only a single woman, the virgin, mother, the fertile maiden. All the others, the midwives, the weird ones, the nutty ones, the Greeks, the goddesses with peacock husbands, the ones who hunted at night, the ones born from paternal shells in the depths of a splendid sea, the ones who frightened sailors with their songs, the Hecates who ruled over crossroads—all the others vanished. I have been told by Michelet that they are not dead, that they have not disappeared, that they revive in every woman burdened with a heart too full of misfortune. And the sorceress is born precisely where the Virgin Mary is apparently triumphant. If I find something really to love in all these torn women, it is because, under the opera lights, they bear the attenuated but recognizable features of a redeeming paganism allowing us to think otherwise. Oh, it is not that paganism triumphs; these women always lose, but that is what they are singing—their resistance to the one god. Christ, Rome, Pinkerton's America, José the cop, or Tristan: the one god clung to by man (who is crucified as well) dedicated to fight pagan women, sorceresses.

Norma's goddess, the chaste Moon goddess, certainly is betrayed by her; Rome wins from the moment Norma has surrendered. Another betrayal is required for Norma to get hold of herself again, finding in her own sacrifice the lost roots. For that is the result: by delivering her own body to the ritual pyre, she regains the forfeited function. From betrayal to betrayal, Norma could no longer waver between Rome and Gaul, between love and defeat. The only one able to save her is the pagan god Irminsul, even if it is at the cost of her life. Rome bows before the god of the people it is colonizing.

Once again they are face to face. Pollione the Roman, driven only by desire, and Norma the druid priestess, the woman torn apart who no longer knows what to do. In this brief moment, in this slow, restrained duet, she is the one in control. She, the priestess, she the possessor of divine power, can kill him or save him. The Roman stands erect; these conquerors have all the eternity of the Empire yet to come, and Pollione does not give in. *"In mia man'alfin tu sei."* Finally, you are in my hands, she tells him. Only the threat against the other woman, the younger, the innocent Adalgisa, will affect the Roman; then he begs, he implores pity, he comes undone. That is all Norma wants. A quick victory song, full of elation, and she is conquered. She will denounce not Adalgisa but herself, the guilty mother, the unfaithful priestess. Around them everything, the Gallic world,

the Roman world, the gods, the other gods, becomes confused. Lost. The lovers
are lost in the midst of a mythical battle. But Norma's voice rises in the silence:
the traitor, the victim who must be burned, is I. *"Son io."*

Finally, the word is found; absolutely simple and alone, with no music, the
old woman's strong voice is found again. The violins' slow quaver returns while
muffled beats give rhythm to the final seconds, the final words of love for this
couple bound by fire. Just a little longer, and the woman of Gaul and the man of
Rome have been burned, united by what Norma's voice calls a *Nume*: a deadly
divinity. This is the flight of the sorceress who finds a way to constrain her faithless lover by fire; the ephemeral victory of the old woman dethroned, of the
waning moon. Once more there is a glow surrounding man and woman, but it is
no longer the Sun's triumphal ascent, it is the nocturnal flame of a pagan pyre.
A young, foresaken woman remains. Adalgisa, young and alive—something
else, no doubt, will happen to her.

Rome. Echoes of the city murmur beneath the romantic rubbish that made Giu-
ditta Pasta, creator of the role, famous. Later, in the history of opera, another
character will become famous in the Rome defeated by Bonaparte. The little
prima donna who holds out, Floria Tosca, is very close to Norma; as if the Pasta
of 1831 bequeathed a bit of tender fury to the character whom Puccini was able
to endow with courage and strength—a Roman woman capable of killing to save
the one she loves. Sunset on the Pincio, golden light on black pines, slow prom-
enades by carriage around Cecilia Metella's tomb revive a pagan Rome and a
romantic Rome, in Norma. And, throughout centuries of myth and history, everything Rome ravished from peoples of the earth: their women, their wealth, their
wheat, their freedom, their Imaginary, finds sweet vengeance, breathing into the
beautiful mouths of tragic heroines regret for a distant past, asleep but insistent.
Norma: the locus where these living histories intersect.

Little Princess Resi, or a chocolate death

Opera has strange geography. Town squares, cities, and countries cut a bed where
conflicts flow, carrying the characters off in the heavy flood of reawakened histories. The Peking of dreams where *Turandot* takes place is the distant reflection
of some heavy, ethereal connections that Leibniz, the philosopher, wove between
Europe of the Enlightenment and China; of the later war of the colonialist nations
against the empress Tseu-Hi; and of the more recent Chinese uprising against the
Legations. Through the intermediary of Prince Calaf and Mongolia, as well as
through the Tartar ancestor who violated the Princess Lou-Ling, it is the stifled
memory of Babour, the huge conqueror, who attacked Trieste with one flank, and
with the other, the coast of Japan. Turandot, the Chinese empress, is dormant
history recounted by an unconscious visionary.

The Gallic forest is the Roman Empire at its birth. All the cities, all the places are full of grandeur and full of ghosts. (Verdi's *Aida*, another foreign heroine enslaved by war, was presented in the brand new opera house of Cairo, built in a few months to celebrate Memphis and reminiscences of ancient Egypt). Run an eye over the spaces that open up on stage to see the history of our various imperialisms: *Tosca*, or Bonaparte invading Italy in the name of the ideals of the French Revolution; *Butterfly*, or Meiji Japan subjugated by the whisky of an American naval officer; *Carmen*, or the yet unfinished Gypsy rebellion, still in the course of history; *Otello*, or the Moor who is traitor to his color in the name of the Republic of Venice; *Tristan and Isolde*, or Ireland carried off by Britain; *Don Carlo*, or the decline of the empire of Charles V. . . . Like a vast unwinding written in passions and daggers, the whole history of a West bound to represent lyrically its own crime—prey to its own mastery, weeping over its massacres—calmly emerges from this limited spectacle reduced to love stories. Class conflicts, power conflicts, family conflicts: nothing escapes the dimension of Western myth told in the scenery—the columns of cloth and cardboard, the background boats, the entire complex apparatus boxing in tiny figurines, prisoners stirring. Until the day the tyrant decides to use a place: Nuremberg, the medieval site of Wagner's *Meistersingers*, became the locus of fascism backed by myth turned into history, by history turned into opera. Until the day opera breaches the ramparts of representation and overflows the containment of audience, stage, and great staircases, to goosestep in the streets.

Vienna. In decline. A city where ghettos give rise to troubled geniuses, where last waltzes twirl in the lost memory of the splendor of Metternich and Sissi. The *Rosencavalier*, despite its title and its reputation of fluffy pastry, hot chocolate and swishing lace ruffles, is the same story as Norma's—of an old, withered skin. Minus the violence and the smothered, exhausted, breathless rages. It takes place in Vienna, in that seventeenth century depository of so much intimate gossip and so much cruel Reason. The story of an old woman giving up on love: with no pyre, no dagger, no resistance, the Marschallin goes to sleep like the old empire in the period when Richard Strauss wrote his opera.

The story: The marschallin of Wertemberg has lovers while her husband travels in distant places. It has always been this way. It is dawn and the man there is very young: Octavian. Everything is fine at sunrise; Octavian and the marschallin emerge from a night of love. When the marschallin gets up, her fat, unbearable, foolish cousin, the baron Ochs, arrives, asking her to find a messenger worthy of bringing his fiancée the customary silver rose: he is getting ready to marry the young Sophie, who, though not of the nobility, has a rich dowry. The marschallin gives the rose to her lover, the promised messenger. And what has to happen happens: Octavian and Sophie—same age, same beauty—fall in love with each other at first sight. Faced with the baron's vulgarity, Octavian revolts, challenges him, nicks him with his sword, and begins plotting to prevent the wedding. To compromise him, Octavian lures the baron to an inn and dresses in women's clothing, passing himself off as a servant-girl. (In the first act he had disguised himself as a woman to avoid suspicion, pretending to be Mariandel, the marschallin's chambermaid.) In this costume he easily picks up the baron, who lets himself get trapped, caught in the act, right in front of the father-in-law . . . and the marschallin. Who understands, gives up, and tiptoes away. Her young black servant returns alone to pick up Sophie's handkerchief, dropped on stage. Perhaps she, or Sophie needs it.[43]

The curtain rises on a bedroom. Full of night love smells. The opera takes place between the sheets. Bodies are undressed; you see their skin as they awake; underwear is scattered about and pillows are everywhere. The woman is the marschallin, a very powerful person in Maria-Theresa's empire. But at daybreak she is a worried woman, despite her very young lover's adoration. Someone still calls her "Bichette"—but not for long. This someone, the young count Octavian, is distinctly unruly, scatterbrained enough and with a good enough start under ladies' skirts to be known tenderly as Quinquin. And Richard Strauss gives him a disturbing woman's voice, the better to express the youth and androgyny of a hero who is barely adolescent: the lover's role is sung by a contralto. His voice is scarcely lower than that of the older woman. Older: you will be told she is thirty, if that . . . and that times have, indeed, changed. But casting fifty year olds in full bloom in the part is no mistake; directors make up for social progress. The great marschallins, Régine Crispin, Elisabeth Schwarzkopf, and Christa Ludwig leaped at the chance to play the role in their maturity. The whole opera pivots on the woman's age: the real drama, the crux of the plot is there.

The marschallin: a little tender, a little soft, a brioche dipped too frequently in a cup of cocoa. Like Sanseverina, like Madame de Rênal, like every aunt in love, the marschallin does not fight or scream. She cries in secret and walks straight ahead. From the moment Octavian climbs out of her bed she spells out her own end. She daydreams while she dresses, imagines herself as she will be later, when she is old. She has no idea how soon it will be, she has no idea that at the moment when she is dressing, she ordains it will happen. She brushes her hair calmly and, submerged in daydreams, puts on her makeup.

But then what she sings, in a small, desolate voice, is dreadful. How did it happen that she was a tiny little girl called Resi and that she became the marschallin? And the music limps on ahead of her, while she gets used to the idea: the idea that one day she will be the old princess Resi. They will call her by the name she had as a little girl, the way they do with hobbling old women who walk with canes. She will no longer be the marschallin. Between the little girl and the old woman, between the two Resis, there will have been (in the future perfect) the age of loves. And this all takes place before our very eyes. In palatial, baroque splendor, a great lady gets out of bed to an untidy dawn in Vienna. "I cannot control my dreams," she tells the frightened Octavian. "The day will come, today or tomorrow,." He will hear none of it. Time does not exist; there is no future, that dreadful day does not exist. Then, infuriated by his youth and innocence, she firmly sends him away. He must go, since he does not understand; let her stay there alone. . . . She gives him permission to ride at her side in the afternoon, the way one who is the "marschallin" might give a poor man alms or candy to a poodle. There, that is all for today. And just minutes before, there were embraces, half-naked bodies, and night's tenderness. Day has no tenderness for women.

Scarcely has he left, scarcely has he said a sad good-bye, still calling her Bichette, when she realizes what she is doing. She thinks better of it, wild with anxiety: "I did not even kiss him!" And the music follows on the heels of Octavian to try and bring him back. Too late. He really is a young man. He is quick, the valets testify—gone like the wind; they phrase his flight. Gone—the young man with the woman's voice, and gone too is love. Youth has flown, Resi's youth is lost already. The end. The rest dispassionately puts the finishing touches on the death of a woman's body. Little Count Octavian, commanded by the marschallin, will carry the rose to a very young girl. There will be plots, waltzes, mistaken identities, small acts of refrained from violence, and dowries in question.

It will not take the curtain long to fall. Octavian and Sophie are engaged, their fresh beauty a perfect match. The ones left out are the baron and the marschallin—this other couple standing behind the young people. Sophie's father, good father that he is (capable first of selling his daughter to an old nobleman and then capable of handing her over to someone even more noble) is touched as he watches the exemplary young couple, joined by a silver rose. Next to him is Resi, a sort of mother, who suddenly realizes she is almost as old as Sophie's father. Faninal, the father, comes out with one of those stock phrases—paternity putting up a good show when there is nothing else it can do. "That is what they are like, young people . . .". The lovers are embracing, strangers to this world. Resi answers with two calm notes, "Yes, yes."

Her voice sinks. She has just made the passage to old age. The day has come, the day that could be tomorrow or some other day, but no, it is today, now. Never again will there be an Octavian in her life: he will have been her last love, and before her eyes, he is in the arms of another. Calmly the marschallin faces up to it. With dignity, she holds still. Life is what is left, life without sex.

For an instant, just before this decisive passage, Octavian remembered a tune from the first act. It is one of those suspended moments that make opera great; in it, death and loss, everything worth getting upset about, is at play. For an instant, in fact, Sophie can lose Octavian who still hesitates between the two loves, both present. But you have not yet heard what he will call the marschal-lin. He calls her Maria-Theresa, her real first name as a woman. He calls her, that is all; he names her, as if he had never named her before, not Resi, not his love, no, just a first name (which is also the empress's) that names their truth. "Maria-Theresa, truly, I do not know how . . .". And she replies, in a serene and tiny voice, sung into the thin air, a cappella: "Nor do I know anything. Any-thing at all." That is it. With this she kills her own image, she finishes off the past, she withdraws from all sexual life.

But afterward, oh how she sings, and all the while the two younger voices mingle with her voice, which is finally suffering. She sings the past—the past spinning out before her eyes—but really, how did it happen? "I did not think I would have to bear this so soon." And she sings, in an abandoned voice, banal-ities that are the very stuff of life. "Everything in this world is unbelievable when you hear it talked about. But when it happens to you, then you believe it, and you do not know why. This young man is standing here, and I am here, with this strange girl, and he will be happier—with her—than any other man in the world." Surrounding her mature, subtle voice, the two other voices are inter-twined. The higher one represents a man's voice when it reaches maturity. The very young Sophie sings as if she were in a church, blinded and petrified in the presence of this great lady who gives her precedence; and Octavian understands no better. Something has just happened, something very important.

Indeed it has. One woman has happened to come to his arms, and he has hap-pened to send another woman away from them, into the age of renunciation. Three female voices singing on their own behalf, each has its own discourse in a moment that has stopped to weigh all three destinies. The three voices are ampli-fied to the point of ecstasy: an ecstasy of suffering for one, a shared ecstasy for the other two. The one left out finishes the song, "*In Gottes Namen.*" Be it as it must, God's will be done. And she tiptoes away. To be seen no more. But while the two children sing a music box duet together, a little black boy in livery comes back—to pick up a dropped handkerchief. For whose tears? Shrunk from bed-sheets to a handkerchief picked up by a cliché opera negro, the marschallin's space has shriveled up as grievously as a *peau de chagrin.*

That is not death. Nor is it Turandot's marriage under duress. It is a sad little death of the sort one might expect from Vienna—a death with no external drama, an entirely inner death, just an end. The shattering finish to a woman's sexual-ity, the definitive passage from little Resi to old princess. In opera sweetness is deceiving: it masks the deep cruelty of generations passing, who erase every-thing with their passage. Sometimes the young pay for the old; sometimes the old grow weak and give in, their nobility all the greater when it is without pretension.

Mélisande put to the question, or the men's secret

Sweetness lies. Other heroines will die of it, of their lie, their luminosity, their deceptive tenderness. From sorceress to sorceress, from the unleashed Furies to the tender marschallin, the thread leads me to the little, unknown sorceress, the woman without origin, the woman who comes from nowhere, the most deceptive, the most moonlike: Mélisande.[44]

The story: It opens beside a well in the forest. Prince Golaud, who is the grandson of Arkel, the old king of Aldemonde, becomes lost while hunting. In the darkness he hears weeping. It is a lost young woman who is wild, Mélisande. He takes her away with him and marries her, despite his family's reservations. Mélisande is bored in this dark, sunless country; her only distraction is playing with her brother-in-law, Pelléas, who is as young as she is. And what has to happen happens: the young people fall madly, incestuously in love. Golaud, who is jealous, has them watched by his son from an earlier marriage, the boy Yniold. But in vain: there is nothing questionable that one can see about the young people's relationship. Mélisande is pregnant. One evening, Pelléas, who is about to leave, asks her to meet him outside the castle grounds. There Golaud surprises them, kills Pelléas, and slightly wounds Mélisande. She gives birth to a baby girl and dies in silence. Old Arkel takes the baby in his arms, saying, "Now it is the poor child's turn."[45]

The simplest language, a banal story, a familiar triangle: husband, wife, and lover, an adulterous affair. It is *Tristan and Isolde* and its underside. In *Tristan and Isolde* everything is right side up and blindingly visible: there is true love, a couple uniting, the narcissistic mirage of two subjects who kill each other. In *Pelléas* everything is upside down; you will never know what is going on. You know nothing about Mélisande's age, or where she comes from, or even if the two lovers are guilty. Uncertainty is Mélisande's tune, secrecy her cover. You meet Mélisande just when Golaud does, you never know what she says or thinks, whether or not she tells the truth, or why she dies. She resists right up to the end: reticent until her very death.

Like Isolde, Mélisande comes from somewhere else, carried off forcibly, half-violently married for lack of a better choice, a conquest, what else can a lost girl in the forest do other than follow the terrifying man? The first sign of sorcery is this: she has fallen from the heavens, come from nowhere; an inherent troublemaker, Mélisande is free and she is a sorceress. She is found wild, like an animal, deep in the woods; she is caught beside a spring, the mythical heiress of virgins with unicorns and of women who wander in woods. "From the moment of her appearance the Sorceress has neither father nor mother, nor son, nor husband, nor family. It is a monster, an aerolith, come from who knows where. Who, Good God! would dare come near?'' exclaimed Michelet as he set his sorceress in the hollows of nature. The sorceress with her long, disheveled hair, her answers that are not answers, her eyes that are too bright. A sorceress—this woman who comes from the unknown. The mystery is so powerful that sometimes people have wanted to reknot the broken thread, virgin wisps flying away on the North wind. They have crudely tied Mélisande's story to Bluebeard's. The lost blond woman beside the well would be none other than the seventh wife of that phallocrat with his closets and closed-off rooms. Joan of Arc, perhaps—burned to death, brought back to life. But no, not even her, she is just a conventional little victim, a rose in the shadows. Her wigs are tow-colored braids, and she is everything Pierre Boulez calls ''silly, anemic postcards.''

But Mélisande is free. ''Where is she?'' Michelet again wonders about this supreme woman. ''Where is she? In impossible places, in bramble forests on the moors, where tangled thorn bushes and thistles allow no passage. At night, under some ancient dolmen. If she is found there, she is still isolated by a horror that is shared, it is as if she is surrounded by a circle of fire.'' She is captured, letting the hunter catch her instead of the wild boar who has escaped; she is the prisoner of a skyless, sunless world, but one free in her instants of freedom. Her hair is free. Oh, Mélisande's beautiful hair! Pelléas watches from a window: she is blondness itself, a comet, a shooting star like Berenice's star in the skies of Egypt . . . astral woman, star woman, mystery woman, symbolizing men's desire; gently, carefully, she will turn this desire away.

That hair is animal hair. Via sublimation of the hair principle Mélisande gets back the silky fur of the animal-woman she has never ceased to be. Michelet's sorceress is transformed into a gentle she-wolf whose leg is broken by her hunter husband. Mélisande beckons men by the fur all around her head. Golaud does not see her face; Pelléas, his brother, is deeply moved, seeing her blond hair fall into the well and touch the water. He dives in, hiding his head in her flowing locks, the way a lover dives somewhere else into the fur of the woman he loves. This is far from any little, innocent girl. We are closer to the most brutish of physical eroticism. It is hardly surprising that Golaud later grabs hold of her by her sinful hair. He hangs on, shaking her back and forth, and chastises her, saying that all this hair finally has some use. That is all he could say because, up to that moment, for him it has been useless. Mélisande is both devil and animal, something high and something low, very close to those primitive feelings that only hair evokes bodily for men. When Golaud finds her he does not know what it is that is moaning beside the well. Whatever is crying is not entirely a woman, not entirely human: ''a little girl weeping next to the water.'' Some indeterminate, undefined thing is weeping. Something secret.

But she has a use for her hair—at a moment of her own choosing. She lets it down and brushes it in the only moment she is finally alone, and, in a gesture of self-love and freedom, she sings to herself. She combs her hair, she sings and speaks of it. "My long, long hair reaches to the foot of the tower."

After describing her hair, the glory of nights, she tells of her patron saints, then the day and hour of her birth. Daniel, saint of the fiery furnace, Michael the dragon-slayer, Raphael the archangel who defeated Satan. Flames, diabolical animals: her heaven has an air of hell about it. This otherworldliness quickly reveals its underside. Mélisande invokes the archangels who defeated both serpent and woman, and all the while she is letting down her hair, an unconscious Lilith with demon eyes. And then . . . "I was born on Sunday, midday on Sunday." Is this a pious reference to the Lord's day and the sacred hour? Yes. But it also the hour of pagan madness. In the South of Italy, where transient Greek voyagers earlier established Magna Graecia, in the center of Apulia, there is a bizarre collective phenomenon. Women are bitten by tarentulas, those venomous spiders that produce the wild dance with a practically identical name—the tarentella. But these spiders do not exist there, nor do their bites; it is all made-up. Still, the women, stung to the quick in a body that suffers somewhere else, give the sacred hour, day, and moment that they were bitten. Often Sunday, at midday. This is the hour of the lion-sun, a holy, mad hour. To escape the strange, depressive languor that the spider caused them, these women have no other choice than a wild, rampaging dance that goes on forever—the way Golaud shakes Mélisande back and forth. Sunday at midday: you can hear the madness returning, beneath Mélisande's torpor, the unspeakable unhappiness, the body incapable of more, the body of the little Bacchante with her wild hair loose.

Mélisande is very like another prostituted yet innocent sorceress, Madame Edwarda, produced and created by a showman of women, Georges Bataille. Discovered by chance in a brothel, she is a woman whose body has been worked over by men before, like Mélisande. She too does not know where she is or where she comes from. "Her voice, like her slender body, was obscene." In its original sense, the obscene is what brings the bad omen: this unyielding voice, this pythian voice, is the voice that always says what is true while never telling the truth. This voice drives Golaud crazy, this voice that speaks only of itself. She barely manages, at the moment of death, to speak of the tiny scrap of body dropped from her without her noticing, her little newborn girl. "I am sorry for her." Her last words, perhaps the only marks of humanity, are the only words in which she concedes. Madame Edwarda pursues the same quest after her secret identity, taking sexual climax to extremes to uncover and simultaneously thoroughly disguise the same feminine secret. The two slender girls finally escape men's gaze; for Bataille, Maeterlinck, and Debussy have made dream creatures for us, these subservient child-women, so that these guilty, seductive images will be reflected to us. Fictions, men's fantasies: "The cold of dawn was coming from her, a transparency where I read death."[46]

Because she is the fantasy of generations of men, Mélisande is put to the question. Notice how insistently, from the first meeting when he barely sees her because it is so dark, Golaud questions her, throughout the opera. It is always dark when questions are asked. First Golaud meets a voice that weeps like a violin. And from the start he questions: "Why are you crying? Why do you cry like that? Has someone hurt you? Who, what did they do to you? Where do you come from? Where did you run away from? Where are you from, where were you born? What is that shining at the bottom of the well? Who gave you a crown? Did you run away long ago? Do you never shut your eyes? Why do you look so surprised? How old are you?" He certainly is curious, this man who asks every question about genealogy and birth, social questions of good taste, the questions of a lord trying to classify and define. Unanswered questions, except the two that finally capture the girl: "Will you come with me? What is your name?" Golaud keeps on asking right to the end, the ultimate question that will have no reply: "Have you been guilty?" Ah, it has been the same question all along! Before Golaud, was Mélisande guilty of having that crown gleaming at the bottom of the well, a crown some other man gave her? Who? Mélisande, guilty of being from nowhere, of having fled without anyone knowing why. Who?

She is wary. She deflects the questions. Will you come with me? Answer: "I am starting to feel cold." Her first words are completely defensive: "Do not touch me, do not touch me, or I will jump in the water." One time, however, she answers. Or rather she acts as if she is answering. When Pelléas asks her "How long have you loved me?" She replies, "Forever, since I saw you," and her voice trails off very gently. But Pelléas is immediately worried, "You will not run away from me? Where are your eyes?" Her eyes are gone. "You are looking somewhere else," he says, already reproaching her autonomy. The true Mélisande speaks, "I saw you somewhere else . . .".

Too late. Here is the accusation; the crime is flight. To show whether a woman was a witch or not, in the days when they were burned by the thousands (that old story about cleaning up the Christian world), the inquisitors' task—it is recorded—was to watch especially the gaze, the language, and the voice of every accused woman. "Thus, when a soul is strongly inclined toward malice . . . this person's gaze becomes poisonous and harmful . . . the eyes look out into space to some unfixed place." The gaze transmits the diabolical infection by contagion. Diabolical literally means deviant. Golaud holds Mélisande's face in his huge killer's hands: "These eyes, I have seen them at work. . . . You would think there were angels in them, eternally celebrating a baptism." Angelic, diabolic— Mélisande's bright gaze condemns her. So does her voice: "A liar by nature, her language also lies, she charms as she stings," the inquisitors wrote in their medieval manual *The Witches' Hammer*. She speaks a language that is made for being accused, a charming, guilty language. A secret, lying language.

This secret is entirely the projection of questioning men. "The insatiable pleasure in asking questions," wrote Freud, "which characterizes a certain stage of childhood is explained by the fact that they have one question, which never passes their lips, to ask. Thus the loquacity of many neurotics is explained by the pressure of some secret which is working hard to be communicated and which, however, despite every temptation, they do not betray." One simple question: where do children come from? Where does Mélisande come from, without parents? And what did she do with the man who gave her the golden crown? Golaud questions her, and so does Pelléas; they do not know what it is that pushes them to make a woman found by chance into the object of all their desires. Mélisande, the mirror of two brothers who fight for her and who both pass over her body as if to encounter each other. Mélisande, maidservant of the men's projections. At the end of the round, Golaud remains alone with his one question, and the living answer, the baby girl, and Pelléas has died of it. Only old Arkel, no longer of a sexual age, can treat himself to the philosophical luxury of assertive statements about life, love, death, and destinies, without questions. There is always some old man on stage who bears witness to transition, who assures the continuity of life that is not contained within this tragedy. Arkel picks up the baby and carries her out of the death chamber: "Now it is the poor little girl's turn." Norma's father, the old druid, gathers up the children of the guilty priestess; the old emperor of China hears the first confessions of his daughter Turandot when she rejoins the ranks. Furies, witches, and waning Moons deliver their rages transformed into affection, their living children, and their deep weariness into the hands of compassionate old men.

Two men and a sorceress have blocked the passage of life, according to a family structure in which the woman, as object of exchange, the prisoner of men's questions, is nothing in herself. Anyhow. Anyhow, they never got an answer in this opera. Mélisande is an Isolde who escapes the union of love, an Isolde who sneaks off. The inquisitors loudly proclaim: "A woman who thinks alone thinks of evil."

Mélisande, little nonexistent sister, when as prima donna you comb your fake hair on the top of a cardboard tower, when your solitary voice unbacked by orchestra names your patron saints and the hour of your birth, something is starting to sing alone, to think alone, to think well.

Once again we are in a forest.[47] A dark, Russian forest in the vicinity of Moscow the Terrible, heiress to Ivan's rages. It is the last act of a long history of rivalry between boyar bands, the populace, and a very young czar from Europe with his well-disciplined soldiers. Peter the Great is hunting down the Old-Believers, a powerful, heretic sect, in the forest. They have all decided to set themselves on fire in a great isba that is ready for the sacrifice. All around them the sound of the new czar's European trumpets are sounding. It is time; already the old boyars are dead, the Khovanski protect them. A woman is leading them into death, just as long ago she had predicted she would.

Yes, long before, Marfa, the faithful peasant woman, had sung an inspired threnody describing this scene: a collective holocaust, a gigantic fire for the Redemption of the World. The Old-Believers are dying for a symbol: instead of making the sign of the cross with the whole hand, they use only three fingers. But they are dying also for the old, torn Russia, while the strong man who will unify it is coming. Before, when Marfa so sweetly sang the song of the future, the pope stopped her: "It is too soon, my dove." The sorceress is never there at the right time. And Marfa is a sorceress. She predicts the future in a cupful of water, she frightens men. Now is her time.

And Marfa, all in white, leads her terrifed lover to the pyre, with sweet words, while the cabin full of men burns and while Peter the Great's soldiers stand guard around a disintegrating world.

Throughout the eternity of a culture permanently covered with the dust of its own tombs, Aida falls asleep in the arms of her Egyptian lover. Underground in a huge temple, at the roots of the lotus-shaped columns, white now, bleached and colorless, the little Nubian slave sings. Her lover, a general, is to be buried alive because he loves the forbidden slave and refuses the pharoah's daughter. He betrays without even knowing it, he accepts his fate and the death to which the priests condemn him. In the open tomb, where Egypt knew only "shores to land on" and the subterranean soil where the sky played no part, the voices sing together of heaven and earth. A third voice sings as well, the voice of Amneris, violent, strong, and rebellious.

Mariette-Bey, an archaeologist adopted by an Egypt grateful for his revelations of its past, helped put together the libretto of *Aida*.[48] But scholarly restoration sometimes is less creative than myth when one is willing to let it act through stubborn, unconscious minds. And this dream Aida is more a Christian than a Nubian. Her chivalrous Radamès is Christian as well. The only Egyptian is the lofty Amneris, the pharoah's daughter. Her violence, her dignity and her anger are Egyptian. The mournful lamentations during which she has thrown herself on the floor of the temple are Egyptian. Animal-headed gods dwell in Amneris, and, while the lovers sing together about resignation and the virtue of taking leave of the earth, she retains the inflexibility of those standing queens with the graceful arms, those eternal girls whose smiles still light up the walls of tombs, columns of ruins, and capitals where the goddess Hathor, with her cow's ears, signifies desire, intoxication, and happiness.

Opposite the strong, savage Amneris is Aida, black, weak, and gentle, a slave. In the long history of ancient Egypt there were two very real conflicting women like the two, Amneris and Aida, in conflict in this single opera. The Egyptian queen Hatshepsut, the king's wife who went through two successive husbands, calmly took the supreme power for herself, wearing the false beard and two crowns of Egypt. Nefertiti was the betrayed wife of Akhenaton, a resigned and passively exiled woman, who died deserted in the High Castle deep in an abandoned city. Her husband, Akhenaton, was the ancestor of monotheism, wishing to destroy the many gods who watched over Egyptian life. In his wish to impose a single sun God, western intellectuals of today delight in finding the future figure of a Moses (like Freud)[49] or a Christ. But he condemned his wife to banishment. Hatshepsut, on the other hand, leaned on polytheism to establish her power; like any good pharaoh she built temples so the gods would guarantee, as they did every year, the flooding of the river Nile and the fertility of the land. Notice: we are in an inner space now, populated with history, where gods and nature exist. Notice: these two heroines, created after a fashion by men of the opera to inaugurate the Suez canal amid imperial pomp, Aida and Amneris (thanks to the faithful memory of a passionate archaeologist), are somehow the heiresses to the two greatest figures of women that Egypt has left us. But one of these, Hatshepsut, ruled powerfully, in a world where gods lived and took care of both everyday life and the wonderfully prepared life on the other side of mortal shores. The other, Nefertiti, the beauty with the bent neck, paid the price of her royal husband's monotheistic madness with her freedom. From the confines of the desert, conveyed from memory to memory, surmounting the ridicule of sumptuous restorations with golden trumpets and paper palm trees, across the thousands of years separating us from it, this struggle between gods comes down to us. They are both locked up in the temple, both Amneris and Aida. The Egyptian is condemned to live, an authoritarian queen, defeated by the opera; and the Nubian woman is condemned to die. The first one finds herself back with the Egyptian gods, the second carries out her death, thanks to heaven.

On the banks of a river.[50] On a funeral pyre lies a dead man. It is Siegfried, the joy of the world. Before the silent, powerless onlookers, a woman is caressing the neck of his horse. A woman knows all about this story that is ending; she knows also what she still has to do. Then, while two crows fly off into the flaming heavens, Brunhilde lights the pyre and with a single leap jumps into the fire. The river overflows, a world ends.

Good Friday, in a clearing.[51] A young sacred hero has just won sainthood and the Grail. In a springtime mystery, Parsifal frees the woman clinging to his knees. This woman, who has long been a sorceress, and enslaved for centuries, committed the greatest of crimes: she laughed, one of those rash laughs witches can find to ridicule the gods, when Christ passed her. And when Parsifal has finally brought her the long-awaited Redemption, Kundry collapses, dead, returning to the Nature that she was deprived of by her crime.

Chapter 6
Madmen, Negroes, Jesters, or the Heroes of Deception

*In which we finally speak of men; but not real ones. In which
we see a black man in love with a blonde; in which an old
child is saved by English fairies; in which a poet-shoemaker
makes shoes for Eve's feet while giving her Adam's hand. In
which the gods threaten to die . . .*

How easy it would all be, how neat and clean, if this break between men and
women neatly separated the world into two antagonistic halves, one persecuting
the other since before the dawn of time. . . . But opera is the reflection of our
historical reality, and this mirror breaks in those places where the image is split
with a sudden incongruity. I thought I saw two figures, as if on two panels of a
triptych: Adam on the left, gazing off into the distance, stretching his brand-new
limbs and his evil virility; Eve on the right, shy still, in a cloud of light, blond
and damned. But I forgot the central panel: Nativity, Virgin's Family, Christ's
Family. I forgot that the only thing separating the two sexual halves is the central
representation of conception without fleshly intervention, in which the union of
two distinct beings never happens, in which the divine family is the only thing
keeping man and woman apart indefinitely, each in his or her panel.

Opera is more real. Of course, there, Eve is undone as a woman, endlessly
bruised, endlessly dying and coming back to life to die even better. But now I
begin to remember hearing figures of betrayed, wounded men; men who have
women's troubles happen to them; men who have the status of Eve, as if they
had lost their innate Adam. These men die like heroines; down on the ground
they cry and moan, they lament. And like heroines they are surrounded by real
men, veritable Adams who have cast them down. They partake of femininity:
excluded, marked by some initial strangeness, they are doomed to their undoing.

They are mad, prey to frenzies of mysticism or love. They are black, their
skin is not the same color as others', and their powerless rage makes them roll
on the ground. They are misshapen, their hunchbacked bodies make straight men

laugh, and they are the court jesters. They are fat and short of breath, ridiculous and mocked by everyone. They are named Parsifal or Tristan, the young rejected heroes, innocent or marked by death; Othello the Moor of Venice, the foreigner in love with Desdemona, who is too blond; Rigoletto, the Duke of Mantua's jester, monstrous with anguish and laughter; Falstaff, the old youth, drunk on beer and vanished dreams. They, more than the men playing women's roles with their ambiguous charm, more than young Octavian or charming Cherubin, join the women, defeated and undone.

Because, they, like witches, have gone beyond the limits of being merely one of two sexes. Sorceresses, unengendered and androgynous, escape the feminine role, on which they confer an autonomous majesty beyond any standard limits; but madmen, Negroes, and jesters, for their part, are not real men. Their male stature may seem solid; but they each have one disfiguring feature that makes them vulnerable and touching, almost mortally wounded. For Tristan this feature is the death of his mother, predisposing him to raving madness, deadly halluci-nations, the suicide he dreams of and finally commits; for Parsifal, it is medieval innocence, the debility of a child unable to speak, the psychosis from which only mysticism can deliver him, on condition that he remain chaste, abnormal in his purity. For Othello it is the color of his skin, his exclusion, his anger, and his epilepsy; for Rigoletto it is his hump, his ugliness, and his daughter; for Falstaff it is his excessive rotundity and his slobby, unconscious sweetness.

They are disconcerting and troublesome. They are different, uneasy. They arouse either anxiety or laughter, which are the same thing. Across centuries and histories, across worlds and seas, they are the heirs to forgotten gods, as are pagan witches in the Christian world. They are heirs to Greek gods, African gods, whose now blurry features Western memory, busily trying to recall a well-be-haved Pantheon decorated with familiar gods, has been unable to preserve.

The African demiurge Legba can throw bridges and throw words: God of lan-guage and pranks, he excites laughter and danger.

Baubô, the little old woman from the Corinthian countryside, was the only one able to make the goddess Demeter laugh. Mourning, Demeter sought her daughter, Persephone, whom the god of the underworld had carried off, and noth-ing grew on the earth; it was winter and there was famine. Baubô lifted her old woman's skirts and showed her ass to Demeter, who began to laugh, bursts of warm, living laughter; and the plants began to germinate again, it was Spring.

Tiresias, the seer, was given his power of language because he honored a god-dess with his favors. He could live for seven years as a woman and seven years as a man; but, because he was unable to keep the secret of feminine sexual plea-sure (he told Zeus it was seven times greater than men's pleasure), Hera pun-ished him and made him blind.

Now follow the thread on the warp, now weave together the amusing sprite, the obscene old woman, the androgynous and blind seer: a child, an old man, a hermaphrodite. They are what are called tricksters: carrion crows, vixens, demiurges, a divine countersociety that proceeds by sacrilege and provocation. They untie, they break, they cause short circuits and zigzags; they divert dogged, straightforward thought and break it into so many splinters that all placid oppositions and shortsighted classifications disappear. In their place appears a jubilant and perverse disorder, the opening up of thought, the impossibility of closing or confining. These beings set free, give birth, and wander. Without them the limits of the world would always be the same. With them horizons move, mountains change shape, bridges appear, hands reach out. On the opera stage they are doomed to be defeated, like women, because the world represented there cannot put up with any social transgression, any drifting off not harshly punished. But their song, whether sad or amusing, is like women's song. Dreadful in their madness or brilliant in their gaiety, they escape the game of man-and-woman and, one by one, become heroes of deception. The anthropologist Roger Bastide said of the tricksters that their nature is simultaneously dangerous and funny. From laughter to anguish, in opera they occupy the position always allotted to marginals—they are thrown out into our locked enclosures. Madmen are doomed to asylums, blacks doomed to racism, and clowns doomed to everyone's ridicule.

Thus it is that, one terribly cold day in Moussorgski's old Russia, a poor simpleton, endlessly tormented by children, is thrown to the earth and beaten black and blue despite his sweetness and his high voice—nearly the voice of a hoarse woman. But this simpleton is the only one who can tell the truth; and when the omnipotent czar, the master then of all the Russias, appears, the simpleton says in his high voice, "Boris, assassin czar." Everyone thinks it, and it is whispered, but the simpleton says it, because his position in the world is to tell the truth. Boris Godounov[52] lets him go unpunished; "God's fools," those inspired men marked with divine madness, are not to be touched. Along with the ridiculous load of hardware dangling from his back, the pathetic simpleton carries divine danger inside himself. Tricksters: sinister jokers, desperate rogues, jesters, lost forever, outlaws. Yet the fathers, the kings, those holding symbolic power tremble, before them. Even if it means losing everything, these characters defy the supreme command and hold all authorities up to ridicule. They bring rebellion; they are revolutionaries in body and flesh; they are undefined and hazy beings, the seeds of the future.

The savage with big lips

Down there everything begins at nightfall. You cannot see a thing. Like they said in colonialism's finest hours: it is black as a nigger's ass. What one can make out is lit by glimmers of a storm: a sail, a standard, the lion of Saint Mark. The Moor of Venice in all the shades of lightning.

The story: Othello, a Moor by birth and color of skin, has dedicated his life and his strength to the defense of patrician Venice. On his return to the city after victorious battle, he carried off Desdemona, a daughter of Venice, and married her. On a night so stormy that the boat almost does not make it, they land at Famagousta. Iago, one of Othello's lieutenants, is not satisfied with close calls. To finish off the hero, he chooses to rouse his jealousy. It takes nothing at all for him to succeed; a handkerchief stolen from Desdemona becomes the only proof of her infidelity. Desdemona powerlessly watches the shipwreck of her happiness. Othello becomes madder and madder. When a Venetian delegation pays a visit, he throws Desdemona to the ground and then rolls there himself in an epileptic seizure. The next night he strangles and kills Desdemona; then, when Iago, finally unmasked, confesses his hatred and plots, Othello kills himself with his sword and dies reunited with Desdemona's dead body.[53]

We will try, however, to forget Shakespeare; there will be only vague reminders, pale traces of the initial text. We know (how?) that the handkerchief Othello gave Desdemona, the accusing handkerchief, belonged to his mother, who was perhaps a magician. . . . We think we remember that a woman somehow figures between Othello and Iago (Emilia, married by Iago and possibly had by Othello). But the opera runs its own course—asks to have its own listening. It forgets, it no longer knows, and in the bare plot that leads the hero to his death float musical remains of a lost dramatic art.

But somewhere, in some corner of the retina, if you will, we also have obsessive images rising from this story's past. We will not be able to lose sight of the figures of Negroes in D.W. Griffith's nationalist films, white faces wearing shoe polish and a three-quarters view of Orson Welles descending the staircase of the citadel at Mogador. White dipped in black: the tenors who sing Othello wear blackface.

We will try to understand why so many men have taken pleasure in identifying with the black-skinned Moor. In *La Mise à Mort*, Louis Aragon played the writer and his madness through *Othello*. The character staged by Jacques Prévert in *Les Enfants de Paradis*, Frédérick Lemaître, a romantic actor, found at last in his own jealousy of Garance, veiled in black and watching from her box, the jealous voice with which to play *Othello*. For all the men who situate themselves in some mobility, for the actor who changes skins, for the writer who changes narcissisms, *Othello* represents desirable and dangerous mutation. *Othello*—driven to build himself a white statue, with black makeup.

Not the slightest division is apparent between Othello and Venice. The Lion of Venice, the one bravely raising his paw on the battle flag, and Othello are the same. Venice is present emblematically and in the white skin of the wife he took from there, the blond Desdemona. But later, when Othello is lying on the ground, the victim of a seizure, while the Cypriots outside are shouting, "the Lion of

Venice," their chief, Iago, sets his foot on the shuddering body and cries out, "*Ecco il leone!*"

Here is the lion! On the ground, drooling, groaning, without his claws.

Because the lion, as in the fable, is in love with a beautiful woman, that love is his weakness, the hold Iago has on him. That is Othello's flaw. For a marriage to take place within the kinship system, one must know how to keep the right distance according to the laws of exogamy. Too close and it is incest; too distant and it is war. Too close, it is Jocasta, or Isolde: death. Too distant, it is Othello: death again. In the twinkling of an eye, he and Desdemona overstepped all distances: skin color, the differences of class and age. And, since all this happens on an island, it is all exposed: there is no longer any family or home base. The two of them are united in an elsewhere that is the symbol of their transgression. Desdemona, however, is on an island belonging to Venice; this is marked space. Othello is absolutely alone, an illusory king on his island, lost in the midst of whites.

The men, the other men, do not forget who this different man, Othello, is. Iago is the first to pronounce the words of racist exclusion. "*Di quel selvaggio dalle gonfie labbra.*" This savage with the big lips. This excluded man, in the position of master, decked out in the plumes of the corps of engineers; this clown, talking like a white man, this Negro. . . let's make him roll his eyes and writhe on the ground: grotesque Othello. So dizzyingly close to the Othello in love. The opera begins with a storm, followed by an orgasm. Night has fallen, utterly. The last clouds are frayed. The drunken lieutenants fought with each other; Othello made them put away their swords. Desdemona appears, awakened by the sound of arms. She has left the bed where she soon will die. There, next to the bedroom, with fresh memories of the lightning and the crash of arms, they will make love, their first night of love.

How, knowing the end of their story, can one not be moved? Look at these beautiful lovers who give themselves in a sublime duet in which nothing concerning desire or its sources is hidden. It is all there already. How near the danger is! Desdemona's first words of love: "My glorious warrior." Their lover's exchange travels in a warlike rage. At the end of a long passage, where, says Desdemona, "the soul's fear and the heart's ecstasy" meet, they reach their climax. Danger. Othello loves war, storms, and violence: "War can thunder and the world come to ruin, if after immense anger comes immense love." Anger, love; Othello stems from these two words. He moves from one to the other, from anger to love; that is all he knows, he has no idea of moderation because he comes from elsewhere and no one ever really taught him good manners or the proper distance to keep. And he has no distance in either violence or love. That is really what seduces Desdemona: the tales he tells about his battles, the attacks, the shouts, the odors still pervading his body. . . . How quickly the little sleeping

Venetian got out of bed when she heard the men fighting! He told her about his wars, his deserts, his slavery; she wept and sighed while she listened to him. Then they return again to the exchange made at the beginning of their lovemaking; they sing together the "I" and "you" of gift and countergift that they call "their love." And we see them pass from war to tears, from pity to atonement, and attain utmost desire.

"*Venga la morte*," sings Othello at that precise moment. There is nothing beyond this; let death come. The pagan Moor has no alternative, but Desdemona, the good little Christian, corrects her oaf, her badly baptized bear. He does not know it, but heaven lies beyond. Desdemona's Amen, fastening the slow fabric of his pagan desire to her Christian otherworldliness, completes the calm transition. In a give and take between the very high and the very low, Desdemona's voice joins the Christian heaven of her childhood to the pagan earth that Othello knows.

This loving baptism becomes his great moment, one he will endlessly seek to repeat. The moment of bodies and union, of the black body and the white body intertwined. What winding detours he takes to repeat this scene! The first time he sings frantically the inconsequential words of love, he is mad with love, already mad. "*Un bacio, un bacio ancora*," a kiss, another kiss. The second time, when it is all over, he repeats these happy words on Desdemona's dead body as reality dawns. How could he, the wretched Moor, have kept the blond white woman? How can one make the charm of war stories last after becoming a husband? How can he retrieve this so distant distance between him and her, the paths of passing comets intersecting in the sky, the trajectory of tremendous movements across the universe? Surmounting, mounting, he sings, higher and higher. He straddles her. And the astonishing tenor voice rises to the limits of possibility, to Venus shining above this Greek island. And Desdemona's voice harmonizes, lower by a third. Their order, above and below, is the order of men and women; unless this voice—that is too high—is the symbol of its own failure. For the Moor of Venice, men's order is untenable.

Just imagine this warrior, his battles finished, shut up on his island. So Iago puts on a show for him. *Now Showing*—a possible lover vanishing around the corner. *Now Showing*—Desdemona all smiles, like a fisherman's madonna, without her handkerchief. *Now Showing*—the handkerchief. . . . Iago is right behind him, pulling the stage curtains. "*Vigilate, scrutate*." And the murderous objects of desire that the divided Othello carries within, those objects of desire that come from his desert and his magician mother, those objects that have taken on for him the glorious form of spears and battle flags, now brandish him and throw him down.

A man would have sufficed; but a man was required. One like Othello but different; someone with a phallus, white-skinned. The real difference is blond, passive, Venetian, and deceptive. The difference between Othello and Iago is more disturbing and Othello does not even see it. According to the Venetian trap, one warrior is the same as another warrior. Othello has forgotten that he is black, a savage. He is like a crazy compass, oscillating between an impossible contact with the white woman and the utmost rejection of this blondness. Propped up by the pugnacious homosexuality in the atmosphere at Famagousta, he goes from loving the distant princess to slaughtering her. The instant it touches the shores of jealousy, Othello's statue crumbles. Bugles blow no more, flags stop flying . . . as if the whole panoply, the masculine trinkets, dropped from the wall where they hung: feathers and plumes and swords dumped on the ground. This is the desert savage in his black jealousy. "*Della gloria d'Otello e questo il fin.*" It is the end of Othello's glory. It was quick in coming, as if he had to drop a load that was too heavy.

From that moment on, the men and women take sides: the Negro and his white double, Iago, the white woman and her attendant, Emilia. Othello and Iago kneeling together vow to be avenged. These two men swearing before their gods, are the shadow of a male couple guarding themselves against woman. This is the final trap that ensnares the savage with the big lips: what he is preparing to destroy is a dummy, a manikin of a woman. Once again it is nighttime in a Christian bedroom, crammed with things signifying prayer: the prie-dieu, the image of the Madonna, the white wedding dress spread out by Desdemona on her bed (as if the situation were not dangerous enough); and her timid song invoking the Virgin. The act itself, the murder, is quick as lightning; a dream that becomes reality in a gasp.

The real end, the aim, the goal: "*Niun mi tema.*" No one fears me. The savage is calm after his madness. This time, finally, he can speak of himself in the past; he has brought himself where he had to go, into that symbolic desert where no white man can understand him: "*O gloria! Othello fu.*" Othello was. Negritude is written in this funeral oration that he delivers for himself. He, the Moor, the living statue, has indeed done his work as a Moor; he fought for the blond city; he entered into a monstrous marriage of beauty and the beast; he condemned himself to "having been." Othello was. Was nothing. Nothing at all except his forgotten name.

And the other, she too is lifeless, a cold statue; but he will not say so. He calls her "pale" rather than dead. So that his tomb can be erected in a cursed, posthumous glory. So that a bit of his warrior's nature will remain, he still must kill himself. The last word escapes him or remains unsaid; the last note of the score does not complete the loving phrase, *Un bacio, un bacio anc'* . . .''. The final vowel is elided; his voice betrays him, the Negro cannot die singing. There is nothing here that partakes of those heroic deaths, the final tender duet of *Aida*, the gallant notes of *Trovatore*. This is a real agony for a white tenor wearing blackface. As if the missing note and this pitiful tomb marked the passage from heroism to truth: Verdi's *Othello* is an opera of old age. There is no more joking with death, it is not portrayed with the swaggering strokes of youth; the gallant death comes to nothing. Othello dies as a Negro, excluded, stripped, without a voice. His only wealth is his past. He is naked before his masters. The savage loses all, even music, over the memory of a forbidden kiss.

Old John

Just one more step, and Verdi, now past the age for love and triumphant narcissism brings forth a fabulous trickster, whose only deviance has to do with his belly: Big-Belly, Verdi called him, while he was composing the opera. This is the most unexpected opera hero: old, fat, dirty, ridiculous, obscene; this is John Falstaff. His belly symbolizes everything that marginalizes him in the little town of Windsor. Noble and flat broke, he comes from somewhere else, and predates the townspeople who fool him and are very fond of him. He has acquired his belly through years of being broke, years of debts and luxurious poverty, kept alive by tatters of aristocracy. Falstaff's sad undoing finalizes the victory of the taunting bourgeoisie, and something even more exceptional, the victory of a time that old Verdi felt coming; it hails the victory of the gossips. The gossips . . . those disparaged, chattering women, those sweet, sensitive females who make life more livable through their mischief and their gutsiness, are witches who have finally been accepted. They are dangerous—but just enough so that they get around their husbands' schemes and have their way. They are living—but just enough to avoid being burned alive. Their flame encircles Falstaff as if Big-Belly had to pay with his fat for all masculine crime. Gone with the Thames . . . the imperturbable river collects sighs, wastes, and the body of Falstaff who catches cold, far from all the heroics of the old days.

The story: Sir John Falstaff, drunk and broke, decides to seduce two wealthy bourgeois wives, Alice Ford and Meg Page. But, when they receive identical love letters from him, they are furious and decide to fool the fat man, sending an ambassadress to arrange a lover's rendezvous. Dame Quickly duly fulfills her mission and Falstaff goes to the rendezvous in the page's costume he wore long, long ago. . . . In the meantime, Alice's husband, warned of Falstaff's plans, pays him a visit in disguise. Because the husband suddenly arrives during the rendezvous, the gossips hide Falstaff in a basket of dirty linen that is to be dumped into the Thames. . . . John Falstaff climbs back out, soaking wet, disappointed and furious. But then Quickly comes with another message: a new rendezvous is set for midnight in the forest. Falstaff is to go there, disguised as the Black Hunter. We next meet our man topped off by a huge pair of antlers, beneath the fateful oak; he is scared to death. All the more because there are fairies popping out of the bushes, and goblins, a whole phantasmagoria that terrifies the poor old pot-

belly. (It is the gossips again, in disguise). Throughout the story, Alice Ford's daughter, Nanetta, has been plotting, with her mother's help, to marry her lover, against the wishes of Master Ford. And during this magic night the two lovers trick the father and end up united.[54]

On one side, there is the poor, seedy world of Falstaff: the inn where he lives, if you can call this sloppy, endebted stay living, with two insolent servants giving him nothing but mischief and petty theft. In this world there are only men, godforsaken and resourceful. On the other side, is the snug and cozy world of the gossips: bright, orderly houses, with laundry drying and lovers chasing each other beneath the sheets, under the trees, among the screens. Falstaff is excluded from this domestic world; he is an old child without a family trying to find shelter where a woman's body and a well-filled purse will provide him with a bit of warmth. Windsor is a town full of shouts and gaiety, poverty wears lace there, and Falstaff is growing old and fatter and fatter. Not just pudgy, not just plump, fat. "*Pancione*," said Verdi, pot-bellied: he leads with his paunch; his voice, full of illusions, comes behind. The theme of popular magic dominates the whole opera. It takes place in courtyards, vegetable gardens, the priest's gardens, places full of rosemary and sage and the aromatic plants found in the woods. It takes place in houses where nooks and crannies hide stolen kisses, in misty forests where English fairies dance the sacred round that drives men mad. Falstaff, thrown into the waters of the Thames, then subjected to the terrors of nocturnal spirits, will have his moment of madness, his ordeals, his initiation rites. Mystery is all around. The same imposing and savage mystery that surrounded Norma's song in the druid forest finds its colloquial version in *Falstaff*, when a shadow through colored windowpanes deforms reality, when a mug of beer makes you see everything askew, when a big, innocent slob can believe everything he is told—even that two pretty gossips are in love with him. This is the mystery of latticed houses, of furniture where suitors can hide, of secret rendezvous, of women in love—crazy and sensible at the same time, knowing how to play without risk, knowing how to live without dying. Only the old child tumbles through all the levels of despair, but, because he is fat this is not understood. Or maybe just a little, just once.

"Evenings with the ironing, in the sleeping house, the maid is no good but we keep her anyhow . . .". What song on French radio do we hear echoing? Charles Trenet's "Mad Lament" is no doubt the masterpiece of another trickster. His songs are about a world where hanged men come back to life, where tramps go their way in defiance of all law, where ducks have parties with flowers. The maid in the "Mad Lament" is not good at all:

Last night we found her and the sieve making out;

> Grandpa's beard fixed her up,
> But he almost got bit
> By this maid in her fit!

Women make disorder in the house at night; but the singer goes out like a candle. The tired trickster goes to bed and disappears:

> I never could say why my mind wandered . . .
> I walk roads alone, saying neither yes or no.
> My soul has melted,
> My name was Dust.

Falstaff's name is Dust. He is too fat for this world of jokes and bold women. The old child is to rediscover (because this is a comic opera and everything turns out well in the end) the maternal breast and the gossips' warmth; but first he has to suffer—die of cold, of fear, of loneliness and poverty. All of a sudden there is Falstaff, like a Parsifal lost in a bourgeois palace where beautiful ladies cruelly mock him; there is childhood, a protected childhood where the little boy runs to huddle under his mother's skirts and has to be spanked before he is kissed.

They toss him, just like a child, into a basket, a basket full of dirty laundry that is fit only for changing him. Like a child they throw him in the water. And when he comes out, chilled to the marrow, soaked to the bones, dripping with the dirty water of the Thames where they throw the garbage, Falstaff, alone with a mug of warm wine strips his belly and his pride and talks to himself in a moment of real despair. "Go, Old John," he says, "Go your own way." He has found his first name again, the admission of age that he has denied with all his might up to that point. This is Falstaff's moment of truth, the ordeal, the same once again. Even in comic opera where everything twirls and dances, we have the tragedy of someone who, to live, must give up or die. Falstaff is no longer the age for death and he has no stupid, heroic stature. Falstaff, an everyday hero, gives up. And the music trots on heavily, accompanying this hero of fat and sorrow in his sad march. Oh, it does not last long—just time enough for a few grumbles, an orchestral pirouette, a little song that starts up again, and there is Potbelly once more in all his splendor. Ready to believe anyone willing to talk to him.

> It rains in the barnyard
> It rains on the raspberries
> It rains on my love . . .

Dust dusts himself off and begins to yell.

Because Quickly, with her huge black skirts, is back—flying all sails, with her deep curtseys and her regrets for Alice. "*Povera donna.*" Quickly, the only one of the gossips who is not under a husband's authority, is Falstaff's feminine other; just as impressive, just as old, simply a woman and alive. No doubt if she were in Alice's or Meg's place she would take him in. For do we really know? The gossips knock Big-Belly around, but when Alice, alone with him, sings their mockery of a duet, something like a nostalgia for chivalry enters the musical comedy. And what if Falstaff's nobility, despite hard times, still had some of its former seductiveness? With their women's voices, light, piquant, the gossips bustle around the fat thing with whom they have chosen to play ball. Quickly finds the ball and throws it to Alice who tosses it to Meg, and the captive balloon gets away and rolls into the water. Listen to those tamed witches, delightful figures, all speckled staccato notes, like dragonflies on a reed who without warning begin to vibrate with all their wings, suddenly all aquiver with a joyful fluttering. Some of them peck away at the musical notes, another one lifts into a melody, dancing they start all over, they never stop flitting around. Alice and Meg, the two married women, are just at the age when their daughters are growing up, just at the age when love comes to an end for them. They are prime for seduction; they are steady on their feet. Quickly is outside it all; a wise, older woman, she delivers what others desire. And at the other extreme of life, there is the very young, fresh-faced Nanetta, the one just beginning. Four gossips surrounding an old child: a mother, a daughter, and two big sisters.

From scene to scene childhood unfolds, backward. "*Alle due alle tre*": at two o'clock Alice and Falstaff are to have their lovers' rendezvous. The poor fat man has found nothing better to wear than an old pink suit covered with ribbons; his blubber overflows everywhere. And while Alice plays the lute, accompanying the old words he digs up from his vanished youth, Falstaff is annulling time. He forgets the fool, regains his adolescence in the pink ribbons and the rose he carries in his hand. For him, time has not passed. And what he says about himself must have once been true: "When I was page to the duke of Norfolk, I was thin and sweet, sweet, sweet . . .". He says he was "*Sottile*." Him, slender, subtle? This huge hunk of meat? The fast music (which makes him out of breath, prancing like a kid again) says it is true. For the duration of a mocking, artificial duet, there is youth between the two, between the gossip and the fat man.

The lost youth echoing here, a garland, a breeze, finds its true nature in the real youth of the couple in love, the two who pursue each other throughout the opera. Nanetta and Fenton are in that youthful stage before opera is in season, before tragedy exists, or flesh, or broken hearts. Like Pamina and Tamino, they are in an earlier time of counting rhymes and hide-and-seek. And they track each other down in every nook and cranny. Everything is a plaything: words, songs, what they think of as love. They play with glances and hands squeezed on the sly. Boïto, the librettist, wrote to Verdi: "This will be one of those merry and lively loves, always disrupted and interrupted and always ready to start up again. . . . I would like to sprinkle the whole comedy—the way one sprinkles a cake with sugar—with this happy love, rather than concentrate it all in a single moment.'' A love of sugar icing, not a passionate love, no slowly drawn out passionate duet; that will come later. They will end up married while still children, even though, in that wonderful space of games forbidden to adults, they were free as the breeze. From their very first words they stop everything—their pretend quarrels, their sudden disappearances—one foot in the air, when an adult arrives—someone is coming . . .

"*Recominciamo.*" Let us begin again. Something that never happens in opera. But with this love that can put up with absence, that can be interrupted, a love not resulting in death, Verdi takes revenge for all the dead men and women. An about-face from all previous Verdi: this is life where one can see an end to suffering, life that is appeased. It is the wound healing, the scrape that scabs over and then disappears, it is the everydayness that opera always represses, the everydayness that even opera cannot help but die of. And life goes its way. . . . They start kissing under the sheets again, in trunks in the attic, behind raspberry bushes in the garden.

But because opera still lurks nearby, barely exorcised, because it will take almost nothing for absence to turn deadly, they bear the seed of passion. Their password, their song of complicity, is a slow, restrained melody with all the solemnity of love. Fenton sings the first phrase, something about a kiss on the lips, and Nanetta ends it, carrying the long phrase off into the luminous spaces of her bright voice, all the way to the moon, once again the moon—the nightstar for girls. . . . The final act, thanks to the lovers, swings over into a marvelous, fantastic magic.

It is in a forest. Midnight: the fearful hour when the living no longer know how to protect themselves from the dead. Midnight in England: the fairies are not far. Falstaff is costumed as the Black Hunter, as Quickly said he should be. On his head he wears an enormous set of horns: he is monstrous, seeming part of the trees; his ugliness is almost gone. Disguised in this way he acquires a sort of grandeur that quickly emprisons him. There he is beneath the oak. The music is imposing. Slowly the twelve strokes of midnight toll. The fat man counts them, repeating the same note twelve times, utterly terrified. It is the hour for loving, the time when the nascent, nocturnal passion of the young people develops: the glory of the night, the mysterious shadows that favor them, are theirs. A fairy sings, now close, now far away. The world is transformed. This is the redolent Sabbat. Every woman is in disguise, and the Queen, the fairy queen, is the little girl who has not yet known a man.

Nanetta leads the round, encircling a frantic Falstaff who is soon flat on the ground hiding his eyes; and the gossips, obedient to the voices of their youth, spin with the fairy, dance the round, trample the damp grass. Tomorrow there will be a magical circle drawn by their dancing feet. . . . This is the Sabbat, where sacrilege and incest take turns, where they kiss the Devil's backside. Michelet described a "great masquerade ball where every union was permitted,'' where separated families were reunited, cousins who were little boys and girls together, who had not seen each other for such a long time, finally find satisfaction. The dreadful hunger is indulged in secret. Freedom discovered, this is the reverse side of the harsh medieval existence. And in the midst of the round, in this Sabbat of bourgeois folk behaving like peasants again, take a look at the nobleman. Watch the delayed vengeance on the part of those who in the previous century suffered feudal harshness. The fat nobleman is down, but as soon as the ordeal is finished, when Falstaff gets back up and the fairies reveal that they are really women, he is part of the same world. The rite is over; so is the comedy. The lovers go off married and everyone goes home at dawn. There is nothing left in the forest except the fairy circle and the veils that served as disguise. Even those the gossips will pick up and fold sensibly: it is the household linen. The marriage and the bourgeois wives are sensible as well. But, thanks to the clown, they will have known their night of madness and dream.

And he, stripped of his ribbons and his haughtiness, will have joined the gossips in their capacity as the subverters of Master Ford's grave order. Alice's suspicious and jealous husband, the bourgeois father who wants to marry off his daughter, Nanetta, against her wishes, is the only loser in the comedy. He thinks he is marrying her to an appalling old man of letters he chose for her. But he is deceived by the gossips and witching night, and it turns out to be Fenton beneath the black mask.

For the opera finally to overthrow the order of fathers and kings requires both resolute comedy and Verdi's old age. Through the unconscious intermediary of a fat, pathetic trickster, women win; they marry whom they wish and love in freedom; witches are transformed into fairies and girls keep the power of infinity, to the detriment of their society and the benefit of their lives.

Paradise anew

Hans Sachs, the main character in Wagner's *Meistersinger*, seems to have none of the qualities of a trickster: no physical deformity, no flaw, nothing strange. There is no one better integrated in his city and his society than this shoemaker whom everyone respects and whose musical authority no one doubts. And yet, he is someone excluded; something eludes him as the opera develops, something is forbidden to him. He is not to have the love of the girl he was promised because he is too old. This is what sets him apart, that is how he will perform as best he can the role of smuggler and go-between. Sachs, seeing that Eva loves someone else, gives up and makes the young lover, his rival, one of the master singers so Eva can choose him to be her husband.

For the real tricksters, the eternal clowns, the poor suckers, are smugglers. It is in their presence that the necessary shifts and disruptions are accomplished. It can happen that they embody disorder and die of it, like Othello. It is also possible for them to be the plaything of women, like Falstaff. But these men, who are unlike other men, further madness, by means of which, at their expense, an opening can be forced into the social fabric. They provide the dialectics of the opera, they are its anxiety and its endless movement between a peaceful life and places where society suddenly cracks apart.

Thus, during the opera, conflictual spaces open and close where the ones who are weak (women, children, madmen, clowns, old men), clash with the powers that be (fathers, husbands, lovers), the ones who are strong because of the laws of civil society and numerous prohibitions. For any individual, woman or man, to become the hero of an opera, he must in himself represent enough deviance and reckless power to create another, antithetical gathering around him. His story will be called fate, chance, a curse, a conspiracy, a plot. There is no "normal" opera hero; and the women fixed upon by the beams of light from positioned powers are only joined in this crucial combat by those men who have left their own world, who lay down their weapons, who are already somewhere else.

Hans Sachs is one of these. Although ordinarily he would be someone who has made the transition to old age, he will betray his fellows for the love of a woman and the unclear future that he senses taking shape around him. Like Falstaff he makes himself into the hero of a forbidden celebration, of a disorder that is quickly over, of a transitory counterorder. Order, after having digested a foreign element, closes back up immediately. Falstaff, poor, oblivious man, smuggles himself in: he is the one who manages to integrate himself into the social body that refused him. Hans Sachs, because he understands his own exclusion from the world of lovers, will smuggle in a stranger, a knight errant who is not a member of the same society.

The story: In the fifteenth century, the bourgeois city of Nuremberg reveres the guild of Mastersingers, a solemn brotherhood governing the art of music according to severe and ancient laws. Master Pogner's daughter, Eva, is to be the prize in a contest. Her father will give her in marriage to the winner of the competition. The dreary Beckmesser and the gallant Walther, a noble knight who looks down on the Mastersingers but loves Eva enough to compete, are in the running. Secretly, Hans Sachs, the most famous of all the Mastersingers, dreams of winning the contest and Eva's hand. As a prologue the Masters, who do not know Walther, ask him to pass a preliminary test, which he completely fails, thanks to Beckmesser's watchful malevolence, "marking" his rival's mistakes on the blackboard according to the rules. Eva, in despair, confides in Sachs, who decides to help the lovers. On St. John's Eve, while Beckmesser sings a serenade to Eva, Sachs plays the same trick on him that Beckmesser played on Walther, "marking" Beckmesser's mistakes by tapping his shoemaker's hammer on the anvil. The banging wakes up the neighborhood. Everyone goes wild, running outdoors and fighting in the streets, but the night watchman restores order.

The next day Sachs broods, listening to Walther's account of a dream he has just had: it would make a marvelous piece for the contest. Sachs helps the young man perfect his song and leaves. Beckmesser steals the paper on which Walther and Sachs jotted down their notes for the contest, and Sachs, seeing him do so lets him have the competition piece because he is sure Beckmesser will make a mess of it. And it happens. Beckmesser produces a ridiculous text before the very solemn competition; he is not even able to figure it out. Walther wins easily and Sachs does not compete. . . . Walther will have Eva and will reluctantly become the Master Singer of Nuremberg.[55]

Like *Falstaff*, *Die Meistersinger* takes place in a peaceful, orderly city; and, as in *Falstaff*, a night of madness reveals the disorder latent beneath the good behavior; a night of dream turns everything upside down. The marvelous St. John's Eve of *Die Meistersinger* corresponds to the fairy's night that strikes fear in the heart of fat Falstaff. All is calm, all are sleeping. Everyone wears their nightcap and long underwear—they go to bed early in Nuremberg, especially because tomorrow is a feast day and they have to get up early to dress, to lace their corsets, to fix their headdresses and hairpins, and to arrange the girls' ribbons. Everybody is asleep except two or three civilians going about their business: two or three civilians with disorderly souls. Hans Sachs, the dreamer, is enjoying the peaceful night, and, because he is a poet, he is waiting for the moon. Eva, the young bride-to-be, awaiting her chosen one, is worried and wandering in the dark, while Magdalena her attendant would like her to consent to go to bed. Walther, the young knight, furious over his defeat, not knowing how he, a von Stolzing, will be able to obtain the hand of a young bourgeois woman whom a rich and proud city refuses him. The idiotic Beckmesser, trying to take advantage of the night for a serenade, serenades. And over them all, surrounding them, hangs the summer scent of an immense linden giving off its fragrance . . .

Solos, duos, trios, whispers, rages, each one thinks and dreams in the midst of a general sleep; each one dreams rather loudly, voices rise. Luckily the watchman's horn is there to bring things back to order. He goes by, lantern in hand, and calls out the time of night so the good folk can sleep in peace: "Glory be to God." And, blowing a monstrously false note on his horn, he continues his round, the professional nightman. Behind his back the shouts, the rages, the trios and duos begin again. They are all upset again, in an uproar.

This is it! Windows open, shutters bang, in serried ranks the bourgeois come out in force, wearing nightcaps and nightgowns. They beat one another with bolsters, they play with pillows and mimic an attack and a defense. What evil enemy is invading the city of Nuremberg? No army, no bandits, no horde of mercenaries: just two lovers who seek each other, two old men who argue, and Saint John's Eve. Here they are, all outdoors, all down on the ground, head over heels—listen to them, they shout, they screech, the moon and the smell of the linden tree have made them mad. Then the night watchman's horn sounds. *Pfft!* They are all back at home. In the twinkling of an eye, *Augenblick*, this madness will have been a dream; shutters close, nightcaps go back to bed, candles are extinguished. In bed nobody breathes, they listen. . . . When, drawn by the noise, the watchman arrives, all is peaceful again, everyone pretends to sleep. Not a living soul. The watchman rubs his eyes. He must have been hearing things; and he resumes his calm refrain: "Glory be to God." The next day some of them will look a bit drawn.

In the morning, Hans Sachs, who scarcely sleeps, is the first one up. He has taken Walther and his anxieties to heart, but the young man has slept like a log while the old man, knowing that his dream of love is getting away, secretly ponders his calm despair. There is no to-do over his renunciation. Some majestic chords are there, just barely to mark it. Hans Sachs's greatness is created without thunder or lightning. The two young people will gradually understand the old man's sacrifice.

Here is the scene that is sublime. Look. Listen. Eva coyly brings him two little golden shoes to be repaired, pretending that one of them pinches, but she knows perfectly well her knight is there, in the shoemaker-poet's house. And Hans Sachs knows perfectly well she has come because of that. Then, without saying a word about what he knows, he kneels before her; see how the gesture of love is hidden in the posture of a shoemaker. For it is to fit her shoes that he kneels, and he busies himself with just her foot. Like in the old French song: "'Twas a little shoemaker, deedee, she chose, dedum, she chose. . . .". But he knows he is not the chosen and never will be. The only tragedy of this antihero, this Hans Sachs who puts all his heroism into fitting shoes for the foot of his love without ever mentioning that he loves her, is this gesture. While Sachs is on his knees, Walther appears. He is young, handsome, and noble, completely the opposite of Sachs. Walther, whom Hans Sachs has just taught the ritual song so he can win the competition; Walther who, while Sachs is still fixing Eva's shoe — it is hard to sew up a little golden shoe; it takes a long time — starts to sing his song of love and victory. That is how Eva understands, foot in the air, what Hans Sachs has done. She is to have her knight, and, overcome, she falls onto the shoulder of the old man, holding her by the foot. He clasps her long and hard. The most difficult thing still remains; he does it, letting Eva slip from his arms into Walther's. Then, just to emphasize who he is, he grouses: what a job, being a shoemaker! No peace, no quiet, people tell him all their secrets, and he always smells like tar, and nobody helps, and . . . Eva, Eva, daughter of Eve, is going to tell all: everything they know so well, everything so well conveyed by the gestures, the shod feet, the silent embraces, the linden tree, the mad night, and the childish scramblings of the bourgeois.

And what she says makes it necessary for Hans Sachs to express himself. Since she sweetly confesses that she would have taken him as her husband if this young love had not made its appearance—sheer luck, you see!—he replies—and the music changes key. The music becomes something else, it comes from somewhere else; the music in this opera is astonishing. And you will recognize, like an echo in your puzzled heart, themes taken from another world, from a previous opera, *Tristan and Isolde*. Because Sachs knows this old story: "Child," he says to Eva, who still has a lot to learn, "I know Tristan and Isolde's sad song, and Sachs leaves his happiness with Marke. I took the right path in time, otherwise the story would have had the same ending." In Hans Sachs's heart, the funeral music sounding King Marke's anguish repeats the story Sachs dreamed on Saint John's Eve, alone under the linden on the square in Nuremberg. All the work of mourning is completed in three phrases spoken to the love who is renounced; all the wise work of an old man who knows, sees, and renounces. The right path is one of order regained, but not even that; because the order Sachs authorizes violates the Masters' laws.

For no one can be a Master if he is noble, and Walther will enter the brotherhood not because he is a knight from Stolzing but because his song conforms to bourgeois art. Sachs knows what he is doing; the old man renews what is new. Walther's unruly inspirations, which he claims to have borrowed from the ancient Master of the Birds, a German *Meistersinger* from the thirteenth century, will give the overstuffed art of the Nuremberg singers a new life. The old man, whom young Walther involuntarily smuggles in, is going to renew Nuremberg. In return Nuremberg will disennoble the knight and turn him into one of the bourgeois: a double strike, one for song and one for the bourgeoisie. Sachs knows what he is doing; and the allusion to Tristan and Isolde is a clear reference to this old world that, two centuries before Nuremberg in all its commercial power, is to beget this bygone world of myths, kings, and knights, which are just that—myths. Secular myths must remain myths, King Marke is no longer around and Sachs is not a king. Hans Sachs, or opera's lesson demonstrated in an opera: or how to lose one's fondness for myth while letting it sing its songs deep in one's heart; or how to keep it at a distance in one's own life the better to learn its lessons. Yes, opera is the reflection of a very ancient and dead code; yes, the stories of ancient times do not apply to the one now taking place; yes, Tristan, that was before, not today. There was so little keeping those ancestral scenarios from happening again. It was a matter of one night, one linden tree, and one young knight who arrived in time to hand Hans Sachs the mirror of his age. Isolde-Eva sets her foot down, Walther-Tristan takes her in his arms, and while the apprentice David and his young fiancée Magdalena leave the house, Walther's song is christened.

A marvelous quintet, all meditative love and grace. A marvelous moment of rest and peace, in the clear morning where conflicts are resolved. But look. Two young couples, women's voices and men's voices, married according to the nature of their social classes and ages: the wealthy Eva and the knight on one side; on the other the apprentice and attendant. Two happy couples and a fifth person who is excluded from the happiness. (*The fifth voice* is always that of the person excluded. Remember in *Cosi fan tutte*, two couples sing together and the fifth person, faced with all this happiness, mutters furiously: The fifth is that lout, Don Alfonso, who hates women and love.) Sachs does not mutter or protest; but his song is not the one the others sing. Where the others speak of love, what does he say? He speaks of his martyrdom, from which he emerges the stronger. . . . Here he is old, here he is in the world where there is help; gone are the loves, gone a life of this poetry that was so much his song; from now on he will have to sing it without living it. . . . Like the marschallin of Wertemberg described by Richard Strauss, he moves on to the other side. And, stretching out his hand, he helps Walther cross the bridge with an elegant leap.

The competition is still to come, and Sachs's triumph. No, not Walther's triumph: of course, Walther wins Eva and definitively eliminates Beckmesser. But it is Sachs whom the crowd acclaims. Although unaware of his sacrifice, it rewards him with a spontaneous song: a song that Sachs composed. Here he is now, becoming a legend, moving into immortality. A harsh lesson in sublimation, but at least Sachs will have earned the utmost bonus of seeing himself acknowledged by a whole city in its celebration. Think about the marschallin who took the same path of age and renunciation: she got nothing in return, nothing, except the certainty of living alone. It is true that women are neither poets nor musicians, is it not?

Hans Sachs, the hero of sublimation, will have one final act. He will crown Walther through Eva's intermediary, and crown him against his will. Because Walther does not want Mastery: Eva is enough for him. This way the young noble is to be deprived of the dangerous origins that provided his daring and his genius; this way, as a Master Singer, he will become part of the city. All is order, all was disorder, and through the power of an old man who is enough a poet to draw myth's lessons, everything is arranged into a new order, at the end of a rite of initiation that will clip the stranger's wings. If King Marke had had the wisdom to give Isolde to his nephew Tristan, there would never have been a story of love and death—there would never have been an opera. And Wagner, after having written *Tristan* and having sung as no one else the genius, the potency and cogency of the myth of love, thwarted his own intentions by writing *Die Meistersinger*.

But after *Meistersinger* came the *Ring*. That is to say, myth all over again, incest and the death of the gods. Hans Sachs acts as a turning point, between *Tristan* and the *Ring*, demonstrating to all the antidote to the western myths that have come from the limits of the Christian world. Myth against myth: Hans Sachs opposes Tristan and the lovers' incest with Paradise. That is his song, the story of the imaginary shoemaker who made the first shoes.

> When Eve was chased from Paradise
> Her pretty feet were chafed, alas,
> By stones that hurt . . .
> God himself felt sorry,
> Who loved her rebel foot,
> Telling his archangel
> "Make her two stout shoes."

Eve, Eva . . . Sachs, the gentle archangel whose business is to cut and sew shoes for the first woman. . . . The scene of Eva's foot was Paradise anew; and as the song prescribed that the shoemaker must also shoe Adam who suffered from the pebbles in the road, Hans Sachs makes shoes for both halves of the original couple. Far from Paradise the road is long and the pebbles are sharp, Sachs knows something about it. But in his *Meistersinger's* heart, the sacred has won out over the profane; Eve and Adam are victorious over Tristan and Isolde, and that is why order returns, sweeping away the paganism unleashed for a moment in the city.

But the *Ring* is the story of paganism's return, its slow, twilight waning back to origins regained: the gods are dead, cries the opera, but it never stops showing their eternal resurrection, over and over again. Christianity against paganism. Church against woman. And the madman who ferries between them, whose flesh and heart and sometimes life are crushed, and no matter what, the triumph of order, of the order that, in the *Ring*, is to overcome the last gods.

Chapter 7
The Tetralogic of the Ring, or the Daughter Done for

In which we see waters and river battle fire; in which a one-
eyed god surrounded by women prefers incest to the law of the
family; in which he sacrifices the daughter he adores. . . . In
which, finally, a woman who knows all, puts an end to the
power of the Gods.

Just suppose we were listening for the first time to the ponderous *Ring*. Suppose
there were no textual sediment weighing down the Wagnerian text, suppose no
interpretation screened this text from us anymore. And suppose this impossible
fantasy of transparency finally became possible when listening to Wagner.

Impossible. You see, the prelude to the *Ring*, to this imposing masterpiece
(that takes four long days), is a specific desire. A desire for the "first time,"
roused by primitive cosmology and demiurgic hope. As we listen, we are going
to follow the genesis of the world. . . . And, from the first chords of *Rheingold*,
the endlessly developed harmonies fulfill this precise function: they force the illusion of an origin that is renewed with each hearing. Each time it can all begin
again in the deep waters. It all dawns on you; it is the first time.

All, but all what? The traps of transparency, the waters of the Rhine, the
flames of the fire, which you know perfectly well are simultaneously ineffectual
and inescapable. Inescapable: you will plunge into the music, you will be born
with it at dawn, you will drown with it in the final twilight flood. Ineffectual as
well: you will be unable to forget the latent and disguised effect of the masses of
writing surrounding Wagner. Yes, we might want not to know any more, to hear
this story the way Wagner tells it to us. But too many parades, too many noxious
shadows have come to weigh it down with history. Even before Nazism and the
tyrant's suicide to the accompaniment of *Götterdämmerung* in the Berlin bunker,
there was the history of a contradictory Germany and its dreamed of national
unity; there was the life of a Wagner who was prey to bourgeois morality and its
obligatory transgressions. There was the history of operatic form and the history

of the notion of myth. The *Ring* was conceived within this universe; any transparency is simultaneously necessary and illusory, and we will be hard put to sort out the tangle.

And that is just the beginning. The form Wagner chose is hard to pin down. He himself composed both the text and the music; the words are his, he wove them with music, it is the same operation. It is simultaneously a myth constructed of words and music telling the same story in a text of sound. The two registers, the two languages, share the same world; and there are such rigorous connections between the two that it becomes impossible to separate the story from what is around it. Right from the beginning, borne by the great musical springs that overflow to fill my spirit, I cannot tell you the story without interpreting it. No longer can I be content with a little italicized text to provide the fabric of the story—the story is also music; the story is still myth—if you are to understand the deluge of words surrounding this work of Wagner's; understand the inevitable idolatry of those faced with a text that is too powerful, like the Bible at the time of Gilgamesh, like the anonymous texts that, from time immemorial, have circulated in our minds. Understand also the tangled undergrowth of Wagnerian circles, shot through with a fierce desire to forget its Nazi seizure. Finally, understand the fierce hatreds, the caricatures (a mongol Wagner, Wagner the gnome), whence the derision surrounding him that, in some ways, is right. He was adulated: Lavignac wrote a *Pilgrimage to Bayreuth*; a kind of religion raised its temples throughout Europe. And Erik Satie made fun of him with his *Wagnerie Kaldéenne*, in which he had grotesque and gloomy characters hopping in time. Both are *true* readings.

So, an additional "reading"? Even if I want to keep to the barest fact, I shall never succeed. I prefer an illusion of my own devising. Very early you heard the "Ride of the Valkyries." It is always being broadcast. Through comic strips you already know the shape of the woman on horseback among the clouds. Somewhere in your memory you have a paternal character, bearded and one-eyed; spears and armor, a whole warlike, primitive display. Somewhere there is fire, a living and evil fire; a dragon that is huge and green; a gallant hero, Richard the Lion-hearted, Rahan, Robinhood. . . . That's all you know. In your head you have the essential castoffs of the Wagnerian imagination, and you have no idea how it functions. You have the correct preparation to be heir to a good metaphysical and theological tradition, which, however, we know can turn out very badly. So listen to the story of a god who was too clever, of a hesitant, one-eyed god, and of his darling daughter.

You are going to meet women who are overwhelmed the way they are everywhere else in opera. Warrior women, goddesses, magnificent and omnipotent; one by one they lose the instruments of their glory. A mortal woman and a Valkyrie will be the instruments of the gods' ruin. Because of two women, who are the excuse for hiding their flaws, their greed, their pride, and their blindness, they will die. These god-men are the same ones that opera depicts for you every-where; but this time they are not to escape.

Entering into the story of disobedient women who violate the laws pro-claimed by Wotan is the story of the gods as a whole and the end of a world. When the whole, long circuit is finally complete, a woman, a woman alone, knows the whole story. She is the devoted guardian of a knowledge for which she has paid dearly, but she still has one more act to perform: the lighting of the pyre that will burn a whole people. No one will come through it alive, neither women nor men. And in the *Ring* the tricksters and the women come together to put the finishing touches on the story of a dead paganism. Monotheism with its inflexible cruelties will be able to rise on its rubble. Look: you are going to hear the dawn of opera.

A real prologue, starting from scratch

It starts in the water. In water that is deep and dark. Very low notes sustained for a very long time, then an arpeggio, then another; it wells up from the depths, it pushes higher and higher; the light, an indefinable light shines from above. And then it flows endlessly: "The waves flow continually from right to left." Louder and louder, the spring bubbles up its chords until . . .

A woman's voice rises. Then another, then a third. Even if you know nothing about them, you will guess (because they are underwater) that they are water sprites. Their songs follow the rising chords and accompany the water's flow. They play. They are fish-women who play in water. Their words are full of waves and "*w*"'s: their names are Woglinde, Wellgunde, and they sing liquid "Weia"'s and "Wallal"'s. It is all very happy; these sprites, who are called the Rhine maid-ens or Nixies, have an explosive laughter. Women who laugh in water—this is the first image of first origins. But, see what a funny father the Rhine is—a river!

A rhythmic, heavy sound signals the appearance of the first man. He is a dwarf so ugly that the sprites tease him cruelly. They flirt with him, but he cannot catch them. He cannot catch the prey with a hand that can never grasp—this is impor-tant. The poor man can catch nothing by hand because sprites' tails are slippery and he is a human barely able to stand firmly on the rocks. He cannot follow them into the water. He slips, that is the first drama, the very first drama of all, it is a matter of a *hold* that cannot hold. Listen to what he sings, all anger and sadness: "Smooth schist, slippery and dirty! How I slide! Hand and foot, I cannot grab or hold onto the slippery stone! The liquid element fills my nose; damned sneeze!" One man, chasing three sprites who tries his luck underwater: already an impossible love. Punctuated by the laughter of women.

In the depths of his despair, the central character intervenes, silent and deci-sive. Gold. Already it was there (although you could not know it) in the indefin-able brightness shining above, right above the water. A sort of coppery sound, vague and diffused, signals the light that begins to grow now on stage: the gold is waking up. Its daughters greet it happily. All is still well in the now golden waters. The poor man stands, fascinated by the brilliance of the stone; clearly he has never seen anything like it. We learn, at the same time he does, that it is the "golden eye, that sleeps and watches by turn." So the gold is a living, organic being, endowed with an elementary life, capable at least of sleeping and watching. But to take it—to catch it, to wrench it away, a little like wrenching an embedded shell from a rock—a fearful vow must be made. Then the silly sprites tell the dwarf what it is, because they are so sure he is not dangerous. For the vow is to renounce love and this lecherous fellow seems decidedly not one to give up the joys of love.

But the initial aberration of the Christian version of Adam and Eve's original sin is still found in the myth. Alberich is going to take the gold the same way Eve takes the apple: out of aberration, out of necessity, out of desperation. He renounces love—listen hard to his melody, it will punctuate the whole story and be passed from hand to hand like an echoing curse—and is able to wrench away the living stone. The gold has become a human object; the gold is to become a ring—that is a wrought object, an object that can be given, exchanged, put into circulation. A curse of commerce: Alberich is going to use his ingenuity to transform the formerly dead stone into precious metal. The Nixies laugh no longer; they mourn. Alberich bursts into an evil laughter, you know, the sinister laughter of the bad man. The waters have turned dark again. Old Father Rhine has been robbed.

In the beginning was the paternal water and the daughters guarded the gold. Terrestrial man, a clumsy lump on the rocks, by stealing the gold, committed a human deed. But you are going to see that love—love: sexual, emotional, heart and sex—the love he had renounced to do this (remember how the mythical American millionaires all said exactly the same thing: money does not make happiness, love cannot be bought? old romantic jingles) will circulate at the same time as the golden ring, and in return for it. And then, one more blow, this all happens through feminine weakness; for if those foolish sprites had not given it all away, no man would ever have known there was a way to get the gold.

That is where it all starts. The next scene takes place somewhere else; literally, in the clouds. It is apparent then that the story that begins at the bottom of the river is not the only one developing and that, at the same time, far above another is taking place. The first part of the *Ring* will see the meeting of the water's tale and the cloud's tale; and you will see that the end of it is a physical encounter between the two elements in the form of a rainbow: water refracted in the air.

A city rises in the clouds along the Rhine. It is the dwelling of the gods. Like the gold, the gods are asleep when the curtain rises. The sun wakes them up. There is a couple (we were lacking the couple element, a marital union). At this point they have an old history; this is even an old couple, you will get to watch them tear each other to shreds from one end of the tetralogy to the other. There must have been some love between them once, but you would not know it now. Love, therefore, will be outlaw love. The woman—she wakes up first—will always be right there to recall that there are laws. The man, the king of the gods, Wotan, has only one eye. When Fricka upbraids him too vigorously, he gravely reminds her that it was to get her, his wife, that he lost it. That is all you will know for the moment. You have to wait two operas to hear the final word on this story of the eye. They have reached the point now in which each reproaches the other's existence. It is the depths of a conjugal love's agony; in the cloud king-dom it is the equivalent of the drama played out at the bottom of the river—a misunderstanding between man and woman.

But they never mention this misunderstanding. There was some deal made. Fricka wanted to keep Wotan in a magnificent castle; Wotan therefore asked the giants (wait! you can hear them stomping) to build a fortress in exchange for Freia, the goddess of youth; and Fricka, who seems to have gone along with it at first, now fears for her sister, Freia. Wotan is unalarmed; he is waiting for Loge, the misshapen and wily god of fire. It is Loge who advised him to make this compact; it is Loge who promised to get him out of it when the time came. And what does Loge want? That is a sore point. Remember the images of fire sur-rounding the sleeping woman? Remember the flaming fortress and its twilight glow? This is already being played out in Wotan's expectations.

For Wotan seems indifferent. It is not entirely his affair. Of course, he is going to have to get involved in it because he is king and it is his responsibility to settle conflicts. All the more when the conflicts are his own. But he speaks to Fricka, casually—if only she would listen—and tells her plainly that he cannot remain a prisoner in the conjugal castle. And, if that is how it is, he is going to go off and conquer the "foreign" world, the world outside. "That is why I am unable to pass up the bet." So he is a gambler? To the point of losing first an eye and then all he possesses. Wotan is a flaming gambler, who will burn the candle at both ends, ecstatically.

No doubt he has already dreamed of this. But the immediate problem is pre-sented by the twin giants' heavy tread. They are Fasolt and Fafner (Footit and Chocolat, Laurel and Hardy). Brief quarrel: Wotan refuses to let Freia go. Some other gods intervene, ready to fight the giants; Wotan separates the combatants with his spear. It is not an ordinary spear. On the wood are inscribed the laws, the Runes, as if the entire civil code was inscribed on a stick. Moses carried a whole culture on two engraved stones. The basic law is absolutely simple: one must respect contracts that are made. That is precisely the case here, therefore, Wotan is obliged to let Freia go. There is a power above him that is greater than his desires, than all human desires, and he will have to cede in every instance to his own spear. A prisoner. He is emprisoned by his spear, his fortress and his power.

Loge, also known as Lie, *Luge*, appears. But this time he tells the truth, to divert the giants who have already wrapped Freia in their arms. He says no one is crazy enough to give up a woman and that there is no woman who is equal to Freia. Only one madman has dared to do this: Alberich, in exchange for the Rhinegold. Now he, Loge, has come to Wotan (who does not understand the trap being set for the giants) bearing the Rhine maidens' complaint. But everyone surrounding Wotan—Fricka, who thinks that gold makes fine jewelry (even a ring, the symbol of fidelity), and the giants, whose thinking is labored—has been listening. Wotan, enticed by something Loge says, gets into it in the end. The Rheingold, says Loge, "is a plaything in the water's depths for the pleasure of happy children," which, forged into a ring has unlimited power. And Wotan begins to think. It is the gold's free play, as much as its power, that attracts him. Here the circle closes and the ring is forged: Wotan wants the ring, he will steal it. Just as the gold was stolen. The fundamental equation remains: whoever has the gold has no woman, has no love. The giants, for their part, are going to settle it: they would happily take gold instead of Freia, but to persuade Wotan, they carry off the beautiful goddess. Results are not long in coming. We now learn that, in addition to her charms, Freia cultivates the apples of youth that protect the gods from aging. Hardly has she taken to her heels when skin starts wrinkling, eyes become sunken, and hearts stop beating.

This is no time to falter; Wotan takes off in pursuit of the gold. Loge follows him, precedes him, and makes circles around him. But look: although everyone else suddenly grew old, Loge did not. He tells us in grating tones that Freia rarely gave him any apples, and he knows he is not quite as much a god as the others.

Well? No one seems to see that Loge wants the gods, his more powerful brothers, to die. They are all too busy with this aging emergency. Loge will circulate always and everywhere, throughout the universe of the *Ring*, and he will bring it to an end, he will be right. He will get the better of those fools who trade a woman for gold. For what is really at stake is twice laid out, deep in the water and high in the sky: either woman or gold, but not both. That is the choice, and they choose gold, first Alberich, then Wotan and the giants.

No one yet has won the gold, and the next phase of original conflicts is played out beneath the earth. That was, in fact, the only missing element.

Alberich rules the subterranean realm. We plunge into a sulfurous cavern to find once more the special light of the Rhinegold: the darkness of the waters, the gold's dazzling glow; the mist of hazy skies, the sun rising over the fortress; the gloom of Alberich's empire, the reddening glow of his boundless industry. Everywhere there is forging, hammering, striking—a thousand little metallic sounds: sounds of a shop, of antlike workers, of weapons. The place is called Nibel-heim. It is an inferno of ghastly labor. There the laborers, working under Albe-rich's orders, are the Nibelungen, who once were charming dwarfs, like Snow White's. In the old days they forged baubles, jewels, toys; now they make iron and weapons for their master's force. This is gold's burden. The anvils striking rhythmically, in tune, with a beat, brand these dwarfs with the metal that is, as you now know, accursed. This is a mine full of exploited miners—exploited by Alberich. It is as if, when he renounced love and got the gold, Alberich simul-taneously learned the power of exploitation and acquired a talent for enslaving. There is, therefore, a necessary connection between gold and exploitation; it is a simple fable, but its simplicity makes it no less true.

And there is Alberich. No longer is he the desiring creature who—just now, on the river—awkwardly tried to hold onto a slippery sprite with his tight fist. Boss now, he holds some sort of apprentice by the ear. Listen to the mysterious motif rising amid shouts and the sound of hammers: it describes a magical helmet, a prop that will turn up later, that can make one invisible. Now we enter a realm not too far removed from Punch and Judy, with sticks shaken behind people's backs, childish tricks, kids' quarrels. But do not forget: these are gods and in Wagner's mind they are acting out the fate of humanity. To become invisible one has to say (as in fairy tales) "Nacht und Nebel"—Night and Fog.

It sounds funny to us, you see, to hear that as part of a myth; but that is an entirely different story.

With his helmet Alberich turns into smoke; he takes advantage of his invisi-bility to whip the apprentice—Mime—who whines in a voice pitched way up high, a young voice, a ruined voice already. The miners scream; listen, chil-dren's voices. And when Mime tells his misfortunes to Loge and Wotan, they laugh. Yes, they laugh; that is not their concern, they have come as thieves. From this point on you are going to be watching quarreling robbers, gods who cheat and lie, gangsters. It will be played out between Alberich and Wotan and the fire power they pass back and forth between them: from one power to another power. The poor dwarfs are the manpower. Pay attention to that word; you will see it is right on the mark. Wotan asks a few questions, and Alberich hides nothing because all the power in the world is his. He is going to have them—these gods who laugh and love (the violin sings high and sweet)—he will catch them with his gold, he will bring them down by force. Everything that lives will renounce love, he cries out in his madness. Wotan would fight Alberich if Loge were not there to stop him. He would raise his spear, but Loge uses flattery, just as he did with the gods in Valhalla's clear skies. And his trick is so simple: what would happen if someone came to steal the gold at night, eh? Alberich tells them about the helmet, but Wotan and Loge already know the story because Mime has told them. What is Loge after? He wants to trap Alberich, compelling him to transform himself. And the idiot does just that. He puts on the helmet and turns himself straightaway into a monstrous dragon. Unaccompanied brasses play the rings of the serpent uncoiling. And you have read this same story a hundred times. Remember the oriental genie who goes back into his bottle out of bravado, just to show he is telling the truth? Alberich turns himself into a grey toad. And is caught. Just like that. The gold, the ring, and the helmet do not add up to cunning.

Once again we hear the bright sound of anvils through a smoke screen. Wagner loves to construct great voyages, immense musical vistas. In *Parsifal* we also wandered like this through the harmonies that bit by bit reconstructed a scenery.

Now Loge and Wotan and their prisoner climb back up slowly. See how the mist thins. They emerge from the subterranean darkness, climbing bit by bit back to the light of day they had left behind. Loge is delighted, he has won again. He jumps with joy around this cousin of his. Loge is kin to everyone in that sort of provincial kinship that is so dangerous. But take a good look at him in his human (or at least anthropomorphic) form—the only way you will see him later is as fire. Alberich is indeed compelled to give in; he has his dwarfs bring up the treasure, but he still counts on keeping the ring—the essential. Here come the dwarfs bearing jewels and gold. They pile it high. But Wotan wants the ring. Alberich shouts and screams, he defends himself, he even argues: because really he paid a high price to get the ring. He did what no one else could bring himself to do: he completely renounced love. He appeals to justice, in other words, to Wotan himself who is the holder of justice (it is written on his spear). He makes no threats; no, he speaks of the gold instead. Wotan is already caught in the accursed circle; deaf and blind he is unaware of any powers that surpass him. And he takes the ring. That is, he steals it, right? From now on the god is guilty. "Now I have the thing that makes me exalted; I am master of masters."

Alberich punishes the god's wrongdoing. The ring became his when he cursed love; OK, so he curses the ring. And words of malediction and benediction are so powerful in this archaic and childish age that malediction will circulate until the very end, until the twilight of these divine robbers. And the expressive force of this music is so strong that whenever the curse theme reappears, you expect some catastrophe, even if you are not consciously aware of it. These notes are to be repeated even in the most powerful of those rare happy moments in the myth, and something in you will know that from then on the curse prevails. Happiness is to be illusory, leading to even more unhappiness, and it is already played out there, in the music.

Wotan hears nothing. He thinks only of his ring. The sky becomes brighter; the gods return, the giants as well, and Freia, youth, accompanies them. Everything is calm and quiet. You might think it is all over, it could stop there. Moreover, that is what happens, in part—a false ending. You know those stories that seem to end, but then someone knows one more episode and tells it and the myth continues; it uncoils its rings until the moment when every element is in place and finally stable. We are making our way to the end of the beginning.

One more episode is missing. The giants take the gold—a pile of gold—and jewels as high as Freia is tall. It has to be high enough to hide her, and the gold piles up and up until she is concealed. All that remains is the gleam of her hair; then the giants demand the helmet to cover her golden locks. But her eye can still be seen sparkling through the heaps of gold. Now all that remains (just as, recently, it was all that remained for Alberich) is the ring on Wotan's finger. The same story starts up all over again, so quickly; why so quickly? Wotan is unyielding. The ring fascinates him—so too bad for Freia. What was recently at stake is now remote; Wotan who set out to free Freia won the ring. Violent conflict erupts. Wotan is unyielding.

Then the mother appears. Do not try to figure out who her children are; it is the eternal mother, the mother of the world, Erda. She can appear, suddenly, from anywhere at all, from the depths of sleep, a mother dream. Wotan himself has no idea who she is. She knows and sees all concerning the gods. If she is there it is because the danger is extreme, and Wotan senses this. The curse lingers in her words. Those broad, broad arpeggios (as if the waters of the Rhine ran slow motion, that slow, majestic rhythm) are not part of the gods' time. Eternity is singing. A new passion takes hold of Wotan, who is caught up in Erda's rhythm: he wants to know, he wants to follow her and catch her. . . . That becomes his most urgent task (see how fast this god switches desires!). He gives up the ring; Erda's warnings worked. But Wotan will not forget the mother's seduction.

The giants get the ring. Oh, but watch out, there are two of them. This is the first time you notice it, because up until now these twins had just one body. It is the ring that divides them. They both want it and things turn out badly. One of them, Fafner, kills the other, Fasolt, and takes the ring away. One thrust of the stake, another: one dead. The music sounds the curse. This time Wotan understands, and he also understands his pain and anguish. Wotan has been touched, stricken with fear. He sees only one refuge from this fear that is irrepressible and coercive—the castle. Their castle of pleasure, their main dwelling will now serve another purpose; it is going to become a fortress, a place meant for defense and protection. Wotan does not know exactly what he has to defend himself against; he calls it "night." Night is rising, rising against the gods; Wotan has understood. But not the other gods who dream they will finally enter their sacred castle. Wotan speaks again of Erda: Erda . . . maybe she could, perhaps . . .

The only thing needed to enter the fort is a bridge to reach it. A burst of magic; the thunder god strikes his hammer—a cloudburst. And through the thick clouds, through the metallic clash, through the din, a huge rainbow unfurls. This is the bridge. It is dawn. Wotan decides to enter and to live with Fricka. The gods begin to cross the bridge; this time they are really gods, they are walking on clouds. Finally they are superhuman; finally you can see a proof of their divinity. And yet their ruin is guaranteed. And yet it is the story of their ruin, through all its passions and divorces and endless rifts, that is being told. Because Loge threatens them under his breath and dreams of burning them. The sprites' laments below rise up all the way to the gods' above. In accusation: there are nothing but lies up there. Purity and truth live in deep waters. Water and fire are in league against the gods; Alberich has cursed the ring that Wotan then put on his finger. If only for an instant of pleasure, he touched the accursed object. They are lost.

Carefree and magnificent they troop in procession onto the rainbow and enter the sunny castle.

Interlude

The curtain closes; the lights go up. You are completely dazzled; you are in a theater. The rainbow is a set, and the gods, exhausted, take their bow. This myth is an opera. It is told by singers and an orchestra, and if it suddenly captures you as if someone was telling a story, it is because voice, reduced to roles, surrounds you everywhere and makes a narrative visible for you. This story begins, *Rheingold* was a prologue. The pieces of an immense puzzle had to be set out, and even if the whole story was strung out for you, when the citadel burns and everything returns to the waters of the Rhine, you still will have been carried away with the passing hours, the harmonies, the outbursts, the melodies, to the absolute end of the tale. To be carried away requires a fabric woven of threads without your knowing, in the unconscious. Or rather, no. The unconscious works to construct this narrative. And the pattern remains invisible, imperceptible, and for that very reason it is effective. When the music is silent, you can try to understand.

First, there is a sequel; and there will never again be a beginning. Everything to follow comes from this story. You will know this is true because the music never stops reminding you of what has happened, things of which the characters in the sequel themselves are sometimes unaware. That means you, the spectator, know more than those playing their parts, and, from that moment on, you enjoy an extraordinary feeling of power. You know and you follow the gods' ruin, which—despite them—was foretold. You are involved in the music, you understand and look ahead; you forget that this is a work that has been composed and that it is all thought out in advance. You watch, you listen, you give orders; seated and still, you see everything. Without the music's articulation, you would not have a clue.

Then the story is traced. It is told elliptically, with blank spaces that the music fills in for you, to help you understand. The next days, *Die Walküre*, *Siegfried*, and *Götterdämmerung*, are often better known than the first. You will meet *Walküre* fanatics who are satisfied with the love story, for whom that is enough, but they enjoy only part of the emotion. Because it is twofold; simultaneously a narrative emotion and a musical emotion, and then an emotion of the narrative constructed in the music. *Rheingold* sets it all in place starting with its first chords, in the river waters. What is played out is also a method and a spectacle unlike any other, interlocking ear and eye, at the same time as the unconscious takes over the weaving of something soon to affect you. But never again are you to have the illusion of an origin, the pleasure of beginnings. You will discover as you go along that the first threads of the story are the most beautiful, the most powerful, and the most true.

To understand this original complexity, one must know the whole story, and set out once again from the beginning; so that in each one of the three operas remaining to be heard, there is someone who recounts it all from the start. In *Walküre* Wotan tells it; in *Götterdämmerung* it is told by the Norns, three goddesses who spin the rope of time. With each opera one learns more and goes farther ahead; in the Norn's tale you will find out why Wotan lost his eye and what he did before *Rheingold*. So that the farther the narrative progresses toward its end, the more it regresses toward an unsuspected beginning. You thought that *Rheingold* was a beginning; but no, it was already the consequence of something else. Thus the tetralogy is known as the *Ring of the Nibelungs*—the *Ring* as you will often hear it called. This circular ring also has the sense of an endless turning and returning on its tracks; it is a story that never stops canceling out the events it produces, right up until the moment when the gold forming the ring is returned to the waters' depths. So you hear two stories relating to the *Rheingold*: one is progressive, carrying the narrative toward the twilight of the gods; the other is regressive, going deeper and deeper into the previous causes of this unerring curse.

Let me go back through the whole length of the story, to show it in a way unlike the crablike progress Wagner provided and unlike the way the music lights it from behind. And let me spin out the story with the three Norns at the beginning of the fourth day, in *Götterdämmerung*.

There are three sisters: the eldest, the middle, and the youngest. Three sisters —Freud would have said that they are also three women representing three phases of a single woman who is always the same, who accompanies man throughout his life. The eldest would be the mother, the middle the wife, and the youngest the daughter: all are figures of woman accompanying a male existence. The story—at least, this story—does not mention the three ages of man that exist for a woman. But, in fact, look: in the god Wotan's existence there are indeed these three sorts of love: Erda, the eternal mother, Fricka, the sister-wife, and Brunhilde, the daughter. The three Norns, therefore, clad in gloom, are weaving the thread of time on a rock surrounded by flames. "No matter what happens, I twist the rope and sing," says the first, as she attaches the golden thread to a pine-branch.

Formerly, she spun beneath the earth's ash tree; that is the origin of the origin. Under this sacred, womblike tree a spring flowed whose waters sang of wisdom; that is the origin of words, the murmur of a spring. Until the day when the god Wotan—the first troublemaker—comes to drink from the spring. But that requires some exchange; it is not an act that will go unpunished: Wotan is to leave an eye at the ash tree's spring. That is why he is one-eyed, just like the other maimed heros—Oedipus or misshapen Hephaestus. Their power is acquired at the cost of some physical deformity. And the other way around (because the myth controls things in every direction) when a human being has some sort of physical peculiarity—whether it be threatening eyes like Socrates or greenish eyes like the legions of witches burned in the seventeenth century—he or she is seen as possessing supernatural power. That is what happens to Wotan after the episode at the spring. Now Wotan goes further and violates the order of nature even more: he carves himself a spear (you have already met it) from a branch of the ash tree. That is the first wound. After that the ash slowly withers away. The leaves fall, the tree dies; the spring dries up. The Norn's song becomes indistinct and confused; their alternative shelter is a pine, where they take refuge so they can continue their work as weavers.

Empowered by his knowledge and his spear, Wotan first conquers Fricka. But one day he stops being in love and wants to conquer the world. That is when *Rheingold* begins. Wotan gives his own version of this at the beginning of *Walküre*. He sadly takes the blame on himself: yes, he was disloyal, yes, he broke treaties, although he was supposed to be their guardian. He let himself be seduced by Loge; he wrought his own ruin. Yet he was unable to do something someone else had the courage to accomplish: renounce love. Love, revived in the strange figure of Erda, suddenly awoke to alert Wotan. Wotan pursues, charms, and magically seduces her, and "worries pride with his knowledge." It does not have to be spelled out for you to know he makes love to her. Next thing you know Wotan is the father of eight daughters, the Walkyries, daughters of Erda the Wala. His is not a pure love: Wotan loves in order to know and then to defend himself. He makes these eight daughters into warrior women, fighting virgins, whose sole mission is to perform a strange collection service. These girls, galloping through the clouds, go into battlefields where they gather up dead heroes for Wotan, so he can form an army that is worth something. What does Wotan say then? Those who have been absent from the story now intervene: "Those whom once we ruled as masters with our laws — men." . . . Men? Up to now there were nothing but gods and gnomes and giants; now there are men. Somewhere among the waters, the clouds, and Alberich's subterranean inferno. And they are going to play a greater and greater role until the final moment in which, as low wage earners, they will win their own future through the ruin of the gods. Men were subjugated, says Wotan, "by shady agreements and deceitful connections"; and the Valkyries push them into battle so that, after they are dead, they can defend the gods. This is a wonderful form of slavery, arrived at through war and death.

Erda has told Wotan the entire future: to escape the curse of Alberich (who vowed ruin to the gods), a free, absolutely free hero must take back the ring from Fafner, now transformed into a dragon, guardian of the treasure. But this is an insoluble contradiction: how can one find a hero to fight both for and against Wotan? "How can I make this other person who would no longer be me and who would accomplish on his own the only desire I have?" Wotan then has the idea of disguising himself. Dressed as a man, he wanders through the woods and makes love to human women. One of them gives him twins, whom he raises in ignorance of his divine nature. He claims to be "wolf," and gives the boy a magic sword; the twins are named Siegmund and Sieglinde. During this time Alberich is preparing to wage battle; he must use exactly the same weapon — Erda has said so. Alberich must father a human child, and that indeed happens, thanks to the power of the gold. Siegmund and Sieglinde are children of love; Hagen, Alberich's son, is a child of hate. The curse has crossed into fathering. So this is now the story of sons, following the story of the fathers.

It is the beginning of the second day, *Die Walküre*, in which you are going to see how Wotan's son will meet his downfall because of some concrete tactics and for reasons beyond any control. Bearing the name, Wehwalt — the only one he knows, the name he took after having lost his father, the name that means woeful — he arrives in exhaustion at a rustic chieftain's dwelling. There he discovers a woman who has been married against her will to the bearlike Hunding; the stranger and the captive woman fall in love at first sight. They do not know who they are; details gradually will tell them. There, embedded in the trunk of a tree, growing in the center of this abode, is a sword that no one has been able to pull out. Sieglinde tells of how a stranger plunged it into the trunk on the day of her sad wedding — a stranger wearing a hat pulled down to hide one eye. (This tells you it is Wotan.) Wehwalt, who says he is also the Wolf's son, sees the sword lit by the moon; he pulls it out easily — this paternal sword stuck away there for him. Then Sieglinde recognizes him: it is her lost brother. Everything would be fine. But the moonlight, bearer of every moon's troubling and evil spells, meddles. The twins embrace, disregarding the greatest taboo — incest.

Wotan is delighted with this affair, which of course contradicts the laws carved on his own spear. Fricka, magnificent and powerful, intervenes to call him back to order, and Wotan (just as before in his confrontation with the giants) is completely constrained by the law, which is stronger than he. He has to sacrifice Siegmund, his son, the free hero who could save him. The occasion is near: Hunding, the deceived husband, wants vengeance, all the more because his human tribe and the Wolves have an old grudge. And Hunding pursues the incestuous lovers. Wotan, in deepest misery, tells all this in great detail to his favorite daughter who is not Sieglinde but the eldest of the Valkyries, Brunhilde. Brunhilde detests the haughty, sterile Fricka and adores her warrior father. But she obeys Fricka's command: Siegmund must perish in Battle and Hunding must win, despite Wotan's wishes.

Siegmund is lost and with him goes Wotan's hope. And yet, no, for the daughter's desire will make up for that of the weakening father. The Valkyrie goes to find Siegmund, watching over his wife who has fainted with weariness and fear, in the middle of the forest, in the middle of the night. She tells him he is going to die and that he will go then to Valhalla to join the troop of dead heroes; but Siegmund asks an unexpected question: can women have this honor? You guessed it, it is impossible. Then Siegmund, who is truly free, renounces the citadel and its pomp and glory for the love of his sister; and to make sure of it, he raises the sword Nothung to kill her before he dies himself. What turmoil for the Valkyrie, shaken by the power of love! She has never known it, yet suddenly she has a sense of it. She stops Siegmund's arm, telling him (she has the power from her mother, Erda, to foretell the future) that Sieglinde is pregnant. Even better, she promises her assistance in combat to Siegmund as well as her protection for Sieglinde. So now she is disobeying her father's orders. Order comes apart at the seams very quickly; first incest, then the Valkyrie's disobedience. From then on things happen fast. The battle begins between Siegmund and Hunding. Above them, in a roar of thick clouds, Brunhilde comes to fight alongside Siegmund. Wotan fights too, taking Hunding's side against his will. Wotan raises his spear; Siegmund dies. Wotan looks daggers at Hunding, who falls dead at his feet.

There is still some business to be settled between father and daughter. Brunhilde gathers Sieglinde up onto her horse and flees in terror to join her seven sisters. They have come back from riding on earth, and each returned with a dead hero. Each, that is, except Brunhilde, who comes back with a woman who is both alive and pregnant! Scandal! They take Sieglinde into a deep forest, near where a terrible dragon keeps everyone out. Brunhilde informs Sieglinde that she is pregnant and offers the future mother the broken pieces of sword for the child. Sieglinde then stands up and sings a unique melody, one you will not hear again for a long time, a song of life and hope.

But here comes Wotan, furious and threatening. He will pass judgment on the disobedient Valkyrie and condemn her to the worst possible punishment; at least, they all seem in agreement to pass this judgment. She is to be stripped of her divinity, to lose her powers, and to spin wool like any ordinary woman. What absolute horror for a warrior virgin to be subjected to the submissive fate of all women! Brunhilde rebels, she begs, and finally persuades her father at least to protect her, at least to surround her with a curtain of flames. Thus the man who will take her virginity to transform her into a woman will have to be brave, "fearless, and supremely free."

Nothing could be closer to what the god most wanted: a free man who would defy his divine plans. He yields, and at the same time reveals all the love he has for his daughter. The real (perhaps even the only) love scene in the *Ring* takes place there, between the regretful father and his punished daughter. He embraces her for a long time and looks for one last time into the bright eyes that upset him so, then lowers her lids and puts her to sleep. He lays her on the rock and summons Loge, fire, who raises a wall of flames around the sleeping Valkyrie. *Die Walküre* ends on this double hope: the child of Sieglinde and Siegmund, and Brunhilde asleep.

Their meeting and their love will be enacted on the third day, in *Siegfried*.

The story continues, Wotan bit by bit vanishes from it. The child is born, its mother dies, and Mime—the little gnome with the voice way up high, the whiner—has taken him in and raised him; oh, not out of the goodness of his soul, but because he counts on using this child's power for his own purposes. Siegfried has become a free hero, akin to the birds, completely fearless; and Mime is timorous in the extreme. When Siegfried catches a bear and leads it around by a leash, Mime is terrified. Siegfried cannot understand how he can be Mime's son and yet be so unlike him. He never stops trying to find out who his parents are and why Mime is so determined to put the broken sword back together. It is because Mime expects Siegfried to go fight Fafner, the dragon, for him, conquering the treasure of the Nibelungen, which has lain idle so long in the cavern. An old man enters, wearing a hat down over one eye; this tells you once again that it is a god disguised as a man—the god Wotan, who has become a vagabond, the wanderer. He and Mime have an enigmatic conversation during which Mime tries to trap him with questions. Wotan has no trouble answering. The final question is about the race of gods: who lives in the sky? Creatures of light, Wotan replies, whose ruler is the "Alberich of Light," Wotan. Now you know that Wotan is the luminous reverse of that creature of gloom. Wotan, as he speaks, strikes the ground with his spear, thunder roars, and Mime recognizes the wanderer. And the wanderer tells the answer Mime cannot give: only one who is fearless shall forge the sword.

Then Mime teaches his blacksmith's craft to Siegfried the child, who merrily makes the sword while the gnome mixes a poisoned drink to be used on the young man once the treasure is his. Alberich on one side, Wotan on the other, Darkness and Light, pursue the stakes of the battle; Siegfried confronts Fafner, who yawns and sleeps at the entrance to the cave, and he mortally wounds the dragon. But before he dies Fafner tells Siegfried whom he has killed and warns him: someone drove him to this murder he committed out of sheer bravado, someone seeking to kill Siegfried himself. Fafner's death brings the child and the monster together in a strange sort of tenderness. Siegfried inadvertently sticks his hand into the giant's blood; inadvertently he licks his hand and suddenly he can understand the song of a bird that calls him to follow. But the magic blood gives him yet another power: the power to understand everyone's thoughts. And when Mime sweet-talks the heroic child, offering the deadly potion, Siegfried hears the truth of what he secretly thinks, and kills Mime. The warbling bird tells Siegfried about the maiden who lies sleeping on the rock; and Siegfried, still ignorant of fear, even the ancestral fear of fire, goes happily off to find her.

Wotan makes his last appearance before vanishing into the mists hanging in the wings and over the citadel. He calls Erda and wakes her with great difficulty to tell her something: he gives up. It is all over for the gods; what Wotan now desires is for their end to come, and he joyfully calls for it. Now it is the turn of others to put their lives at stake. Erda, the mother, goes back to sleep wrapped in clouds. However, Wotan still tries to take action, doing something as contradictory as his murder of Siegmund: he is going to try to bar his grandson Siegfried's way (yes, he is the son of his son Siegmund). Their encounter is amazing: the grandson, who is as innocent as the warbling bird, takes the strangely dressed old man, who is missing an eye, for a ride and ends up breaking his grandfather's spear. He is unaware that he has just broken the divine spear, the guardian of law. The old man picks up the broken pieces: the spear is in bits, the sword back in one piece. All Siegfried has to do now is to waken Brunhilde. It is then, as he uncovers her, taking off her helmet and armor, that he will know fever and fear; at that moment he calls his mother. Brunhilde awakens to the sparkling sound of brasses; her mind is confused, she has lost her powers of divination and lets herself become a woman. In her turn she now calls for the gods' end to come.

The end of the gods—let it come so men can love: that is what they call their love, "joyful death." From the moment the god Wotan declared that he had lost the fight, there has been suicide in the air, a joyous and baleful suicide such as that hanging in the air of the times when Wagner wrote the *Ring* cycle.

Götterdämmerung, the twilight of the gods, finishes off the suicide. For once there is hardly any ellipsis between the end of *Siegfried* and the beginning of the last day. Time shrinks, narrows down to the god's final end. The Norns have spun and spun the story's golden thread, when suddenly it breaks, snagging on a sharp rock. The thread is broken . . . Siegfried and Brunhilde appear; they are going to be separated. Siegfried, driven by a fatal necessity wants to go off "on new adventures.'' Understand that this means the story has to come to an end. Siegfried's departure is a reference to an entirely different universe than the one in which until now we have been existing: the universe of humanity, the subjugated humans who lift their heads again in the darkness. And before leaving, Siegfried gives Brunhilde a ring: the Ring. You see, he knows nothing at all about the ring; all memory of it is in the consciousness of the gods, and neither Siegfried nor Brunhilde are gods. The former Walkyrie has some vague memory in a hidden corner of her dreams, but it is so hazy. . . . She takes the ring as a wedding ring, a human marriage. But the curse is still there, Alberich's ancient curse recalled in bits and pieces, snatches of music, as vague as the lost memory. Siegfried and then Brunhilde are therefore to inherit, one after the other, the evil power of the omnipotent ring, which they have converted into a ring of love. In exchange, Brunhilde gives him her beloved Grane, the horse she rode as a Valkyrie. Of course, Grane no longer flies through the air, but he is still a special horse. Then off he goes, leaving Brunhilde surrounded by flames, a frumpy, homebody Brunhilde now, patiently waiting for her man to come home. She has become a woman.

And Siegfried goes away by boat. On the Rhine. Once again the music describes the changing spaces, and the old river whose surface we see bears the young hero to the scene that will give it back the ring. This place is a human palace inhabited by some country squires unheard of until this moment: the Gibichungs. There are three of them engaged now in a family council: Gunther and Hagen, two brothers, and Gutrune the sister. But one of them, Hagen, is a bastard, the son of Krimhide and . . . Alberich. That is the real connection with the rest of the story. He is the one spoken of by Wotan in *Valkyrie*, this child that Alberich (for a fee) had managed to father. So he is the enemy, or rather the agent of the final action. Hagen devises a villainous scheme. He proposes to marry Gunther to Brunhilde and Gutrune to Siegfried. But how can it be accomplished except through trickery? Gutrune is to use a magic potion to seduce Siegfried and above all make him completely forget his wife. After that they will persuade the hero to go, disguised as Gunther, and conquer Brunhilde. Which is what in fact happens, but it is not Hagen's real objective. Hagen wants Siegfried to die. We have not quite reached that point. Hagen is the only one, in *Götterdämmerung*, who knows everything. His father, Alberich, cleverly keeps this knowledge alive during Hagen's dreams, so that he holds the sovereign power of memory over all the others. Everyone else is unaware, or has forgotten because of the love potion. The plot of the black Alb, Hagen, unrolls as planned: Siegfried drinks the magic drink, falls in love with Gutrune, forgets Brunhilde. He leaves with Gunther, and, aided by the magic helmet he had taken from Fafner, reconquers—although for him in his clouded consciousness it is for the first time—the Valkyrie. He gives Brunhilde to Gunther, his brother-in-law. Then everything really goes wrong.

Because, upon arriving at the Gibichung's palace, Brunhilde who was overcome by male strength, Brunhilde, who now knows the whole burden of paternal condemnation, and who, is this time truly dethroned, conquered by force, sees the ring on Siegfried's finger. Could it be that Siegfried came to get her and not Gunther? Betrayal! Brunhilde knows nothing of the potion and its forgetful spell; and Brunhilde reacts as a woman deceived. She becomes outraged and swears on her solemn oath that Siegfried has betrayed her; Siegfried in good faith swears just as solemnly in his innocence that he has not. Brunhilde goes even further; she plots Siegfried's death with Hagen, who is ready and willing, who could hope for nothing more. She tells him that the hero is invulnerable except for his back. Then Hagen prepares a hunting party during which it would be easy to use his treachery to kill Siegfried, all the easier because the hero's prestige has been tarnished by the burden of suspicion posed by Brunhilde's oath. This is a universe of men: confused, complex, contradictory, traversed by ancient ancestral hatreds that no one even remembers but that continue to exist unbeknownst to all.

The gods are far, far away. Not a single god puts in an appearance. Twice, however, they send signs and messengers. The first time, while Brunhilde waits alone on her flame-encircled peak, a Valkyrie comes down from Valhalla to speak to her; she tells her that Wotan returned one day from his wanderings, holding his divine spear, broken into pieces, in his hand; that he commanded that the ash tree of the world be cut down and made into an immense pyre surrounding the formerly sumptuous ruling citadel. And there, surrounded by the terrified gods, he waits. All that he has said is that if Brunhilde would return the ring to the Rhine maidens, all would be saved. Brunhilde refuses: for her it is a ring of love, she could not return it, even if keeping it dooms the gods.

A second time, when Siegfried goes hunting, he walks along the banks of the Rhine following some escaping prey. Suddenly the Rhine maidens appear from the river to have a chat with him. Jokingly they ask him, these merry maidens, to give them the ring as a present. It is just a game between the naiads and the young man fascinated by the grace of these siren-women. Because he refuses they accuse him of being greedy; and Siegfried, cut to the quick, holds the ring out to them. For an instant anything can happen; for a glancing moment the ring, perhaps, is finally going to return to the river, then the gods will be saved. . . . But the sprites change their tune and tell Siegfried the curse of the ring: he must return it or he will die. The Rhine maidens are the divine essence; they are part of the waning troop of those who know. Then Siegfried is spurred on again, but in the opposite direction. So, they are trying to frighten him? Fine, he will show them that he does not know what fear is. And he will keep the ring. This time the die is cast. Then the Rhine maidens swim off to find Brunhilde, to tell her—remind her—of everything.

Siegfried's death approaches. The hunters stop to rest in the woods on the banks of the river. Hagen gives Siegfried a drink of a potion that progressively restores his memory and asks him to recount his exploits. Siegfried describes how he forged the sword, killed Mime, followed the bird, awoke Brunhilde. . . . Awoke Brunhilde? The armed men surrounding him, and especially Gunther, who had no idea, are startled. So it was true, he betrayed her, at least as they all see it, since none of them knows anything about the double-dealing of the two cross-potions. Hagen wastes no time and thrusts his spear into Siegfried's back. Two cawing ravens fly overhead.

Ravens are Wotan's appointed birds. It is all over. The free hero who acted on behalf of the god, against his own desires, is dead. As he lies dying he dreams of love; he relives Brunhilde's kisses. Once again he has forgotten, but this time it is his mistaken betrayal that he has forgotten. He dies knowing nothing. He will never have known any of this: who his parents were, what kin he was to Wotan, who his wife really was, why he was killed. Siegfried is a completely innocent hero; the only one who, from one end of his life to the other, will have known absolutely nothing. Except two things: that he was fearless and that he loved Brunhilde.

The body of the dead hero is carried to the palace. Siegfried's two wives await him (the polygamist in spite of himself); one of them knows nothing and the other, whom the Rhine maidens have told, knows all. Gunther, terror-stricken, is killed by Hagen; Gutrune says nothing. The two opposing forces are still there: Hagen, Alberich's son, and Brunhilde, Wotan's daughter. Hagen wants to take the ring from Siegfried's finger, but the corpse raises its hand to stop him. Then Brunhilde intervenes; motionless, she gives the orders. A pyre is to be built on the banks of the Rhine; her horse is to be brought to her there beside the heap of wood. Now she knows all, she even knows why she, a woman, is the one to know all. "The purest one had to betray me so a woman could attain knowledge." She speaks to Wotan beyond the clouds; she hears the wings of the two ravens who are going to tell Wotan to light the pyre surrounding Valhalla at the same moment she lights Siegfried's funeral pyre. The gods will be able to rest in peace. She takes the ring and tells the Rhine maidens to take it from her finger after the flames subside. She mounts her Valkyrie's steed, lights the pyre, and with a leap joins Siegfried's body in the midst of the fire.

Everything burns: the palace, the entire world, the citadel of the gods. The waters of the Rhine rise, overflow, and flood everywhere: water and fire rage together. Loge has won and so has the old river. The three sprites take the ring, which Hagen tried to snatch away one last time; they drag Alberich's son into the depths. Everything has collapsed in ruin. In the deep waters the gold shines again, back where it came from at last. But far, far above, in the clouds, a red light flares. The music tells of something beyond the death of the gods: the sublime melody uttered by Sieglinde when she learned she was expecting a son now rises above all, snuffs out the flames, and brings peace. The river waters have washed everything clean; the world of humankind is ready for another future.

Some minor fugues on kinship

Now you know the whole story, in its linear narrative, like the thread spun by the Norns, which they hang on the branches of a pine. We ourselves have been the thread itself. That is the first and most immediate function of the spectator. To be carried away by the story and to go out into the night with one's memory full of figures who are not oneself but who have inhabited one's life during this very brief period of the *Ring* cycle. Now you are no longer a spectator; the moment of emotion, that moment of musical time, is over and done with. All that remains is its trace.

The trace is what we are going to work on. Work: because, in itself, this show has not been work for you, although it is exceedingly so for the actors, whose singing and acting has cost them great effort, and also for the musicians, the technicians, and all those who have worked for your emotion. However, in another sense, a sort of work (not for money, but work all the same) has been produced in you—the work that made you understand and experience something. For us to work on its traces is to analyze and to try and explain an operation after the event. This is a secondary, fundamental, and reflexive time, beyond what is immediate. I would dare call it philosophical because that is my background. This formation never goes away, and I am never more conscious of exercising it than when I explain the functioning of an opera. Because becoming aware of a complex whole that is made to move and carry one away allows one, first of all, to take the necessary distance, and then to grasp the threads, other threads than the one spun by the Norns.

I will start with the family. Always, everywhere, it is one of those structures that never stops functioning in everyone's unconscious. And there are things so aberrant about the family of the *Ring* that the way the music echoes is even more remarkable. Its beginnings are extremely vague and shaky: there are gods, there are black gnomes who are their brother-opposites, there is the river and its daughters. And there is only one mother, Erda. Now what does Wotan do? In order to "know," he sets off to seduce the mother—hence, his mother, because she is that for all the gods—and has eight daughters by her. In the world of men, you know, that is forbidden. It is called incest. If you look hard in the mythical tales borrowed by Wagner to make his own myth, you will find that Wotan has already committed incest: Fricka is his sister. But that is just a "slight" incest, commonly found among gods in all of the tradition inherited from Greece and often from other places as well. The "grave" incest, all the graver because it harbors another sin, is the incest with Erda. It is gravely burdened with the "sin of knowledge," which has always been felt to be somehow dangerous, scandalous, and forbidden. This god is always trying to know something: to get Fricka he had to drink from the spring, which cost him an eye; to know more he would even commit the utmost incest. For Freud that is the basis of the search for all knowledge, even scientific knowledge. If men are confounded seekers, it is because they want to "know" the real key to their history—that is, according to the first psychoanalyst, where they came from, where babies come from, about this mysterious sexual connection that is hidden from them. And Wotan has no father. It is logical that he learn no more and that this will bring him to his death. Freud, you see, did not escape the religious threat concerning knowledge; it is indeed a fearful critical weapon, which it is often the function of families to neutralize.

I will reel off the incestuous thread; you will see where it takes us. The twins, Wotan's son and daughter, go to it happily, and this beloved child, Siegfried, the bearer of all their hopes, is the child of a brother and sister. In fact, notice that right up to and including his death, he will be ignorant of his origins. One might think, perhaps, that the incest is so close and so ticklish that it prohibits Siegfried's seeing anything at all about his own history. For an instant he evokes his mother—when he is standing beside the sleeping body of the Valkyrie. Who just happens to be his aunt, because she is the sister of his parents and the daughter of his grandfather. Of course, when put like that, a whole poetic side disappears in favor of those old stories by babbling women whose familial function it is to know and pass on the genealogy. And yet, this tetralogical structure is so powerful and so glaring that it generally goes unseen. It is as if, rather than exchanges between men and women taking place from generation to generation, there are leaps accomplished and things sealed off to such an extent that the structure, rather than opening up on itself, closes back down until it reaches the twilight of the gods. Here we have gods who did not follow the human norms necessary to the basis of all culture; normally a father gives his daughter in marriage to another man, a brother exchanges his sister. Wotan tries hard, in his wanderings, to open up the divine structure by fathering the children of a woman from somewhere else, a simple mortal woman. But it was a waste of time: the curse that doubtless brought death and incest simultaneously, quickly gains the upper hand, and the two children, rather than opening up with marriages that were not of consanguinity, close back on each other to produce Siegfried. Ethnologists have something instructive to say about this: if the prohibition of incest were not respected, society would end up in giant families, closed back on themselves, with kinship ties knotted one on top of another; and it would be family war. You can read the entire *Ring* as the progressive disappearance of a family that refuses exchange. There is nothing but refused exchange, with the false pretext that "they" are too ugly, or too rough; but Alberich and Hunding, the "villains" of the story, are really normal. Alberich runs after sprites; Hunding carried off his wife as one of the spoils of war. Somehow they are right, and love, the sublime love on the part of the gods, is a mortal love. That is why, when they first begin to love each other, Siegfried and Brunhilde embrace and sing of joyful, suicidal death. Furthermore, take a look at something strange yet nonetheless coherent: divine marriage, the marriage that is the law, which Fricka and her husband, Wotan, are in charge of guarding, is a childless marriage. Sterility afflicts the gods when they act within the norm.

I will move on to the end of the story where men, with systems doubtless too complex for a divine nature, come in. Gunther and Gutrune are perfectly within the norm: they each seek a wife or a husband in a "regulation" exchange. One of them will conquer his wife violently and the other will take a husband in a chance encounter. Fine, but it is at the price of magic, because neither one seems capable of going about it any other way. That is where Hagen has a hold on them. He is the relative who is the evil genius: the line of Gibich, their father, still has no offspring. Consequently, the potion's magic powers, Gunther's hateful ruse, will be the final means to guarantee the lineage. But Hagen is Alberich's son, and Siegfried himself is damned for having put the ring on his finger. The poor men are minor instruments of the curse; furthermore, at the death of the gods, they will disappear as if by magic, transcended by a death that has nothing to do with them. We are in a sort of foggy and archaic prehistory, where matters of life are not yet solidly in place. Things happen as if, for them to begin, a world had to vanish. Death of a culture. But do not forget that this is a text written within our system, one sending you, as the spectator, back to very old fantasies tucked away in the system of your unconscious—and that is where the work is working. It recounts a so-called past, a so-called origin, telling itself, and presenting itself as something it is not. For it is not a true story; it is a myth, an imaginary projection of a real situation. For example (and what an example), when Hitler and his family, and a few other families closely connected with him, shut themselves up in the bunker in Berlin, and they all committed suicide because defeat was imminent, they played music from *Götterdämmerung*, the twilight of the gods. That was their imaginary construct, and you know what their reality was—carefully masked by myth, among other things. That tells something about the seduction and danger of myth, and why, at all costs, one must *know* and keep one's distance. The threat is that one take oneself to be a character and give oneself the right to act like a god. Myth always has political potential, and it is impossible to look at it in isolation as if it were reality.

See! Now we have another thread, another network, as if we were playing string games, passing the threads under one finger then onto another, stretched between two hands, and other figures appear. Still working in the family, but this time according to function: fathers, mothers, sons, wives. . . . And these functions, when precedence is taken into account, are not overlapping. Wives, for example, are not mothers.

There are two *fathers* who are perfectly complementary, the white Alb, Wotan, and the black Alb, Alberich. They have offspring, of course, but they have offspring to accomplish something specific; they are not content to breed merely for love or merely to perpetuate their lines. This *merely* is the clue to Wotan and Alberich, because they seek something *more* from their children. They make them instruments of their power, or their defense, or their attack. Alberich sleeps with a human woman *for the purpose* of making a man descended from his race who is capable of destroying the gods: that will be Hagen. Wotan sleeps with Erda, his mother, *for the purpose* of creating a legion of warrior women to protect him; and with the mother of his twins, *for the purpose* of trying to produce free beings who are independent of him, because he knows that could be a possible defense against the death of the gods. All the children are defensive bastards. Wotan knows this well and laments this basic incapacity: how can he get a child who is free and yet comes from him? That is what is impossible for him. He himself will have to kill Siegmund, and Siegfried will have to die.

The *mothers* are the great sacrificial victims in the story. Two of them are more or less unknown to us; Sieglinde's mother just passes through, Wotan's children "hardly knew her."

The same is true of Hagen's mother, Krimhilde. They are bellies, just barely of some use for childbearing; after that they disappear, having fulfilled their function. And even when Siegmund and Sieglinde recognize that they have the same eyes, like looking in a mirror, these eyes are Wotan's, with their incomparable sparkle. Nothing remains of their mother, except her absence. The other two are scarcely better treated. Sieglinde is present a bit more, but as a sister rather than as a mother, and when she is a mother she too becomes a passerby. As soon as Siegfried is in the world, Sieglinde dies; it as if divine seed cost women their lives. Finally there is Erda, but what a curious mother she is. A mother before giving birth to a child, an ancestral, immortal, and sleeping mother. She emerges and is present on the stage only to prophesy misfortune, or to sleep. Mothers are doomed either to silence or to death; they sleep. But a dialectic progressively develops between Erda and Sieglinde. The former, mother of the gods, goes back to her twilight sleep; after having warned Wotan, she is no longer able to fight against being buried. The latter is the first to utter the love motif that is to end *Götterdämmerung*, at the end of the end. One of them begins the children of the gods, the other finishes them. They are mothers dooming to death their progeny, who are used by the father in certain strategic moves.

The *sons*, with the utmost reliability, accomplish their fathers' desires, since they were conceived for that purpose. But the desires are spun out of insurmountable contradictions, and, just as reliably, the sons destroy their fathers' desires.

Hagen, however, came very close to achieving the stubborn, straightforward aims of Alberich. It is true that Alberich has a firm hold on his son. He haunts Hagen's dreams, leaves him no peace, fans his actions into flame, aging him and depriving him of any joy. Hagen exists only for Alberich; but that does not take the Rhine maidens into account. They take their revenge, transmitting enough knowledge to Brunhilde so that she lights a double pyre, one in Valhalla and the other in the Gibichung palace. Hagen is drowned in the waters of the Rhine, which is what did not happen to his father when he took the ring, but it is the logical conclusion of a story of a gnome and a river. A son in the place of a father, drowned by the water sprites. As for Siegmund, he above all carries through Wotan's contradictions: free, but dependent on Fricka's law, brave, but destined to lose the battle, the beloved son of a father who is prepared to kill him. Siegmund is endlessly "repressed" by Wotan: repressed the way police hold demonstrators in check, and repressed the way the unconscious represses things it wants no part of. Repressed the first time because he is abandoned by his father, and the second time because his father kills him for standing in his path. Like all sons, he is his father's unconscious. Hagen, too, is a simple version of Alberich's unconscious. Wotan is crossed and plagued, hesitant and inexplicable; and Siegmund puts his indecisions into action. Nothing better dramatizes Wotan's destiny than the incest between his two children. Siegfried, the fruit of this incest, is like the "return of the repressed": that which, after all, emerges from the unconscious anyhow, and returns all the more powerfully when the repression has been powerful. Siegfried is so violently impelled by an unconscious resentment, the legacy of his father's death, that he in turn places himself across Wotan's path and breaks the divine spear. That was the end of it: the son's son has defeated the father. He has only to kiss the daughter to accomplish Wotan's total defeat. Even better: when all that has been achieved, he will die a stupid, inglorious death, with a hole in his back, thanks to a woman. A paltry end for the grandson of a god; an undistinguished defeat for the presumed savior. Wotan mulls over his loss and does not understand.

The *wives* are nasty old women who bring out the contradictions in their good-natured husbands. You might say that it was sufficient to be in the position of a lawful wife to expose the problems and impose the law. Fricka is the model. She was the originator of Valhalla and was full of reproaches as soon as there was some question of paying the giants for it. Taunting Fricka who comes to remind Wotan of the duties of his office. Greedy Fricka who ogles the gold as soon as it makes an appearance in the hands of the Nibelung. And what happens to Brunhilde when she becomes the lawful wife of Gunther? She "tells," she reveals, she betrays Siegfried and plots with Hagen. She will be the initiator of the deadly hunting party. She has become a woman, at least a woman as Wagner describes them, totally without virtue unless they are sisters. As mothers they die; as daughters they suffer; as wives they are annoyed. As sisters they are sublime, but man has very little to do with that. *Brothers and sisters* are the ones who remain, a whole legion of them, fluttering around as extras. The two giants, Fasolt and Fafner, united to build the citadel and separated by the gold; Hagen and Gunther, united in evil to obtain the two marriages, separated by the ring; one killing the other; finally Wotan and his brothers and the young cousin, ambiguous Loge, who weaves a cloth of fire against kinship—weaving guile and malice into a protective curtain of flames and a devastating conflagration. Cousin Loge grows while the gods shrink, a dangerous relationship. All that remains is for the brothers to kill each other and for fraternity to fall apart. "Sorority" is not worth much: Fricka and Freia, the three Norns, the troop of Valkyries, all have one trait in common—complaint. They complain about one another, they moan incessantly, they are always crying. Relations between the brothers, on the one hand, and the sisters, on the other, are hardly effective. It is not the dominant relationship but a doomed relationship.

But there is *one daughter* who is recognized as such, endowed with a highly privileged position, escaping from the booby-trapped system I am trying to describe. She, of course, corresponds as any child does to some maneuver by a god; like her seven sisters, all created at the same time, she was created for the love of knowledge. But why is so much love invested in her? She is the one in whom Wotan confides when Fricka comes to persuade him (if one can say that) to kill Siegmund; she knows how to make her father talk. She truly has the utmost privilege of a real relationship with Wotan. Oh, there are limits to this, the limits of divinity, since Wotan cannot bear to speak to his daughter unless he is pretending to talk to himself. Even Brunhilde defines herself as Wotan's will. Listen to the dialogue between father and daughter: "Who am I, then, if not your will?" to which Wotan responds in echo: "I am only thinking to myself when I speak to you." And she is the one to whom he tells the story, always the same story, four times over, once for each of the four days. But the thing is that, although Wotan, who seems so stingy with it, has endowed her with this unique love, she is going to deliberately transgress his will by loving love, seduced by her brothers' and sisters' incestuous love. One might say that her legacy is love itself and that the one-eyed Wotan, the god who has one eye with which to see love, is unaware that this eludes him. Actually, he is a fine Oedipus—one eye too few and thinking he knows everything. (Oedipus, you know, the one who married his own mother and killed his father. The poet Hölderlin said he had "one eye too many.") There is an element of misplaced clairvoyance in these stories: Wotan and Oedipus both want to know what is going to hit before it happens. While they are spinning a too distant future, actions and gestures elude them, like tears dropping from their eyes, which someone nearby would collect. This tear, this uncontrolled secretion, semen released by accident, is collected by the daughter: faithful Antigone, faithful Brunhilde. Love, this other figure of fate, goes by way of the daughters in their relationship with the father. And both of them, Antigone and Brunhilde, draw there the power of disobedience that makes them even more dear. For Brunhilde, having betrayed Wotan—but having fulfilled his most cherished desire—is even more cherished herself. And he sings her the most passionate of all the songs, the most loving melody. Listen: "These two twinkling eyes . . . these two beaming eyes, that have often shone for me in storms. . . . For the last time, how comforting these eyes are for me today in this last kiss good-bye." Wotan acknowledges himself in Brunhilde and in no one else. Brunhilde, his only love. . . Brunhilde, the passion that destroys him.

Father and daughter are separated for good, by space and time and by the daughter's definitive fall to womanhood, where she becomes stupid, stripped of all knowledge. However, Wotan still sends her the messenger, Waltraute; and she is the one to whom he finally sends the two ravens of misfortune who hang in flight over the dead Siegfried. The ultimate signal—which faithful Brunhilde clearly recognizes. She responds to the funereal sign and sets fire to the final pyre herself. She burns her father like the Phoenix does when it is about to die. Now, the Phoenix, in fact, in all myths is a bird that signifies something very curious: androgyny, bisexuality, the phenomenon of a nature that partakes simultaneously of man and of woman. Hegel says exactly the same thing about Antigone, who remains faithful to Oedipus; in both stories the sons die in combat, sacrificed for the glory of the father. It is the daughter who inherits the sons' real power, and who ends the story of the family. Reticent and faithful, she ties it all together. A woman is the one in this opera (where, as in all operas, the woman is allotted suffering or malice, where men—Wotan, Alberich, Siegfried, Hagen— carry out the affairs of men) who concludes it. After Brunhilde's death on the pyre, a feminine melody rings out again to bring the opera to an end. The entire *Ring* cycle can also be read as a father's undoing, his defeat by his own daughter.

I pick up another thread here and change fingers, another figure will emerge for you. This story is filled with animals and objects that come to revolve around characters with human faces, who make use of them to accomplish a particular journey. The distinctive feature of the objects is that they circulate, from hand to hand, without anyone's being able to hang on to them; and if someone keeps some object, it ends up being destroyed. That is what happens to Wotan's spear. It is a stable object, basic to the world, the symbolic compendium of written law, and it belongs to Wotan who does not let go of it. But this object constrains Wotan—the object keeps the god—so that, when the young fool breaks the divine spear in pieces, divine Wotan is set free. He is vanquished but relieved. He picks up the pieces of his spear and builds his pyre. The other major objects are all ambulatory, moving from one person to the next. First, there is the ring, the epitome of a circulating and circular object. From the Rhine to Alberich, from Alberich to Wotan, from Wotan to Fasolt, from Fasolt to Siegfried, from Siegfried to Brunhilde, from Brunhilde to Siegfried, finally from Siegfried to Brunhilde and from her to the Rhine maidens. How it goes around! But in the language, the words, it is love that goes around, not gold. You might say that there is a perversion of "normal" circulation: the gold moves from hand to hand, and with it the love curse, and, suddenly, love is no longer going around. Also, the ring is only a ring in men's hands: before, in the Rhine, it was a light; afterward, in the Rhine, it became a light once more. The circle has to break. It only succeeds in doing so only in the give and take between the two lovers: for like pass-the-shoe it moves from me to you to you, but when it lands on a woman's finger, it suddenly comes back, it does not move on. It circulates twice between Siegfried and Brunhilde to finally stay on the favorite daughter's finger. She does not return it; it falls from the ashes of her finger. Brunhilde, her bones burned and reduced to ashes, returns the ring.

The spear and the ring are controlling objects; but there are also the sword and helmet. The helmet, like a face veil, makes one invisible. Alberich uses it first, then Siegfried, always as an object with which to dominate. Alberich uses it to rule and exploit the dwarves, Siegfried uses it to dominate his wife. It is easier to be dominant when one does not let himself be seen. . . . Masked, the power of exploitation is stronger. This fable is easy to decipher. The sword is more complicated. Plunged deeply into the trunk of a tree by Wotan, stuck at first and impossible to take—except by one man, Siegmund, for whom it is destined—its route is the opposite of the one taken by the spear. Initially it is shattered by the spear, and then, reforged, it is the one that does the shattering. A by-product of the spear, Wotan's defensive-offensive weapon against himself, it turns against him to the extent that the hands holding it, that think they are holding it, are instruments of the sword.

And the animals? They are always there, a mute and living presence, duly recorded in the script and production instructions. But they are often, too often, replaced by lights supposed to evoke them, by eyes lifted toward the sky—which says nothing to me. There is no hint of a neck for Brunhilde to lean against, no hint of a flight, no feather, no fur, no odor at all. I remember the childish wonder, an integral part of the pleasure of opera, when I saw for the first time the productions of the Bolshoi theater. Real horses came on stage, an insolent presence, one scarcely under control, and sometimes left their droppings. . . . Their presence is *resistant* and that is the very reason it is essential. Consequently, if it has been suppressed, it is not by accident. The *Ring* has been made into an "eternal" story, an out-of-this-world story, one that is mythical and supermythical and that takes place in the heaven of sublime sentiments. No more armor, no more glow, no more props, everything that could interfere with the Idea has been eliminated. Phooey. Wagner wrote a story full of real animals, perhaps the only real, nonfictional creatures of all those presented on the stage; it has been transformed into a sentimental serial novel for fourth-rate philosophers. I dream of those interferences; they disrupt the order and that is their purpose. An actress who has trouble staying on her real horse, real rams (Fricka is always accompanied by two rams), "real" matter calls one back to order, because disorder is possible there and everyone knows it. These gods are played by men; so show that to us. All in all, and in a totally different register, I prefer Mauricio Kagel's serious farces. *He* take props seriously; he turns them into playful elements. He builds Siegfried's anvil out of styrofoam and has his singer bang on it with a foam hammer. It does not make an anvil sound; but it calls attention to the emptiness, the idiotic emptiness of all those who have transformed the *Ring* into conceptual "philosophy." The emptiness of dead gods. . . . Hear the full sonorousness of it all?

The family story has to remain an unconscious structure, just as it was written, or one risks emptying it of its sense. What we see are characters, wearing costumes, recognizable in their helmets like the woman on the blue packs of Gauloise cigarettes; they wear animal skins, they carry horns to start the hunt; somehow, they are living and affected by the story. If we put shiny leather clothes on them and "eternal" costumes, they turn into vaudeville characters. Of course, they are that *also*, moving from the grotesque to the sublime in the twinkling of an eye. The number of things mocked in the work makes this evident and it is full of indispensable pastiches. But to deprive them of their prehistoric flavor, their childish disguises, is to take away their life. Substituting a visionary, accusatory interpretation, adding intentions to the myth, is to lead it astray.

Little structural pieces

Let us put aside the string games, have our hands completely untied and free, and talk music. Because all that, all the things I have told you, are stories. To be taken two ways: they really are stories and then it is all made up—"a bunch of fibs." Because we are talking about opera, and thus about music essentially. Several times, throughout the narrative, I might have wanted to remind you that "without the music" there would be something you would not know at all. Remember too what Lévi-Strauss wrote: with Wagner, and especially the *Ring* cycle, for the first time we are dealing with a structural analysis of myths. *Structural*: one should not get all worked up over that. It just means that, between the music and the words sung, between one word and another, and between one music and another, there are laws, correspondences and relations put in place that function without your even knowing, and doubtless even better if you know of them. Family relations are an example. But they do not take into account the musical relationships.

The same Lévi-Strauss, when he began work on the notion of *myth*, used the functioning of an orchestra to make his comparison and found that a myth must be able to be read like a score. You have already seen a score, no doubt; you read one direction for the story, the narrative, the melody—the things that are perhaps sung, and are retained, the rest. In the other direction, vertically, you find what the instruments are playing. In a myth it is the same thing. There is the bare narrative told and retained, and then there are bundles of relationships that can be organized in an entirely different order, no longer chronological, and which is combined with the narrative. For example, mothers, fathers, and so on, but also events that are similar: Siegmund is killed by Wotan's spear /Siegfreid breaks Wotan's spear; Wotan puts Brunhilde to sleep and surround her with flames/ Brunhilde procures eternal rest for Wotan and lights the final pyre. In both cases the events resemble and thwart one another, the second both annulling and repeating the first. To see these correlations, one must stop listening to the narrative in chronological order and leap backward, anachronistically.

There is, it so happens, another (but is it really another) operation that functions in this manner. That is, the unconscious, in the relations it has with daily continuity. The unconscious could not care less about time passing and the order of events, and it never stops recalling spots in the past that it places in the present. That can be called a lapse, or an abortive action; more generally it is part of an essential process that Freud calls *delayed reaction*, a reaction after the fact, but also always a reaction in advance, because the traces that are permanently inscribed make you act and make choices that are somehow knowable in advance. There too, bundles of relations are operating, which are opposite and supplemental to the life you lead—that you believe you "lead" but that, in fact, leads you. It is even more simply inscribed in the very functioning of the word, (something I am borrowing from another venerable ancestor, Lacan). Given the linkage of the elementary terms of language, it forms a vector oriented in the direction of time, from one letter to the next, O to I, for example; this connective system does not stop except when you speak it, and does not take on meaning except when you have punctuated it, given it a period. Without this punctuation the chain runs on and means nothing, it is just a reservoir. The result is that meaning exists only *retroactively*, backward, directing the arrows of orientation of this fictional vector in the opposite direction. This is how Lacan put it: "The sentence . . . does not complete its meaning until its final term, each term being anticipated in the structure of the others, and inversely setting a seal on their sense by its retroactive effect." Just like, at the end of *Götterdämmerung*, the waters of the Rhine seal in the return of the gold to the river. But the music of the waters of the Rhine is no longer the same as it was in the prologue to *Rheingold*, and when you complete a sentence, it is no longer the same as when you began it; language has brought you to where it decreed its meaning, just as, from the beginning, the music inscribed its own musical story accompanying or, on the contrary, nullifying the text that is sung.

That is the crux of the matter. The story told by the music in a rather precise narrative system is not entirely the same one told by the myth. It is "on the whole" the same story, they are certainly the same characters, the same events, but the order is endlessly out of whack, shifted forward or backward in time the way the unconscious produces dislocations in life. The music, therefore, is like the word's unconscious, and plays tricks on it, forming another line, opening bridges, rainbows, to some point in the past, while winking toward the future. You will have heard, in any one of the selections one can make from the *Ring*, musical phrases that you recognize. These phrases make a story all by themselves, which informs the ear about the event in process. They complicate the words, restoring to them a risky dimension that appears uncertain but, if one is willing to study it more closely, is cumulative.

This system of "recognition," the return again and again of musical phrases, is something curious. Very early, of course, the system was detected. All around Wagner, and most especially in France, a few gullible, idolatrous smart alecks began to create dictionaries, naming the phrases and giving them titles to make them more "recognizable." It became a real business. Naturally, in naming the music, they did not do it innocently, and with their big words they superimposed on the Wagnerian text, on its words and music, their bungling obsequiousness, their racketeering commentary. Some of these designations (such as naming the Valhalla theme) caused neither harm nor good. But "Redemption through love" is something else again. It is interpretation. "Justice of the expiation" is another such. Oh, it is all done in the most absolute faithfulness to what Wagner *said*; because, indeed he also wrote and composed *Parsifal* on the subject of redemption. He put the mystical and mystifying words Redemption for the Redeemer in the mouth of choirs tumbling from heaven. But, since the Nazi system adopted this particular aspect of Wagnerian thought, to follow Wagner, the individual, in his century-old words, to transform him into a divinity as is frequently done, is to condemn him even more certainly. A century later, we have other work to do rather than listening to the motifs and punctuating them regularly with : "Aha! There is the 'work of destruction' or 'Alberich's power'!"

Exactly as if you ran into "Whosywhat" in the subway.

We should work on an example, starting with a central situation, one simultaneously a point where the story ends and a point of sudden revival. This is the moment when Wotan has just killed Siegmund; Siegmund was shielded by Brunhilde, who as a result clashes with her father and fails in the mission he confided in her (to bring him the dead Siegmund). Wotan appears on the scene, Brunhilde is hidden behind her seven sisters. She has one advantage over her father: she knows that Sieglinde, whom she has just saved, is bearing a child, who is, from now on, Wotan's only male offspring. But Wotan is lord and master and proclaims her sentence. Brunhilde is to be stripped of power and transformed into a woman. That is the end of one story, the story of the Valkyries; and another one begins, the story of Brunhilde the woman, Siegfried's future wife. Wotan makes a tricky and suicidal bet: to let this union, which both are then premeditating, happen. So that the gods will be saved? or lost? Wotan himself does not yet know. A moment of suspense.

Let us begin. Wotan has just told Brunhilde that she is no longer to be a Valkyrie. And he specifically says he will no longer send her on missions. That is all he says: he will no longer point out to her the heroes for the battlefield, she will no longer affectionately give him his goblet, he will no longer kiss her. And the insistent theme beneath these words is the one we heard for a long time, marking an entire scene that has already taken place: when Brunhilde comes to tell Siegmund that he is going to die and that he will be taken to Valhalla in the troop of heroes. A slow theme, marked by muffled, funereal percussion instruments, a theme that for both you and me, has initially been associated with the foreboding of death and with Siegmund's refusal. Associated equally with both these things; for it is this unheard of refusal—and for what a motive, the love of a mere woman—that is going to make Brunhilde teeter and fall into rebellion and then into love. Love, you must not forget, is forbidden to Wotan ever since he touched the cursed ring. Here we are, already back at the beginning, and that is the purpose of this endless back and forth work, which has no affect on the singers but does on the spectators. When Wotan sings these words and Brunhilde hears them, the music thus signifies *the relationship between the two of them*: this action that Brunhilde will no longer perform and all those that, on the contrary, she will carry out as a woman in love, all this will get away from Wotan. Wotan loses what his daughter used to bring him—a smile and dead heroes—and he loses what she will do on his account—her loving as a woman. A little later—but there is a gap—he will bitterly tell her this, that she is in the process of tasting love. But while he is saying this the music says two things that Wotan does not: first the phrase that accompanied Alberich when he was stealing the gold—the one that punctuated his definitive renunciation of love—and then the phrase with which he cursed the ring when Wotan, in turn, stole it from him. Hence, the music gives an accounting that adds to the complaints of Wotan, that it is his own fault—he is responsible for having stolen the gold and beyond that it is the fault of the gods, since it was Alberich who triggered the whole thing. Wotan's muttered contradictions are a historical reminder, contrasting with what Brunhilde is going to sing; she is the physical medium for bringing in new phrases. The theme that from beginning to end accompanies Siegfried's existence is first sung by her when she announces to Sieglinde, who is still unaware of it, that a child is going to be born whom she must name Siegfried. Thus, from the beginning, Brunhilde sponsors even Siegfried's name; she keeps him nice and warm for herself, saves his mother, and preserves herself by going to sleep until the moment he will come to awaken her. In this scene with Wotan, she is once again the one who announces the imminent birth to her father; she is the one finally who has the idea of putting fire around her. These new melodies start the drama again, keeping it alive until the twilight of the gods; the music is the impetus for the action.

Hence, Brunhilde is the basis of new motifs; and Wotan, on the contrary, having attained divine power, utters only old themes musically, melodies that are already ancient. He puts Brunhilde to sleep to Alberich's theme of the renunciation of love: "For the god thus distances himself from you and with a kiss deprives you of divinity." It all takes place as if Brunhilde and Wotan were battling musically, one of them for a future to be saved, the other for a past that he believes is settled, lost, and sewed up tight. Brunhilde wins this game between present and future; and Wotan wins because of the fate of the gods. But at the moment in which he gives in, taking Siegfried's themes, the themes of a child to be born, as his own, the music says something else again, and puts in play the three notes signifying the final fate. The music, always ahead of things, always out of sync, calls one back to order. What order? In every instance, an order written in the combined text of both music and words, an order that dismisses the psychology of the characters to the status of merely one constituent element of the whole tetralogy.

This theme accompanying Wotan's words to Brunhilde: "I shall not send you on a mission ever again" is very interesting. Let us take a look at where it springs from and when. Siegmund and Sieglinde are fleeing Hunding who is fortified by his marital rights. Sieglinde is haunted by a prophetic dream: an ash comes crashing down, Siegmund is dead! — Sieglinde faints. Siegmund holds her in his arms. That is when Brunhilde, the other woman, enters; Siegmund has never seen her and does not know who she is. Throughout the beginning of the scene it is Siegmund who is to sing the funereal theme, asking question after question: who are you? Where are you taking me? Whom shall I find in Valhalla? Shall I find my father? Shall I find a wife? Shall I find Sieglinde there? It is only then that Siegmund tells Brunhilde no, taking what she has said as offers. All Siegmund's questions are punctuated by the announcement of his death. Brunhilde breaks in, picking up the melody. She tells Siegmund that this is a necessity, not a choice for him to make. He has seen the Valkyrie's fatal glance; he will die. Three times she has to repeat for him that he has to die. Always with the same melody, emphasized by the muffled percussion instruments. The theme grows lively. Siegmund looks at Brunhilde and describes her as beautiful and cold. For Brunhilde, the theme becomes the unbearable proof of her own image as it is reflected by a fearless man. She gives in, just as Wotan will give in to her later. But in the last scene of *die Valkyrie* (the one I just recounted), when Wotan decrees that he will never again send his daughter on a mission, something comes to light: what Brunhilde did was not her own desire, but the desire of her father, the patron of this deadly motif, the sponsor of the troop of dead heros. In the scene with Siegmund a man sings this theme; in the scene with Wotan a man does so again. Brunhilde repeats the themes of other's desires: first her father's when she "valkyries" and then Siegmund's when she rebels. Finally, she lets herself go in telling of Siegfried's desire: so when will she be herself?

Never. I told you that Brunhilde ended the business, properly, according to the good old tradition that has women neatening everything up at home. Just a quick sweep with fire, a nice flood, and it is all done. But before vanishing at the same time the gods do, Brunhilde explains, or, rather, the music sums it up. She is there, standing before Siegfried's dead body, and she looks at the one who betrayed her; she tells how no one had ever been so faithful and also so treacherous.

The theme foreboding death rises with these words: "Do you know how that could be possible?" The only possible answer: it is the gods' fault. The theme of Valhalla responds to the question. To come to the final decision, Brunhilde still must address herself to her father who is absent. She announces in turn her own death and sends him the "fearfully desired" message concerning the gods' end. Desire has completed its journey; it is returned to the sender, Wotan. Wotan set it moving when he fathered Siegmund and Brunhilde, each of whom is the bearer of half their father's desire. Each one has performed his or her task, and Wotan gets back what he desired: the announcement of death. Then the ring must follow the same path. Sprites and fire must return to their origins; the music ties the melodies we have heard so often together and suddenly takes one of them, which overpowers the others. This one belongs to a woman, but this woman is not Brunhilde, it is Sieglinde. She sang it when she learned she was going to be a mother. She died of this maternity. So, in the end, everything is deadly: desire and its effects—in the heart and womb of woman and in man's flesh, in his back.

And this is the end of the voyage and the end of *Götterdämmerung*. No more looking ahead, no more possible futures, since finally all is finished. Thus, it is all played out in the interpretation of the past; meaning, of course, the past of what has been played out before your eyes for four long days. The characters vanish, their silhouettes become blurred, giving in to a musical system that takes them, uses them, gives them one meaning or another, according to where they are located in relation to it. It is not what Wotan "thinks" or what he "does" that counts, even if, to understand the story, it all has to be presented like a Punch and Judy show. What would the "thought" of a fictional character be?

No. What may count is the relationship between a particular theme that he sings at a particular moment and the same theme sung by someone else at another moment. Wotan and Siegmund both sing the theme from *die Valkyrie* that announces the hero's death to him; then what counts is this theme making the rounds from one person to the next, by way of Brunhilde. The music thus runs from character to character, weaves their relationships together, makes them and undoes them, and finally kills them all. The music is the *Ring*'s unconscious; for the unconscious runs from one person to another, weaves together and undoes relations, gets hold of human subjects and drives them, just as the music of the *Ring* does for you. It is a difficult notion when you hear it for the first time that the language speaks the subject rather than the opposite; that you speak, that you think you speak, and that in fact *you are spoken*. But the *Ring* is like a fable that would tell you that *also*. Old Lacan also says that a signifier represents the subject for another signifier; a signifier, that is to say, an element of language, represents the one who speaks—who is spoken—for another element of language. A musical theme represents a character for another musical theme; for example, the motif foreboding death represents Brunhilde for the theme predicting Siegfried's birth. The characters—the subjects—are exchange relations among circulating terms, like the gold and its ring which surround you with an immense circle. Watch Brunhilde; she is constantly sent away, from her father to her man, and in between there is Siegmund. But these men are only temporary bearers of other themes, and the characters pass by, from scene to scene, from generation to generation, all the way to the ultimate harmony when all is finally, once again, covered by water.

Some next-to-last thoughts

We are going to stop there. That is one of the rules of written texts. It is a rule that does not apply to stories, to mythical narration—meant to stop whenever you feel tired, but to tirelessly begin again, and never end. What I decided to do in pretending to talk to you, was fill in a bit of your education, which is nowhere near ending. But one must know when to stop that too, or at least when to pause. When one tells a story, something is always forgotten in the process; and when it ends, there is something like a leftover regret, something still to say that maybe was forgotten . . .

What one forgets is never innocent; no forgetfulness is. For example, the things I forgot in this story. I pointed out two fathers: Wotan and Alberich. But Siegmund is also a father because he begets Siegfried, and I never once thought of taking his paternity into account. It goes by so fast, and he pays no (or so little) attention to it. What does he do when Brunhilde gives him the news? He lifts Nothung, the sword, and prepares to sacrifice two lives rather than just one. Brunhilde is the one who acts like a mother. However, doing this, he is no different from the two other fathers, who, each in his own corner, sacrifice their daughters too. But then, where is the difference? In the music. Siegmund's song is a man's song, and it is not a paternal song; it is in his voice (higher) and his figure (which does not have the same symbolic attributes as the figures of the others) and by the relationship of his song with the woman's song. Wotan and Alberich are "in charge of" paternity; Wotan carries a spear and, on the spear, the laws. He also wears a hat that half hides him. Alberich is a hateful master, but he is the boss, and he sets himself up in the middle of roads announcing the curses that create law. Siegmund has none of that, he is a lover and a brother, he only sings of rebellion and love. It is only acts of despair and passion that he carries out: he is a son, he is not to have time to be a father. What counts is symbolic paternity, which is transmitted in the relationship between music and text.

And then, the brothers and sisters. I put them in brother-couples, bunches of sisters, each with his or her own sex. However, one of the central moments of the *Ring* is an act of incest between brother and sister, between Siegmund and Sieglinde; it is certainly close fraternizing — too close to be permitted. It is also a love scene, with the romantic prop that often sets its mark on those who adore that scene: moonlight. No doubt the moonlight and the stereotypes that go along with it are what made me "forget" the incest between brother and sister. It is quick to turn into nuptials; thus Siegmund puts his cards on the table at the end of the first act of *die Valkyrie*: he makes love to his sister, "so the blood of the Walsungs will flourish." So the family will continue. Paradoxically, it is at the height of incest that Siegmund comes in close contact with paternity, in his thorough occupation with reproduction. The playing cards of seven families are all mixed up with this intermediary character who is not a father, nor a husband, not entirely a brother, nor entirely a lover. Siegmund the joker, the unclassifiable Siegmund eludes all categories; he is this but simultaneously that; in Greek he would be called a "demon," that is, he makes transitions that others do not. Demonic; in transit; even in his life he is transitory. Siegmund circulates and, with him, so does the entire *Ring*. It is not surprising that he found no place in an approach that was one of classification. Not surprising that he is rediscovered after one has reflected on the music and on the dislocations, because he is fundamentally out of sync. However, the moment in which brother and sister are reunited is a unique moment; Hegel saw in the brother-sister relationship the culmination of all relations, an unadulterated relationship, meaning also that it was not adulterated by the mixing of blood.

The twins vanish, dragged into the system, disappearing more quickly than any of the other characters. There will be other "forgotten things" like this that you will find. They are the things I have forgotten in this reading, which (like all readings) has gaps in it where one's fantasy blocks something out. Here we are, back at the beginning: too much commentary, traps laid by interpretation, "wanting to say everything" at all cost. It is now your turn to create your own reading, constructing your own grid on the basis of fantasy and culture — which can never be dissociated. It is your turn to read and listen, no doubt you will hear other things and this reading will also have been just a way through, a passage. In all civilizations there exist what are called "rites of passage."

These make the transition between one stage and another in life's progress. A reading and a hearing are both rites of passage, and, as such, they are left behind, forgotten. Music also, in some ways, is forgetting, because it is directly connected to the time of the unconscious, whose vital function is to inscribe things at the same time that it inscribes their forgetting. In your culture, repetitive music pushes this process to a very advanced degree, to the point where repetitive forgetfulness undoes and advances everything. Wagner should be listened to the same way, after any reading — in forgetfulness, leaving this story of a twilight family, these women who are devoted to the point of death, these murderous fathers, and this interminable death, far behind.

Finale
In Praise of Paganism

The gods are dead. Frozen in their final poses, swallowed up in the bottom of the sea, burned on the last pyres, the gods finally fall silent. Against the twilight glow, as their voices fade away, one last image is affixed.

I know it is the last. When the opening curtain went up earlier, I felt my heart beating. Now that I know (because it is customary) that the wonderful box of fantasies is going to shut back up, taking with it the myths seen in their flesh which inhabit me, I cannot help but feel a pang of anguish. I know it is all over. It is not just the completion of a social performance that ends late and success-fully; not just the splendid success of a well done display in which marvelous things were accomplished. The simple pleasure of exploits in sound, the pres-ence of a prestigious conductor, the performance of a star, the intelligence of a production—I leave that to the others. For me it is something else entirely. The last word spoken to someone who is going away, the pain of a separation, the last kiss one lays on the cold forehead of a dead body, the moment when the stupid shroud edged in lace is closed, and the vanishing forever of what had been a smile, eyes of blue, a presence brought to nought. . . . A moment later and there is no one left; the smile becomes a rictus, instead of a body there is a bundle of white linen, and closing it all—a top sealed shut with silver nails. That moment accomplishes, for keeps, the beginning of mourning—that slow, difficult, and seemingly infinite work. Before it was "just for laughs"; before, there was some semblance. Now it is all over; I will have to begin, I will have to begin to come back to life, without . . .

Without them. The end of an opera is a work of mourning. It is ephemeral work, quickly absorbed by little actions. One has to get up, move around, put on a coat, leave, walk, go down the stairs. But, from this moment on, the men's house is uninhabited. Like a huge coffin it lets out the troops of refined, well dressed onlookers who form the funeral procession. How sad it is leaving the opera. The world that has just died on the stage abandons the vast social body, hurrying out through all the doors, all the exits, to its destiny of death. Instead of voices I now hear words, spoken words. The sound of speech clashes in my ears like some strange incongruity; I need silence and to go on into this sleepless night without saying a word.

No doubt one applauds so loudly to bring this buried celebration of the invisible, divine death to an end, to break it up. Before, for one more moment, the appearance is still there, in its costumes, its semblances, its scenery, its figures; a wonderful, fleeting silence still protects the closing scene. Afterward, when the curtain closes, there will always be someone, the first, who will produce this violent, coded noise that gives the signal for the agreed upon wave of sound. The harmonious architecture is broken; the audience all clap their hands to their own rhythms; some stand up and others remain seated. Some shout. An incoherent organization of a sound very different from music is what comes after. It seems that the extent of the success is measured by the extent of disorder it provokes. On stage the dead gods display smiles, bows, and — in a harsh light — their makeup and the wrinkled pleats of their robes. They have not completely stripped away the imaginary figuration turning them into hybrid creatures in whom no man or woman can quite recognize him or herself. They are on their way, minds afire and hearts in commotion, back to their human nature. What are they thinking? What do they feel? What emotion clings to the voices now silent? Graciously, they face the tremendous tumult in their honor. What violence . . . Have you ever measured the roar of an entire theater applauding? Hands clapping, feet stomping, voices out of breath from shouting "bravo" in celebration of the courage, the merit of the combatants (men and women), and the bouquets thrown wildly, like weapons. . . . The legacy of the ancient hired mourners, this wild rite, to make a long story short, gives opera a savage dimension where something other than a simple representation is being celebrated. Listen. . . . This is all we know how to do in reply. Listen. . . . We no longer know how to sing together.

And, in the theater, there always remain, long after the audience has left, a few lone people who never stop wanting to hang onto something. Please, Mr. Hangman, just one more minute. . . . One last kiss, my darling. Just like before going to sleep, the childish part of us tries to stay awake. Just like, before closing the casket, the suffering part wants to hang on to the illusion of life. We have to go. Arms tug on me, sounds talk in my ear; my body moves slowly, as if invisible threads held me to the ground. Any commentary is superfluous. Outside there will be a man who, from the height of his scholarly perch, will think this or that, will do his work as a critic. Since I am more polite than not, I will answer, anything at all: often, contradicting him because I am so annoyed by spoken words at the most painful moment. But I will want to strangle him. Why do they not shut up? . . . Do they not hear the victory of the god of armies over pagan rebellions? Do they not know what a strange mass they have just consecrated? And can they not understand the pain of defeat?

It is cold. Or rather, on the contrary, the night is tender, dawdling. Outside, my inevitable anger calms down. Reason returns—that stinking reason that has me standing now, walking, and accepting a dinner invitation, when what I need is to run straight for the sea. And, while my insensitive mouth speaks these polite words that I ridicule, there are bits of music to nourish me, resounding in a space no one can take away. Going to the opera is like an ethnologist taking a voyage to a strange land: when he comes back home, everything seems incongruous to him, and, deprived of his culture he no longer recognizes himself in his compatriots. He is Lazarus brought back from the dead, he comes from another world, bearing its unerasable marks. When I come home, I no longer recognize myself there; something has happened inside me that makes me wander, lost, for a long time. I never want to come back from this being lost . . . but there is no place in everyday life for delirium. I will have to do the work of mourning in *decrescendo*. I will have to slowly incorporate, without anyone's knowing, these dangerous objects, these women who fought so well, these sorceresses who from now on are part of my life. And at the same time that their music is inscribed in obsessive melodies, the ferment of swelling rebellion passes from them to me.

I am pregnant with them. The work of mourning often includes this surprise; and after long months, the dead makes the living pregnant. They swell my voice in anger, and soften it in love. They spread their powerful arms in my gestures. My mind bristles with strange symptoms like the hysteric's body; I am full of excrescences, I am pimply with ideas and feverish with thoughts. I give birth to yet unheard of words; I delight in producing barbarisms. I am pregnant with them, they have fertilized my images, and restored new pride in me. Nobody notices. It is invisible work, solid weaving, woven by thousands of voices, by thousands of years. Norma passes the silent torch of revolt to Carmen, and it falls into my hands, like a shuttle with which it is my turn to weave. Tomorrow, I already know, I will be singing unconsciously a turn come from who knows where; it belongs to no one, no one will realize it. But way inside myself I shall keep the secret. And I shall be ready for the next encounter with my musical sisters.

You will be told that this is not right at all. Some very learned speeches have been delivered to me. I listened to them respectfully. They concerned the necessity of knowing how to take some distance in looking at artistic forms, yes, go ahead, bury it, cover it with sand, with those vain words, masculine thoughts, lost in the breeze. Keep running for comfort; stick the pieces back together. As for myself, I prefer to get lost in this beneficial going to pieces where my body is no longer mine but is inhabited; as for myself, I choose hysteria, the blessed quality of being other. I identify with them, with them alone, their long battle, their fight; I will not bear their defeat much longer, the undoing that has begun again. For the scholarly gentleman calmly going off to supper, and spinning silkworm spittle from his head, the cocoon will close up quickly. I want to keep open the shell that the butterfly will come from. And I do not want to see it stuck to a board ever again, its wings spread out for the entomologist's gaze. I know they come back to life in me, I will endlessly sing inside myself to keep the trace alive. For the time it takes to do something of which I may be unaware, I will be Carmen, and no one will understand the meaning of a ''no.'' I will be multiple; I will disperse myself from music to music, secretly prey to unknown tenderness. I will turn myself over to feminity without reservation, but no one will know it. And their music inside me will be like night in the middle of day. A perpetual eclipse of the male sun.

They will tell you that hysteria is a sickness. That, since the time of the Greeks, everyone has known about the little hedgehog circulating in women's bodies. That every woman is sick; and that in a family, there is always one woman to concentrate in herself all the misfortune of the others. *The family invalid*: that is Freud's expression. You have seen them, you have heard them, these sick women, moaning, weeping, screaming, and finally falling down in defeat. Do not believe it. Hysteria is woman's principal resource. My friend Diderot made no mistake. ''Woman carries within herself,'' he wrote, ''an organ susceptible to terrific spasms, taking her over and arousing every sort of phantom in her imagination.'' But he quickly added: ''It is in hysterical delirium that she returns to the past, that she hurtles to the future, that all times are present for her.''[56]

For a long time what acted as thought for me came from the head and did not belong to me. For a long time, orderly thoughts, words of wisdom, and controlled arguments crisscrossed the space of something that was not my language but that of others, men. The opera formed an enclave, an Indian reservation where wildness was permitted, a transitory and painful promised land. Music for me was an unthought refuge. One day I became aware that opera did not come to me from my head. And, although I had often used the word heart, it was because of some leftover sense of propriety and prudence in a world where women are still held—in respect or contempt. Opera comes to me from somewhere else; it comes to me from the womb. That is no easygoing sexual organ. The uterus, which is where hysteria comes from, is an organ where the thought of beings is conceived, a place where powerful rhythms are elaborated; a musical beat that is peculiar to women, the source of their voice, their breathing, their spasmodic way of thinking. There and there alone history is expressed in the first person. There buried centuries are revived, just as Michelet, Diderot, and Freud in certain flashes that were quickly picked up on, were able to see. The hysteric knows how to rediscover the rebellions against Rome in her womb, as well as mythical Sabbats; these days the hysteric is able to make herself consumptive, just like in the last century, and die of it if it is necessary. But this past is no bittersweet nostalgia. As the present forms of numerous and disorganized movements in which feminine revolt is incoherently expressed prove, it is the thrust of the future. The projection of the future depends on this return of the womb. And the imitation dead women who haunt me sow bits of a world in which, perhaps, one day I shall feel free.

I will thumb my nose at Leibniz, who will be very surprised to hear something like a burst of laughter that he does not understand coming through the pipes of his magic house. I will splash the gold garlands with red and the red seats with gold. The men will finally wear feathers and colors. They will no longer look like identical policemen, gray, brown, black, drab. I will no longer be afraid to laugh and sing when, for the moment, it is still out of place. And sorcery will be a joyful, everyday affair. Opera will no longer exist. It will be the old reflection of a broken mirror, whose precious shards will be in a museum, where they will still have some attraction, some mystery for school children who will come to see the remains. There will no longer be either a stage or an audience; and women will sing of happiness.

It will be a great pagan festival, paradise regained, before a single, vengeful God had decided that Evil existed and suffering was necessary. The beasts of dread will be soft and fluffy, they will not threaten sleeping children anymore. Man and woman, all smooth and naked, will touch each other without sin, and their two voices mingling will unite in a music that will no longer be love or its romantic sufferings. There will be no more prohibition, no more weapons raised in the air, no more betrayals; God will exist no more than his vanished opera. . . . Ah!

The curtain goes down, erasing my dream. Death remains. The world is not coming apart in that manner, it endures, and with it this God whose shaky images defend phallocratic severities. I know the delirium of mourning. When the dead one with all its gigantic body invades the heart of the one left alive, a savage explosion drives the living to obliterate all limits, in a dangerous intoxication. The immense dead one comes back to life, happy. But unhappiness cannot be replaced by happiness; this is a completely artificial opposition, and I gain nothing from the deal except the word. On the grand opera stage, you saw unhappiness and its opposite; you saw nothing of life, except the derision of figures who were thwarted, whose voices alone sung the truth.

When the Bourgeois Revolution was simmering soups of humanism, the philosophers paid a lot of attention to the education of daughters. For the sons this had been taken care of for a long time. But the daughters were something else. Today the French Revolution dies hard. Its daughters received a harsh education. Its sons are doing fine; all their education remains to be done.

They must unlearn how to be men; they must undo their language and their sniggering; and like a baby who crawls around on the ground so his legs someday can hold him up, they must learn tenderness and forbidden caresses. They have to discover weakness in themselves — or at least what their good education has always called weakness. You, my son, when you found out that your sister was going to have periods one day and that that day was soon, and when we decided we would have a celebration, you were shocked and furious. So where did you get this legacy of rage? From the depths of the ages, you refused to hear anything about it. You wanted secrecy, mystery, and shame. You were distressed by our laughter, and you changed. The story of women in the opera is no different from this true episode. First the sons must be educated. They must be shown their fathers' plot on stage. You saw the traps where women are caught, you heard the marvelous music with which the West is still able to cover up its most intimate murders. . . . This is my story, no doubt. Perhaps you are already part of another world. But, if the hysterics' madness could move from the stake to the opera, and still endures through the overwhelming splendor of their voices, no doubt there are also great unthought myths hanging around in the corners of your head, whose prisoner you are, without your knowing. Opera is the collection of these myths; better than any book, it has been able to display them in all their past grandeur. It makes them live, survive, come back to life; in blind pleasure it maintains the harsh laws of family and politics. One must know how to look its myths right in their dazzling eyes.

Wait. Do not go away yet, do not leave the house. One last story. When one's child's childhood is over, one's own returns. I remember my first tears. I am not talking about tears of need, the ones used by a newborn baby to mean hunger, thirst, or being wet. I mean real tears, the first distress. They came from a book, no doubt my first. Like voices, printed words have the perverse power of affecting something more than just vision. This little picture book told the story of the little match girl. ''Behind the brightly lit windows everywhere one could tell there was joy.'' Once upon a time there was a little girl, lost in the great coldness of Andersen's tale. She sold matches to live, and, I remember, she had bare feet. And she thought about all those roasted geese in the warm houses whose lights she saw. She did not dare go home, for fear of being scolded by her father who would surely beat her.

Then she sat down in the snow. And to warm herself, or maybe just for something to do, she struck the first match. And a huge, glowing stove suddenly warmed her feet; then the match went out and there was nothing. Another match . . . before her there was a table full of food. She went on striking all the matches this way. When she came to the last one, her grandmother appeared to her, young and beautiful again, as she had never known her.

The next day at dawn the little girl was still sitting in the snow, surrounded by blackened matches scattered everywhere. She had frozen to death. Even today, do I know what made me cry? If I knew I probably would not go to the opera anymore. It was no doubt the first clear vision I ever had of my own people dying, when I was a little girl in the winter of 1942, which was so cold. All the threats of the real world went into the pretend death of this very small heroine. But also, think about it, the matches. Struck all at once, in a luminous, ephemeral splendor: all happiness at once, but it does not last. And the result is death, as if every happiness struck a little too quickly would go out right away. That is indeed the world of opera. A great blaze of light and love, and death is the result. Outside it is cold, you have to keep on living. There is no happy love; there is no happy opera. . . . And every time fresh tears. Every time my little match girl dies when she has burned all the lights of her life on stage. Every time the mourning hurts and prolongs an image of suffering that is more cogent than reality.

Now happiness is exactly the opposite. The opera, the matches, or the little mermaid who cuts off her tongue so she can live with the man she loves and who will not love her, is the enchanted world passed on by parents. I like the English psychoanalyst Winnicott. He was an old man who knew a lot about childhood. He noticed that for a long time—sometimes until they are grown up—children go to sleep with stuffed animals or bits of cloth. He called these "transitional objects." Well, what do you expect, after all, he was an analyst and he was not worried about being understood by his peers. A transitional object is a temporary support, a support for the duration. It is an object that the child brings to life when he pleases, one he attacks and destroys and that is strongly resilient. The teddy bear, much beloved, has had only one eye for a long time; shapeless and ugly it is still the cherished object. It guarantees the transition into the world. It is simply there. It helps the time pass; and with time the harsh stages of education.

The matches are the opposite of this transition. They flame and there is nothing left. The women, whose eternal story I have told you, blaze up all at once and there is nothing left. Nothing is left but the music. Yes, finally, the music, like a transitional space; the music that is neither inside nor outside, but elsewhere and surrounding you. The music where love and hatred can interact without vital risk, and where the light of passions burns and immediately goes out. Life is different, nothing in it happens that way. But opera still endures with its limited stories because music plays the blessed role of the stuffed animal in it. Every aggression is possible in the music and every fusion; in it one dies, one throbs, and one is wounded; but the music mends and glues things back together. It is like a great living, membranous surface where the substances for the continuance of life spring back up. It will help you to get through; it will help you to get across. It becalms the patriarchal laws that put women to death. A nurturing grandmother, music obliterates those women whose too real sufferings I wanted to show you. For a long time it has neutralized my rebellions and laid my suspicions to rest. Even today, if I love opera, it is because I know the charm and mending power of the way it beguiles me and puts me to sleep.

Leaving the magical night, I need a long moment for my mind to wake up. One must reconquer the ground, finally leave the motherly arms and get up. And even, you see, one must know the truth about hysterical women. They have centuries of memory, they have bodies filled with memory, they tell the truth about oppression, they bore holes in the family, they are right with *delirious* reason. But Freud was immensely surprised at their resistance to misfortune. Beaten, tortured, defeated, down, the next day the hysteric (all fresh and ready to go) takes on a new battle and produces a new symptom. Another pimple has appeared on her lip. The prima donna, whom you just saw weeping real tears and suffering with all her bodily force, gets back up, smiling, scarcely affected. Hysterics with their beautiful indifference! Misfortune plays on the surface, the matches strike, the skin burns, but a hard core resists and does not die. Indifferent to her sufferings, the hysteric creates new ones.

Men will tell you that women are like that. Their conclusion is that it is not particularly important. They suffer, but not really. I, on the contrary, see it as women's ultimate victory. They suffer, but nothing can affect the resistant center. The opera will not succeed in getting to the end of it. And in these indefinitely repeated murders, it is killing dead women who have already come back to life. The matches blaze again and the sky lights up once more . . . the hysterics stand back up. The great musical flow will not put them to sleep.

Their eyes sparkle, wide wide open. They are indifferent to something and live even in their death. Their skin quivers, their surface sheds a new skin, then another, then another, infinitely. Daughters of the serpent that men have always called their accomplice, they slough off skins. They are more immortal than that hated God who made us women as halves of men. Their indifference is the unconcern of ancient goddesses, serene and giant women lightly touched by passion but unshattered. This God will pass while they remain. And opera, which is doubtless an ephemeral form with regard to centuries to come, will never have been anything other than the deep sleep of their violence, the representation men provided for themselves of their poorly guaranteed victory, in a battle conducted only by themselves, desired only by themselves. Beautiful and alive, the women will continue to sing in a voice that will never again submit to threat. They will say something entirely different than the words breathed in delirium and pain. They will ask no more than that they finally be permitted to die. . . . I do not know what this song will be.

I imagine it as a lullaby. Listen to the heights of coloratura, to the highest uplift of a suffering voice, listen. . . . Singing there, scarcely audible, is a voice from beyond opera, a voice of the future. A voice from before adulthood: the voice of tenderness and cuddling. The voice of a sweet body, one with no distance, one only a real body can make appear. Sleep will no longer awake to a little girl who is dead. Just as you always stretch your arms when you leave the darkness, these women will always sing.

Notes

Notes

Foreword

1. *Contemplating Music: Challenges to Musicology* (Cambridge, MA: Harvard University Press, 1985), p. 17.

2. Said, *The Nation* (February 7, 1987), pp. 158-60, and Sandow, "Roll Over, Opera: Open Letter to Will Crutchfield," *Village Voice* (June 16, 1987), p. 78.

3. Trans. Betsy Wing, introduced by Sandra M. Gilbert (Minneapolis: University of Minnesota Press, 1986).

4. See also the section in this volume, "The hysteric at her midnight hour," pp. 32-38.

5. See especially, *The Raw and the Cooked: Introduction to a Science of Mythology*, vol. 1, trans. John Weightman and Doreen Weightman (New York: Harper & Row, 1970). Various sections of this book are arranged as a theme with variations, a sonata, a symphony, and a fugue.

6. Opera originated, of course, in the early seventeenth century in the courts of northern Italy where it was an aristocratic spectacle. Although public opera houses opened in Venice in the 1630s, it remained an entertainment for the elite for most of the seventeenth and eighteenth centuries. Nonetheless, class politics mark both its procedures (favored plots, vocabularies of musical gestures, etc.) and its modes of production. See my "The Politics of Silence and Sound," afterword to Jacques Attali, *Noise: The Political Economy of Music*, trans. Brian Massumi (Minneapolis: University of Minnesota Press, 1985), pp. 154-56, and José Antonio Maravall, *Culture of the Baroque: Analysis of a Historical Structure*, trans. Terry Cochran (Minneapolis: University of Minnesota Press, 1986). These earlier, aristocratic operas (especially those by Monteverdi and Handel) are occasionally performed today, although they remain for the most part esoteric fare. Clément rightly picks up her discussion of opera with the emergence of opera for the middle-class audience at the end of the eighteenth century, for these are the operas of "our" standard repertoire.

7. In addition to Said's and Sandow's pieces, a few other studies have come out concerning images of women in opera. See especially Jeremy Tambling, *Opera, Ideology and Film* (New York: St. Martin's Press, 1987).

8. I discuss these issues, using both *Carmen* and Tchaikovsky's Symphony no. 4, more thoroughly in "Sexual Politics in Classical Music," a paper delivered at the *Women and the Arts Symposium*, University of Wisconsin, Madison (April 1986).

9. A helpful guide to Lacan and the intellectual community that formed around him is Clément's *The Lives and Legends of Jacques Lacan*, trans. Arthur Goldhammer (New York: Columbia University Press, 1983).

10. Roland Barthes's music criticism often openly explores such images. "Schumann is truly the musician of solitary intimacy, of the amorous and imprisoned soul that *speaks to itself* . . . in short of the child who has no other link than to the Mother" [Barthes's emphasis]. "Loving Schumann," *The Responsibility of Forms*, trans. Richard Howard (New York: Hill and Wang, 1985), pp. 293-94. "But, in music, a field of *signifying* and not a system of signs, the referent is unforgettable, for here the referent is the body. The body passes into music without any relay but the signifier. This passage—this transgression—makes music a madness. . . . In relation to the writer, the composer is always mad (and the writer can never be so, for he is condemned to meaning)." *"Rasch,"* *The Responsibility of Forms*, p. 308. My thanks to Barbara Engh for bringing these passages to my attention.

11. Hysteria over music's ability to appeal to the senses and thus render the listener "effeminate" is a constant in Western music history. Plato praises the manly virtues of dorian music and condemns the more sensual lydian and mixolydian modes "for they are useless even to women who are to make the best of themselves, let alone to men" [*Republic*, trans. Paul Shorey, 398, in *The Collected Dialogues*, ed. Edith Hamilton and Huntington Cairns (Princeton, 1961), p. 643]; John of Salisbury (d. 1180) attacks the emergence of polyphonic practices (now usually regarded as the glory of Western music) thus: "Music sullies the Divine Service, for in the very sight of God . . . [the singers] attempt, with the lewdness of a lascivious singing voice and a singularly foppish manner, to feminize all their spellbound little fans with the girlish way they render the notes and end the phrases . . . .the ears are almost completely divested of their critical power, and the intellect, which pleasureableness of so much sweetness has caressed insensate, is impotent to judge the merits of things heard. Indeed, when such practices go too far, they can more easily occasion titillation between the legs than a sense of devotion in the brain" [*Policratus* (1159 A.D.), trans. William Dalglish in "The Origin of the Hocket," *Journal of the American Musicological Society* 31 (1978): p. 7]; and T. W. Adorno: "The aim of jazz is the mechanical reproduction of a regressive moment, a castration symbolism. 'Give up your masculinity, let yourself be castrated,' the eunuchlike sound of the jazz band both mocks and proclaims, 'and you will be rewarded, accepted into a fraternity which shares the mystery of impotence with you" ["Perennial fashion—Jazz," *Prisms*, trans. Samuel Weber and Shierry Weber (Cambridge, MA: MIT, 1981), p. 129].

12. New York: Franklin Watts, 1984.

13. Ibid., pp. 11-12.

14. See my discussion of this piece in "Getting Down Off the Beanstalk: The Presence of a Woman's Voice in Janika Vandervelde's *Genesis II*," *Minnesota Composers Forum Newsletter* (January 1987).

Opera, or the Undoing of Women

1. A film by Bernardo Bertolucci, 1963.

2. The famous hero of Gaston Leroux's fantasy novel.

3. See Pierre Macherey and François Regnault's sound analysis: "L'Opéra ou l'art hors de soi," *Les Temps modernes* (Julliard, 1965). Ledoux's remarks are about an engraving of the theater at Besançon.

4. Yvon Belaval edited this text for the *Nouvelle Revue française*, no. 70, October 1, 1958.

5. Antonio Garcia Gutierrez, Francesco Maria Piave, and Arrigo Boito.

6. Jean Cocteau, "La Cantate," *Cahiers Jean Cocteau (Gallimard, 1971).*

7. Gaston Leroux, *The Phantom of the Opera* (Laffant, 1984).

8. With the exception of Roland Mancini's work in *Opera International*, in the supplement to the February 1978 issue.

9. A woman has recently carried the singer's ashes back to her native Greece.

10. Pierre-Jean Rémy, however, wrote a brief and perfect text a long time ago: *La Mort de Floria Tosca* (Mercure de France, 1974).

11. *The Death of Maria Malibran.*

12. The detail of all these stories (of Malibran, Sontag, and Falcon) can be read in Olivier Merlin's delightful book: *Quand le bel canto regnait sur le boulevard* (Fayard, n.d.).

13. Opera composed by Jacques Offenbach and Jules Barbier, after a work by E. T. A. Hoffmann.

14. Opera by Mozart and Da Ponte.

15. This is Pierre Jean Jouve's expression, from his book *Le Don Giovanni de Mozart* (Plon, 1968).

16. Henri Barrault, *Les Cinq Grands Operas*, and Jouve, *Le Don Giovanni de Mozart*.

17. Opera by Giacomo Puccini, with librettists Giacosa and Illica, after a play by Victorien Sardou.

18. Opera by Giacomo Puccini, with librettists Giacosa and Illica, after a play by David Belasco.

19. Opera by Bizet, Meilhac, and Halévy.

20. Meilhac and Halévy.

21. Prosper Merimée.

22. Cited by Edith Falque in *Voyage et Tradition* (Payot, 1971).

23. Flaubert, *La Tentation de saint Antoine*. [Translated as *The Temptation of Saint Anthony*, trans. Kitty Mrosovsky (London: Secker & Warberg, 1980).]

24. Opera, libretto, and music, by Richard Wagner.

25. I borrow this analysis from Claude Lévi-Strauss's *Mythologiques*, pp. 67-287 of *Le Cru et le Cuit*. [Translated as *The Raw and the Cooked: Introduction to a Science of Mythology*, vol. 1, trans. John Weightman and Doreen Weightman (New York: Harper & Row, 1970).]

26. *Pelléas and Mélisande*, opera by Claude Debussy and Maurice Maeterlinck.

27. Opera by G. Verdi and F. M. Piave, after a play and novel by Alexandre Dumas The Younger, *La Dame aux camélias* (London: The Folio Society, 1975). [Trans. Barbara Bray.]

28. Opera by Verdi, Méry, and du Locle, after Schiller.

29. Opera by Mozart and Schikadener, after a collection of stories by Wieland.

30. *Elektra*, opera by Richard Strauss and Hofmannsthal, after Sophocles.

31. Opera by Tchaikovsky and Shilovski, after Pushkin.

32. Opera by Puccini, Giacosa and Illica, after Henri Murger.

33. Opera by Donizetti and Cammarano, after Walter Scott.

34. Théophile Gautier turns this into one of the purple passages in *Histoire du romanticisme* (Aujourd'hui, 1978).

35. Opera by Bellini and Pepoli, after Walter Scott.

36. Opera by Bellini and Felice Romani.

37. My italics. This is how the seducer reveals the secret of his seduction: a deflowered woman is good for nothing other than being a man. Then would not man be just an old (former) virgin?

38. *La Fanciulla del West*, opera by Puccini, Civinnini, and Zangarini, after a play by David Belasco.

39. *Cosi fan tutte*, opera by Mozart and Da Ponte.

40. Claude Lévi-Strauss, *Mythologiques*, vol. 2, *Du Miel aux cendres*. [Translated as *From Honey to Ashes: Introduction to a Science of Mythology*, vol. 2, trans. John Weightman and Doreen Weightman, (New York: Harper & Row, 1973).]

41. Opera by Puccini, Adami, and Simoni, after Carlo Gozzi.

42. Opera by Bellini and Felice Romani.

43. Opera by Richard Strauss and Hugo von Hofmannsthal.

44. I am endebted to Vladimir Jankelevitch, who, in 1960, said the first true thing I heard about Mélisande because of his extreme fondness for her as well as for all of Debussy's opera. His philosophical study of this is in progress.

45. *Pelléas et Mélisande*, opera by Claude Debussy and Maurice Maeterlinck.

46. Georges Bataille, *Madame Edwarda* (Pauvert, 1985).

47. *La Khovantchina*, opera by Moussorgski and Stassov.

48. *Aida*, opera by Verdi and Ghislanzoni, after a study by Mariette.

49. Sigmund Freud, *Moses and Monotheism*, trans. Katherine Jones (New York: Vintage Books, 1955).

50. *Götterdämmerung*, opera by Richard Wagner (words and music).

51. *Parsifal*, opera by Richard Wagner (words and music).

52. Opera by Moussorgski (words and music), after Pushkin.

53. Opera by Verdi and Boito, after Shakespeare.

54. Opera by Verdi and Boito.

55. *Die Meistersinger*, opera by Richard Wagner (words and music).

56. Denis Diderot, *Sur les femmes* (Gallimard, bibliothèque de la Pléiade, 1975).

Bibliography

Bibliography

Adorno, Theodor. *Philosophy of Modern Music*. Continuum, 1980.

———. *In Search of Wagner*. Schocken, 1981.

Andersen, Hans Christian. *Andersen's Fairy Tales*. Macmillan, 1963.

Aragon, Louis. *La Mise à mort*. Gallimard, 1973.

Attali, Jacques. *Bruits*. PUF, 1981. [*Noise*. University of Minnesota Press, 1985.]

Barilier, Étienne. *Alban Berg*. L'Age d'homme, 1979.

Bastide, Roger. "Le Rire et les courts-circuits de la pensée," in *Les Mélanges Lévi-Strauss*. Mouton.

Bataille, Georges. *Madame Edwarda*. Pauvert, 1985.

Bourgeois, Jacques. *Giuseppe Verdi*. Julliard, 1978.

Brecht, Bertolt. *Brecht on Theatre*. Trans. John Willet. Hill and Wang, 1964.

Brion, Marcel. *Histoire de l'Egypte*. Fayard.

Chailley, Jacques. *La Flûte enchantée, opéra maçonnique, new edition*. Laffont, 1983. [*The Magic Flute, Masonic Opera*. Da Capo, 1982.]

Chantavoine, Jean. *Petit guide de l'auditeur de musique*. Plon.

Cocteau, Jean. "La Cantate," in *Cahiers Jean Cocteau*, Vol. 2. Gallimard, 1971.

Cœuroy, André. *Wagner et l'esprit romantique*. Gallimard, 1965.

Diderot, Denis. *Sur les femmes*. Gallimard, bibliothèque de la Pléaide.

Dumas, Alexandre (fils). *La Dame aux camélias*. Gallimard, 1975. [Trans. Barbara Bray. The Folio Society, 1975.]

Dumesnil, René. *Le Don Juan de Mozart*. Plon.

Ehrardt. *La Légende des Nibelungen*. Piazza.

Engels, Frederick. *Origin of the Family: Private Property and the State*. Path Press, 1972.

Falque, Edith. *Voyage et tradition*. Payot, 1971.

Fernandez, Dominique. *Porporino*. Grasset, 1974.

Flaubert, Gustave. *La Tentation de Saint Antoine*. Gallimard, 1983. [*The Temptation of Saint Anthony*. Trans. Kitty Mrosovsky. Cornell University Press, 1981.]

Freud, Sigmund. *Essais de psychanalyse appliquée*. Gallimard, 1971.

———. *Moses and Monotheism*. Random, 1955.

————. *Origins of Psychoanalysis: Letters to Wilhelm Fleiss, Drafts and Notes, 1887-1902*. Basic, 1954.

————. *Selected Papers on Hysteria and Other Psychoneuroses*. Repr. of 1912 ed. Johnson Repr.

Gautier, Théophile. *Histoire du romantisme*. Aujourd'hui, 1978.

Gozzi. *Turandot*.

Green, André. *Un Œil en trop*. Éditions de Minuit, 1969.

Hegel, G. W. *Phenomenology of Mind*. Humanities, 1966.

Hergé. *Les Bijoux de la Castafiore*. Casterman. [*The Castafiore Emerald*. Atlantic Monthly Press, 1975.]

Hocquard, Jean-Victor. *La Pensée de Mozart*. Seuil, 1958.

Hoffmann, E. T. A. *Le Conseiller Krespel*. Aubier-Flammarion.

————. *Princesse Brambilla*. Aubier-Montaigne.

Jankelevitch, Vladimir. *Debussy et le mystère*. La Baconnière, 1949.

Jouve, Pierre Jean. *Le Don Giovanni de Mozart*. Aujourd'hui, 1968.

————. *Le Wozzeck de Berg*. Bourgois, 1985.

Kierkegaard, Søren. *Diary of a Seducer*. Trans. Gerd Gillhoff. Unger, 1966.

————. *Either-Or*, 2 Vols. Trans. W. Lowrie. Princeton University Press, 1971.

Lacan, Jacques. *Écrits*. Seuil, 1966.

Lavignac, Albert. *Le Voyage artistique à Bayreuth*. Minkoff, 1951.

Leibniz, Gottfried Wilhelm. "Drôle de pensée touchant une nouvelle sorte de représentation." Ed. Yvon Belaval. NRF, no. 70 (October 1958); *La Théodicée*. Flammarion, 1979.

Leibowitz, René. *Histoire de l'opéra*. Buchet Chastel; *Les Fantômes de l'opéra*. Gallimard, 1978.

Leiris, Michel. *L'Age d'homme*. Gallimard, 1973. [*Manhood*. Trans. Richard Howard. North Point Press, 1984.]

Lévi-Strauss, Claude. *Anthropologie structurale*, 2 vols. Plon, 1968, 1973.

————. *Mythologiques*, 4 vols.: *Le Cru et le Cuit*; *Du miel aux cendres*; *Origines des manières de table*; *l'Homme nu*. Plon, 1967, 1968. [*Raw and the Cooked: An Introduction to a Science of Mythology*, Vol. 1. Harper-Row, 1970; *From Honey to Ashes: An Introduction to a Science of Mythology*, Vol. 2. Harper-Row, 1973; *The Origin of Table Manners*. Harper-Row, 1979; *Naked Man*. Harper-Row.]

————. *Structures élémentaires de la parenté*. Mouton, 1968. [*Elementary Structures of Kinship*. Beacon Press, 1979.]

————. *Tristes Tropiques*. Plon, 1955.

Longchampt, Jacques. *L'Opéra aujourd'hui*. Seuil, 1970.

Lorcey, Jacques. *Maria Callas*. PAC, 1983.

de Martino, Ernesto. *La Terre du remords*. Gallimard, 1966.

Merlin, Olivier. *Quand le bel canto régnait sur le boulevard*. Fayard.

Pushkin, Alexander. *Boris Godounov*. Greenwood, 1976.

————. *Eugène Onégin*. Dutton, 1981.

Prévert, Jacques. Dialogues from Jean Cocteau's film, *Enfants du paradis*. Balland.

Rémy, Pierre-Jean. *Maria Callas, une vie*. Ramsay, 1978.

————. *La Mort de Floria Tosca*. Mercure de France, 1974.

de Rougemont, Denis. *L'Amour et l'Occident*. UGE: 18 October 1962. [*Love and the Western World*. Princeton University Press, 1983.]

Schiller, Friedrich. *Don Carlos, Infante of Spain: Drama in Five Acts*. Ungar, 1959.

Shakespeare, William. *Othello*; *The Merry Wives of Windsor*.

Sprenger, Jacques and Henri Institoris. *Le Marteau des sorcières* [*The Witches' Hammer*: *Manual for Inquisitors*.] Plon, 1974.

Stendhal. *La Chartreuse de Parme*. Gallimard, 1973 [*The Charterhouse of Parma*. Penguin, 1958.]

————. *Le Rouge et le noir*. Didier, 1968. [*The Red and the Black*. NAL, 1970.]

————. *Voyage en Italie*. Gallimard, 1973.

Tranchefort, François-René. *L'Opéra*, 2 vols. Seuil, 1978.

Wagner, Richard. *Die Meistersinger von Nürnberg*: *Complete Vocal and Orchestral Score*. Dover, 1976.

_____. *The Ring of the Nibelung*. Trans. Andrew Porter. Norton, 1977.

Weaver, William. *Verdi*: *A Documentary Study*. Thames Hudson, 1977.

Winnicott, D. W. *Jeu et réalité*. Gallimard, 1975. [*Playing and Reality*. Methuen, 1982.]

Reviews

L'Avant-Scène Opéra
Musique en jeu
Lyrica
Opéra International
Les Temps modernes, 1965: Pierre Macherey and François Regnault, ''L'Opéra ou l'art hors de soi.''

Some of the analyses in this book appeared in an earlier version in the review *L'Avant-Scène Opéra*, edited by Guy Samama, to whom I am grateful. The examinations of the operas *Tosca*, *Pelléas et Mélisande*, and *Othello* have been completely reworked. The chapter on the *Ring* cycle, on the other hand, which was also published in *L'Avant-Scène Opéra* (in the issue devoted to *Rheingold*), has been only partially modified.

Index

Index

Adorno, Theodor, 10
Aida, xii, 107, 116-17, 124
Alfano, Franco, 101-2
Altdorfer, Albrecht, 20
American Musicological Society, ix
Andersen, Hans Christian, 178-79
Anderson, Laurie, xiii
Angelico, Fra, 98
Animals, 163-64
Anthropology, x-xi, 5
Antigone, 161-62
Aragon, Louis, 37, 121

Balzac, Honoré de, 3
Barrault, Henri, 35
Bastide, Roger, 120
Bataille, Georges, 113
Bellini, Vincenzo, 14, 20, 30, 90-92, 102. *See also I Puritani*; *La Somnambule*; *Norma*
Berg, Alban, 25. *See also Lulu*
Bernhardt, Sarah, 41
Bizet, Georges, xiv, 49. *See also Carmen*
Böito, Arrigo, 18, 21, 128-29. *See also Falstaff*; *Otello*; *Simon Boccanegra*
Boris Godounov, 120
Bororo, x, 5
Bosch, Hieronymous, 69-70
Boullée, 6

Bourgeoisie, xi-xii, 70-71, 134
Brecht, Bertolt, 9-10, 20-21
Brothers, 76, 161, 170-71

Caballé, Montserrat, 18, 28-30
Callas, Maria, xvi, 16, 18, 28-31, 104
Carmen: Carmen as a foreigner, 58-59, 67; character of Carmen in, xviii, 14, 103, 175-76; chromaticism in, xiii-xv; death in, 12; as French opera, 16; imperialism in, xii, 107; night in, 102; productions of, xvii; and psychoanalysis, 85; racism in, xii, 103; society's authority in, 10; synopsis and interpretation, 47-53
Casta Diva, 102
Chantavoine, Jean, 90
Chéreau, Patrice, 18-19
Chopin, Fréderic 13
Christianity, 103, 105, 135-36, 140
Chromaticism, xiii, 56-58
Cixous, Hélène, x, 18
Cocteau, Jean, 24-25, 27-28
Commedia dell'arte, 98-99
Cosi fan tutte, 95, 135
Crispin, Régine, 108

Da Ponte, Lorenzo, 18. *See also Cosi fan tutte*; *Don Giovanni*

197

Catherine Clément is a delegate of the French "Festival of France" in India and is currently living and writing in New Dehli. She is also a *maître de conférences* at the Université de Paris I, Panthéon Sorbonne, as a philosopher. Clément previously was the diplomat in charge of cultural exchanges at the French Ministry of External Relations and also was an editor and the head of cultural services for the Parisian newspaper *Le Matin*. She is the author of books on structuralism, psychoanalysis, and Marxism, and co-author, with Hélène Cixous, of *The Newly Born Woman* (Minnesota, 1986).

Betsy Wing has a B.A. in art history from Bryn Mawr College; she also attended Columbia University and Miami University, Ohio, and is currently a candidate for the M.F.A. at Louisiana State University. Her translations include Hélène Cixous and Catherine Clément's *Newly Born Woman* and Denis Hollier's *The College of Sociology (1937-39)* (Minnesota, 1988). Wing's translations and fiction have also appeared in *Representations*, *Boundary 2*, *Argo* and *The Southern Review*.

Susan McClary teaches at the University of Minnesota, where she is associate professor in three areas: the School of Music, Women's Studies, and Comparative Studies in Discourse and Society. She is also a member of the Center for Advanced Feminist Studies and served as acting director of the Center for Humanistic Studies in 1984-85. McClary received her Ph.D. in musicology from Harvard University in 1976. Her publications include articles on seventeenth-century style, on the ideological dimensions of music by Bach and others, on problems in the reception of new music, and on feminist music criticism. She is co-editor, with Richard Leppert, of *Music and Society: The Politics of Composition, Performance and Reception* (Cambridge University Press, 1987). Her music-theater piece, *Susanna Does the Elders*, was produced at the Southern Theatre in Minneapolis in July 1987.

DATE		